"A"

FAISAL

THE M&E HANDBOOK SERIES

'A' Level Law

Barry Jones

BA (London)
Barrister
Headmaster, Avonhurst School, Bristol

SECOND EDITION

Pitman Publishing
128 Long Acre, London WC2E 9AN

A Division of Longman Group UK Limited

First published 1981
Second edition 1984
Reprinted (with update) by Pitman Publishing 1986, 1988, 1990

© Macdonald & Evans Ltd 1981, 1984
© Longman Group UK Ltd (Update) 1986

British Library Cataloguing in Publication Data

Jones, Barry, 1922–
'A' Level Law.—2nd ed.—(The M & E
HANDBOOK series, ISSN 0265-8828)
1. Law—England
I. Title
344.2   KD661

ISBN 0-7121-0192-6

Founding Editor: P. W. D. Redmond

Printed and bound in Singapore

Preface to the Second Edition

To minimise the need for a costly profusion of separate texts, this HANDBOOK is devised to cover the GCE Advanced Level law syllabuses of the Associated Examining Board (Paper I), the Welsh Joint Education Committee, the Oxford Delegacy of Local Examinations and the Joint Matriculation Board. As the last two prescribe contract and criminal law as optional subjects, separate sections are devoted to these. Treatment is also given to relevant sociological and jurisprudential concepts.

The law is stated as at 1st August 1984 and the uniformity in presentation is intended to facilitate the memorising of information. Every chapter should first be read through, with a view to acquiring a general picture of its scope and content. After that, all of the individual sections should be separately studied and only then should the progress test be tackled and checked against the sectional references. On completion of Parts One and Two (or Three), the respective test papers at the end of the book should be attempted under examination conditions, with a strict time limit.

With synopses of 397 illustrative cases, it is hoped that this HANDBOOK will be of use and interest to "A" Level candidates, to students taking examinations in the English legal system, contract or criminal law, and also to those who are not facing such ordeals but who require a general introduction to law.

1984   BJ

Contents

Part Two: THE LAW OF CONTRACT

Part Three: CRIMINAL LAW

Table of Cases

TABLE OF CASES

Table of Statutes

THE FOUNDATIONS
AND FUNCTIONS OF LAW

CHAPTER I

The Nature of Law

THE FOUNDATIONS OF LAW

1. The evolution of law. An examination of the evolution of law necessitates a venture into the field of sociology—the study of the development, nature and relationships of human society—thus one needs to consider:

(*a*) *The attributes of human society.* The fundamental assumption of sociology is the relative helplessness at birth of the human infant, who is born into and depends for his survival upon, a social group. The individual's ways of thinking and acting, also the social order, must therefore be understood as a product of group life. It can be argued that the most significant difference between human beings and animals lies in the fact that the former alone have *culture*—a term used by the anthropologist to embrace all modes of thought and behaviour that are handed down by symbolic communication (language, gesture, etc.), rather than by genetic inheritance. The processes whereby persons are involved with one another are termed *interaction*; thus culture is both a creation of, and an influence upon, interaction.

(*b*) *The regulation of social order.* It is a characteristic of human social life that what is done by the majority of the people in a given situation takes on the quality of what ought to be done. In primitive societies, which are generally small, social order is therefore regulated by *norms*, i.e. rules of conduct which are conveyed as part of the cultural heritage. The American social scientist William Graham Sumner divided norms into two main categories:

(*i*) *folkways* (relatively minor conventions and forms of etiquette); and

(*ii*) *mores* (standards regarded as crucial for the welfare of a group, whose social cohesion, and even survival, might depend upon them).

Mores expressed in a negative form give rise to *taboos*, some of which (e.g. those against incest) may have important social functions, whereas others may have economic effects (e.g. food conservation by the prohibition of fishing at certain seasons). Long-established folkways and mores, oft-repeated by many generations, give rise to *custom*, i.e. practices that tend to be observed simply because they have been followed in the past.

(*c*) *The imposition of sanctions.* Whereas folkways are generally enforced by informal social controls (e.g. ridicule, gossip, ostracism), breaches of mores may be curbed either by the expectation of undesirable extra-human consequences (e.g. illness, death of a relative, lack of success in hunting, etc.) or by permitting the injured party to vindicate his claims by way of personal retaliation or vengeance. If the other party rejects the legitimacy of a claim, he may deny the right to resort to force; hence feud or internecine war might result. The need to maintain a peaceable existence thus creates a requirement for sanctions enforced by a special agency. The distinctive sanction of primitive systems is physical force (e.g. whipping, mutilation, death, imprisonment or exile) and, though damages and fines may be exacted, refusal to pay would result in force. The primary authority for enforcing such sanctions is the kinship group, in support of its individual members, though some acts are recognised as punishable by the society at large or through explicitly delegated officials.

When mores thus come to have some special organisation for their enforcement, they may be called *laws* but, in the absence of a legislative body for the enactment of new rules not previously part of the cultural heritage, they would essentially be *customary* laws (i.e. founded in custom). It can thus be seen that law may be distinguished from custom by the nature of its sanctions and by the status of those who apply it. The acknowledgment of such authority as legitimate is dependent largely upon a sense of moral obligation and the next four sections will examine the role of law in the support of morality, the provision of justice, the fulfilment of interests and the maintenance of social order.

2. The relevance of morality. The attraction or repulsions felt by people towards anything constitute what are termed their *values* and these may be considered in two categories:

✗ (*a*) the *normative* (derived from norms); and

(*b*) the *idealistic* (derived from ideals, which sometimes coincide with the norms but, even when not, provide guides to behaviour).

Viewed from the standpoint of the individual values can be called *attitudes*. The value-concepts of right and wrong form the basis of *morality*—a pattern of norms observed not simply because they are traditional or generally adopted but because they conform to the abstract principle of the supreme good.

Though morals are closely interwoven with *religion*, a distinction must be drawn between the two, as the one connotes a relationship between man and man, whereas the other establishes it between man and some higher power. The principal difference therefore lies in the authority and sanctions of each, and a contrast can be drawn between the moral idea of *wrong* (with its harmful social result) and the religious concept of *sin* (with possible extra-human consequences) but these are not mutually exclusive. In so far as the relationship between morality and *law* is concerned, it is necessary to consider:

✗ (*a*) *The contrasting of morality with law.* Within any society there develops a *social morality* involving certain obligations or duties (e.g. to keep promises or to abstain from violence), which require a sacrifice of private inclination or interest, essential to the security and well-being of the society. Herein lies a similarity between morality and law—but there are striking differences between them and the cardinal features of morality are that:

(*i*) *It is immune from deliberate change*, whereas law may be modified by legislative procedures. Conversely, moral attitudes are perpetually and naturally evolving, whilst law remains unaltered until formally amended.

(*ii*) *It is voluntary in character*, whereas law makes human conduct non-optional or obligatory. The consequences of moral lapses are a sense of shame or guilt and "punishment" by one's own conscience—however, the law provides sanctions for non-observance.

(*iii*) *It is of general application and emerges from particular groups*—whereas law relates only to particular circumstances and emanates from the state.

(*iv*) *It stresses duties and is concerned with motive*—whereas law embraces both duties and rights, and is concerned with actions.

(*v*) *It is not subject to adjudication.* Unlike legal disputes, moral disagreements cannot be resolved by the verdict of a third party.

X (*b*) *The relationship of morality to law.* From Greek and Roman times, under what have been termed the theories of *natural law*, there has existed a belief that man-made laws are valid only in so far as they conform to certain moral value-judgments which emanate from some absolute source (e.g. God's "revealed word") and also that these natural laws are immutable, eternally valid and discoverable by the proper employment of human reason.

As it is not possible to establish moral truths commanding general agreement and as they are relative to time and place (the principle of *moral relativism*) rather than eternally valid, support for the natural law theory steadily declined but enjoyed a revival during the latter half of the twentieth century in the criticism of the legislation of oppressive regimes and in the furtherance of revolutionary ideas.

There has nevertheless been a move towards *legal positivism*—the contention that it is in no sense a necessary truth that laws should reproduce or satisfy certain demands of morality—even though they have in fact often done so; emphasis is therefore placed on what the law *is*, rather than what it *ought* to be.

The moral standards of a community are generally recognised as having a profound influence upon the development of its law but this is not universally accepted and the Scandinavian jurist Karl Olivecrona, for example, has argued that the use of force (underlying the law) is a principal factor in moulding people's standards, rather than the reverse.

Both morality and law are founded in norms essential to the well-being of society and related to the socio-economic structure—thus has theft developed from the concept of private property. Moreover, morality and law both occupy much common ground, as numerous infringements of the law are also morally abhorrent.

Nevertheless, there is no necessary coincidence between the dictates of the two and it can be stated only that they supplement and reinforce each other. Moral codes supplement the force of the law which prohibits murder, theft, etc., whilst the sanctions imposed by the law reinforce the moral reprobation inspired by such acts. Morality and law are thus inter-related and interact upon one another in a highly complex way.

X (*c*) *The enforcement of morality by law.* Nowadays the law regards some kinds of behaviour (e.g. parking offences) as criminal although, in general, they may not be looked upon as morally wrong; likewise other forms of conduct (e.g. adultery) may be morally condemned but not legally prohibited; yet again, some practices considered to be immoral (e.g. lying) are illegal only in certain circumstances (as in the case of perjury or misleading trade descriptions).

It has sometimes been argued that the law should proscribe all immoral acts, as failure to do so would ultimately cause the disintegration of society. The impracticality of this, however, stems from the plurality of values and cultures in our society (whereby there is a total lack of consensus over particular moral issues, e.g. abortion) as well as from the evolutionary nature of morality (whereby what is immoral and criminal at one moment might not be so shortly afterwards). As *deviance*—the breaking of rules—can be said to be created by the very framing of those rules, one should examine the manner in which any particular moral attitude (as opposed to a competing one) becomes embodied in the law; often it simply reflects the views of a restricted section of society (politicians, judges, etc.) at one moment. Legislation of morality "for its own sake" is notably exemplified by the so called *victimless crimes*, which involve only the participants themselves (e.g. smoking cannabis).

Thus there is a school of thought to the effect that, although morality and law are inter-related, there are some aspects of human behaviour which may be considered immoral but which should not be legally proscribed so long as they do not harm other people. Both sides of the argument have been well illustrated in:

(*i*) *The Report of the Wolfenden Committee* (*1957*). The *Committee on Homosexual Offences and Prostitution* recommended that homosexual behaviour between consenting adults in private should cease to be a criminal offence, and stated that "there must remain a realm of private morality and immorality which is, in brief and crude terms, not the law's business" In *The Enforcement of Morals*, Lord Devlin opposed these findings and wrote that

"societies disintegrate from within more frequently then they are broken up by external pressures. There is disintegration when no common morality is observed and history shows that the loosening of moral bonds is often the first stage of disintegration, so that society is justified in taking the same steps to preserve its moral code as it does to preserve its government. ... The suppression of vice is as much the law's business as the suppression of subversive activities."

In *Law, Liberty and Morality*, Professor H. L. A. Hart supported the findings of the Report and wrote that: "the only part of the conduct of anyone, for which he is answerable to society, is that which concerns others. In the part which merely concerns himself, his independence is, of right, absolute. Over himself, over his own body and mind the individual is sovereign."

(*ii*) *The decisions of the House of Lords.* Two leading cases relating to the role of the courts as guardians of morality have been:

Shaw v. *Director of Public Prosecutions* (*1962*): The appellant had conspired with others to publish and sell *The Ladies' Directory*, a magazine containing advertisements by prostitutes, inviting perverted practices as well as ordinary intercourse. The House of Lords upheld his conviction of conspiracy to corrupt public morals (a common law offence resurrected from the eighteenth century). Viscount Simonds said: "in the sphere of criminal law, I entertain no doubt that there remains in the courts of law a residual power to enforce the supreme and fundamental purpose of the law, to conserve not only the safety and order but also the moral welfare of the state". Dissenting from the majority decision, Lord Reid said: "Notoriously there are wide differences of opinion today how far the law ought to punish immoral acts which are not done in the face of the public. Some think that the law already goes too far, some that it does not go far enough. Parliament is the proper place and, I am firmly of opinion, the only proper place to settle that."

Knuller (*Publishing, Printing & Promotions*) v. *D. P. P.* (*1973*): The appellants were directors of a company which published the *International Times*, a magazine containing advertisements inviting readers to meet the advertisers for the purpose of homosexual practices, in some cases for money. Although the Sexual Offences Act 1967 had legalised homosexual acts in private by consenting adults, the House of Lords upheld a conviction of conspiracy to corrupt public morals on the grounds that this offence could be committed by encouraging conduct which, though not itself illegal, might be calculated to corrupt public morals. Referring to the 1967 statute, Lord Reid said: "I find nothing in that Act to indicate that Parliament thought or intended to lay down that indulgence in these practices is not corrupting. I read the Act as saying that, even though it may be corrupting, if people choose to corrupt themselves in this way, that is their affair and the law will not interfere. But no licence is given to others to encourage the practice."

3. The concept of justice. Justice, the ultimate goal towards which the law should strive, is but one segment of morality because, although unjust acts (e.g. unjustifiably punishing one child more severely than another) may be considered immoral, the converse is not true and immoral acts (e.g. cruelty to children) cannot be described as unjust. "Fairness" is the closest synonym to justice, a vital function of which is the attainment of equality. Lawyers who subscribe to the doctrine of positivism are concerned only with the fairness of the legal process and whether a law derives from a valid source (statute or precedent) but not whether it is just or unjust. Laymen, however, are more prone to examining the outcome of a case and its accordance with a subjective commonsense view of fair play. Thus it is necessary to distinguish between:

(*a*) *The concept of formal justice.* This implies fairness in the *application* of the law and in the *conduct* of trials, whereby like cases are treated alike under existing rules which are impartially and generally applied. There must be equality of treatment to the parties—but this does not mean that all persons should be treated similarly, regardless of individual differences—because, where necessary, allowance must be made for mental incapacity or minority, etc. It means rather that everyone classified as belonging to the same category for a particular purpose must be treated in the same way; however, formal justice does not prescribe how such classification should be made.

(*b*) *The concept of substantive justice.* This implies fairness in the *substance* of the law and in the *outcome* of trials, but it is simply an observer's subjective impression. As suggested by Lord Lloyd, there are possibly two ways in which a legal system might aspire to attain substantive, as well as formal, justice:

(*i*) *The infusion of flexibility.* A basic problem in law is the need to reconcile two opposing requirements—uniformity and flexibility. The former is necessary to provide certainty and predictability, whereas the latter is desirable because no rule can provide for every possible case. Sentencing is only one area where totally rigid rules would be wholly inappropriate. For example, formal justice may prescribe that everyone convicted of a particular offence shall be fined, but substantive justice might lead to a variation of fines, dependent upon the wealth of the offender, so that the legal sanction has an equal effect on all. Flexibility also enables the law to adapt itself to social change; as a society alters, so do its needs and the legal system should take account of new social, economic and political requirements.

(*ii*) *The embodiment of value-judgments in a constitution.* States which are newly established, or which lack a reasonably homogeneous population with generally accepted values, may need the incorporation of certain principles (relating, for example, to

8   I. THE FOUNDATIONS AND FUNCTIONS OF LAW

essential human rights) in a formal Constitution. "The value of this
approach is not only that it makes explicit some of the underlying
assumptions of the legal system, but also that it may render these
into obligatory and overriding legal norms capable of being enforced by legal process" (Lloyd: *The Idea of Law*).

4. The fulfilment of interests. The American jurist Roscoe Pound
(1870–1964) viewed law as a form of social engineering, whose
function it is to maximise the fulfilment of the *interests* of the
community and to promote the smooth running of the machinery
of society. He defined an interest as *a demand or desire or expectation which human beings, either individually or in groups ... seek to
satisfy.* In this context, three related problems are:

(*a*) *The classification of interests.* Pound divided interests into
the following categories:

(*i*) *The individual interests.* These involve claims related
to an individual's life and comprise interests of *personality* (e.g.
protection of physical integrity; freedom of will, honour and
reputation, privacy, belief and expression; freedom from deception; free choice of location), *domestic relations* (e.g. parents,
children, spouses, claims by members of a family against each
other and against third parties, also the protection of marriage) and
substance (e.g. livelihood, property, freedom to carry on enter-
prises and make contracts, ability to rely upon promises, protection
of contractual relations, immunity from interference and freedom
of association).

(*ii*) *The public interests.* These involve claims related to the
necessities of public life and comprise interests of the state "considered as a juristic person" (e.g. security, freedom of action, etc.)
and as "guardian of social interests" (*see* (*iii*)).

(*iii*) *The social interests.* These involve claims of the social
group constituting the community and comprise (1) *general security*
(security of peace and order, health and safety, transactions and
acquisitions); (2) *security of social institutions* (domestic, religious,
political and economic); (3) *general morals* (security against acts
offensive to general moral sentiments); (4) *general progress* (the
"self-assertion of the social group towards higher and more
complete development of human powers" including, for example,
free speech and cultural progress); (5) *individual life* (the demand
of each individual to live a human life according to society's
standards); and (6) *conservation of social and human resources.* As
individual interests are not asserted in the name of a particular
person, they are all really social interests; it can also be argued that
public interests are merely social interests seen in another light.

(*b*) *The recognition of interests*. Pound believed that interests exist independently of the law, that they seek "recognition and security" and that the law satisfies as many as it can. However, not all interests (e.g. the right to privacy) are fully recognised by English law—particularly on account of the difficulty in initiating legislation and the limitation of judicial creativity. Furthermore, what interests exist in society and which of these are, or should be, recognised are questions of a mixed sociological, ethical and legal nature.

A significant political development in Britain during the past decade has been the growth of *pressure groups*, i.e. bodies of persons not constituting a political party but with the aim of influencing governmental decision-making (e.g. by deputations to Parliament, mass meetings, media propaganda, demonstrations, strikes, squatting, violence, etc.). Resultant influence may well be determined by a group's activities and publicity, rather than by its size or the strength of its case, nevertheless such bodies, together with opinion polls, etc., provide a means of determining which interests merit recognition.

(*c*) *The balancing of interests*. As illustrated below (*see* (*i*)-(*iv*)), different interests may easily conflict with each other and, in order to decide which should prevail, comparisons and evaluations must be made. These necessitate an assessment of the values of society—with the result that legal decisions can be influenced by an ideology.

In some countries (e.g. the USA and Federal Republic of Germany) attempts have been made to identify certain "preferred values", which override lesser ones in the event of conflict, but they relate only to a particular period in time and cannot give rise to any permanent order of priority.

With regard to contemporary English values, "national and social safety override all other considerations and sanctity of the person is superior to sanctity of property but, beyond this, the pattern is kaleidoscopic and not hierarchical" (R. W. M. Dias; *Jurisprudence*). Examples of competing interests exist in respect of:

(*i*) *The freedom of speech*. As shown at VIII, 6(*b*), the interest of free speech can be overridden by that of protecting personal reputation, maintaining racial harmony or preserving state security.

(*ii*) *The inviolability of property*. Property comprises not only land, buildings and goods but also intangibles such as debts, patents, copyright, business goodwill, etc. With regard to land, a conflict can arise between the occupier's interest of enjoyment and that of his neighbour not to suffer interference. Reasonable use of one's property is perfectly legitimate, even though it may cause harm to a neighbour (as in *Bradford Corporation* v. *Pickles* (*1895*); see VIII, 5(*a*)(*ii*)); however, if he suffers material discomfort through indirect and unlawful interference (e.g. by permitting branches, roots, noxious fumes, noise, germs, vibrations, etc., to enter his land) then he can protect his own interest by way of a civil action for the tort of nuisance.

(*iii*) *The right of employment.* The right formerly enjoyed by employers to engage and dismiss persons at will has now been circumscribed by legislation, notably the Trade Union and Labour Relations Act 1974, the Employment Protection (Consolidation) Act 1978, etc. Resultantly, employees are protected from "unfair dismissal", are entitled to lump sum payments if declared redundant, are permitted to join trade unions and to take strike action, also are allowed time off for certain public duties. Discrimination is proscribed by the Equal Pay Act 1970, the Sex Discrimination Act 1975 and the Race Relations Act 1976.

Recently denial of the "right to work" has arisen mainly from trade union interests, where an employee refuses to join a union in a "closed shop" situation; however, under the Employment Act 1980, an employee dismissed for not joining a union can appeal to an industrial tribunal which can award compensation, direct reinstatement or require re-engagement in a similar job.

(*iv*) *The protection of marriage.* The conflict between societal interest in marriage stability and the individual spouse's interest in release from an unhappy union is reflected in the provision of the Matrimonial Causes Act 1973. This enables a decree of dissolution to be granted on the sole ground of the *irretrievable breakdown* of the marriage.

However, to establish this, the petitioner must satisfy the court of one or more of the following facts: (1) adultery by the respondent since the marriage and the fact that the petitioner finds it intolerable to live with him or her; (2) such behaviour by the respondent that the petitioner cannot reasonably be expected to live with him or her; (3) desertion by the respondent for two years immediately before the petition; (4) five years' separation before the petition (but only two years if the respondent consents to the decree).

Except in the case of exceptional hardship (upon the petitioner) or exceptional depravity (by the respondent), petitions for divorce cannot be presented within three years of the marriage. Initially a *decree nisi* is granted and the marriage subsists until the decree is

I. THE NATURE OF LAW

made *absolute* (usually six weeks later); after that date, either spouse may marry again.

5. The maintenance of social order. Every society constitutes a set of human arrangements whereby life is ordered and sustained. In different societies such arrangements are not identical, as they manifest a wide, and often contradictory, range of cultural values. In relatively small groups social control is exercised with minimal resort to formal agencies. The desires to achieve acceptance by one's peers and to avoid ostracism, ridicule or gossip can be coercive mechanisms—with the resultant paradox that the individual may be most effectively controlled in that group in which he feels most free. Growth in population size creates the need for *authority* (i.e. *legitimate power* attached to *office*, invoking the respect, submission or reverence accorded to those who represent the office) and also law. The latter still remains only one technique of social control and, in addition to the resolution of conflict, it has dual functions:

(*a*) *The control of harmful activities.* As a marker of boundaries of "acceptable conduct", the law provides sanctions for breaches thereof and the purpose of these may be deterrent, reformative or preventative (i.e. precluding the commission of further offences). The legal control of activities defined as "harmful" embraces:

(*i*) *The offences against the person.* These are summarised in XXI.

(*ii*) *The offences against property.* These are summarised in XXII.

(*iii*) *The offences against the state.* These include (1) treason (a breach of duty of allegiance owed to the Crown, as defined in the Statute of Treasons 1351); (2) sedition (oral or written publication of words with a seditious intention); (3) offences under the Official Secrets Acts (*see* VIII, **6**(*b*)(*ii*)); (4) unlawful assembly, rout and riot (*see* VIII, **6**(*c*)(*ii*)); (5) blasphemy and obscenity; (6) offences in respect of controlled drugs; (7) perjury (a false or knowingly untrue statement by a sworn witness or interpreter in a judicial proceeding); (8) contempt of court (*see* IV, **2**(*c*)) etc.

(*b*) *The protection of freedom.* The maintenance of social order must be reconciled with the preservation of individual *freedom*, an objective sought by most people and consequently deserving of legal protection. It is, however, difficult to interpret as it is a normative word and valuational in concept—since preference for one particular system, as offering greater freedom than others, stems from the fact that it is free in those things which the observer values most.

(*i*) *Absolute freedom*. At one time the concept of *absolute freedom* prevailed and freedom was viewed largely in terms of *liberty* or the *absence of restraints*.

(*ii*) *Laissez-faire*. During the eighteenth and nineteenth centuries the economic and political background of *laissez-faire* reflected *individualism*—the belief that the individual had supreme value and that society was only a means to individual ends. It was thought the law should interfere as little as possible with individual freedom—thus legislation to limit working hours could be seen as infringing the unfettered right to make any desired contract.

(*iii*) *Collectivism*. As a reaction to individualism, collectivism emerged with its organic view of society as an entity distinct from, and superior to, the individuals comprising it. This has greatly enlarged the role of the state which must, of necessity, impose restraints upon the individual. Where rules are minimal or unenforced, some groups and individuals are able to increase their own liberties and freedoms at the expense of others. Thus respect for the rights and freedoms of some people must give rise to certain limitations on the freedom of others, who become subject to corresponding obligations and duties.

In this way *relative freedom* is sought but, in a society with a plurality of cultures and values, there will always be areas of disagreement as to what conduct is "acceptable" and which activities are "harmful". The role of the state should therefore be that of protecting freedoms of highest general value, bearing in mind that freedom is situational in time and place, being subject to new interpretations and modifications as conditions and circumstances alter.

THE DEVELOPMENT OF THE COURTS

6. The establishment of the common law. By the time of Edgar (944–75), England was divided into shires, hundreds and vils, with two main "communal" courts—the *shire moot* and the *hundred moot*. From 1066 William I began the policy of centralisation which led to one government for the whole of the country, one legal system and one body of law. Being the national law of the country, as opposed to local laws and customs, it can thus be called *common law* but, confusingly, this term has two other possible meanings.

(*a*) In the first place, it is used to describe case law arising from

the decisions of all courts (including those of equity (*see* I, 7(*a*));
and

(*b*) secondly, it can connote the law applied in the common law
courts (*see* 7(*a*)(*i*)–(*iv*)) (as opposed to those of equity).

After the Norman Conquest, the chief central administrative
organ was the *Curia Regis* ("Court of the King"), which dealt with
legislation and also big trials. As time went on, it took over much
of the administration of justice from the local courts, because it
could enforce attendance and judgments: it could also offer a
rudimentary form of trial by jury, which was preferred by many to
the old methods of proof (ordeal by fire, water, etc.). As its work
consequently increased, the need arose for a division of functions
and thereafter the principal elements in the history of the common
law were:

(*a*) *The development of the common law courts.* Over a period
of time, the judicial functions of the Curia Regis were divided
among the following courts:

(*i*) *The Court of Exchequer.* This broke away from the
Curia Regis in the reign of Henry I (1100–35) and its officials were
termed Exchequer Barons. Originally their jurisdiction was purely
fiscal (e.g. deciding questions between the Crown and the tax-
payer). From about 1320 it gained common law jurisdiction by the
use of the writ *Quominus*, whereby a plaintiff could plead the
fiction that he was a debtor of the King and could not repay his debt
because of the defendant's failure to pay him.

Fictions have played a significant part in English law and are
statements or suppositions which are known to be untrue but which
are not permitted to be denied, in order to overcome some difficulty
and to secure substantive justice.

(*ii*) *The Court of Common Pleas.* In 1178 Henry II
appointed five justices of the Curia Regis to hear pleas between
subjects not involving the King, also *real actions* (i.e. those
concerning land). This court was less popular than that of the
Exchequer or King's Bench (*see* (*iii*)), which derived benefit from
association with the King's own rights and also the use of fictions.

(*iii*) *The Court of King's Bench.* This separated from the
Curia Regis in 1230 but for a time it remained closely connected
with the affairs of the King and travelled the realm until 1400, after
which it remained at Westminster. The court exercised civil and
criminal jurisdiction, both at first instance and also in an appellate
capacity.

(*iv*) *The Courts of Assize.* Henry I established the practice
of periodically sending to each country *itinerant justices*, who

derived their authority from royal commissions. The *Commission of Assize* covered civil cases, the *Commission of Oyer and Terminer* related to grave criminal offences, and the *Commission of Gaol Delivery* was a direction to try all the prisoners in a certain gaol. In a modified form, this system existed until the implementation of the Courts Act 1971.

(*v*) *The Courts of Exchequer Chamber.* These were constituted to establish a system of appeals and initially they comprised merely informal meetings of the King's Bench and Common Pleas judges in the reign of Edward II (1307–27), to discuss cases of particular importance or complexity. Subsequently *Courts of Error* were created and in 1830 a Court of Exchequer Chamber was set up to hear appeals from all the common law courts; from this court appeal lay to the House of Lords. The courts of Exchequer, Common Pleas, King's Bench and Exchequer Chamber all existed up till the implementation of the Supreme Court of Judicature Acts 1873–75 (*see* 7(*c*)(*i*)).

(*b*) *The development of forms of action.* When anyone wished to seek the aid of the royal justices, it was first necessary to obtain a writ from the Chancellor. This specified the injury complained of and directed the sheriff that the person named should right the wrong or state his reasons before the King's justices.

These *original writs*, which started proceedings, were quite separate from the *judicial writs*, which were issued during the proceedings to bring parties before the court, settle subsidiary questions and enforce judgment. Injuries of common occurrence gave rise to common forms of original writs and, in its turn, each original writ attracted towards it certain judicial writs.

This practice gave rise to separate *forms of action*, peculiar not only in their original writ but also in the relevant procedure. As no action could be started without a writ, the common law was forced into a very restricted mould.

(*c*) *The development of mercantile law.* The growth of trade, internally and externally, involved contact with legal principles not always embodied in the common law. There thus evolved a separate body of law administered in two principal types of court:

(*i*) *The Pie Powder Courts.* These were created by franchises (royal grants) which entitled a borough corporation or a lord of the manor to hold a market or fair, the name is derived from *pieds poudrés* (dusty feet). Their jurisdiction covered actions for breach of contract, petty offences and almost all matters arising in the area of the fair. Procedure was swift and the courts were not hampered by the technical rules of the common law. In a modified form, exercising civil jurisdiction, some (e.g. the Bristol *Tolzey Court*) existed until the implementation of the Courts Act 1971.

(*ii*) *The Courts of the Staple*. These were created by the Statute of the Staple 1353 in the staple towns (i.e. those designated by Edward I to be exclusive markets for certain staple products such as wool, tin, lead and leather). The jurisdiction covered debts, breaches of contract and trespass but the influence of the courts declined as the staple system decreased in importance. In the sixteenth and seventeenth centuries the jurisdiction of the common law courts embraced actions based on merchants' customs and in the eighteenth century Lord Mansfield CJ established the recognition of mercantile customs as part of the common law.

(*d*) *The development of the High Court of Admiralty*. After the Battle of Sluys (1340) the admirals and their deputies held courts which sat at the main sea ports, but, early in the fifteenth century, these were absorbed by the *High Court of Admiralty*. This enjoyed criminal jurisdiction in respect of piracy and other offences at sea and also a wide civil jurisdiction over maritime and mercantile affairs.

Its popularity led to opposition from the common law courts, which envied the profits of its business, and by 1660 its influence had greatly diminished. However, its prize jurisdiction had been left untouched and this became important in the Napoleonic Wars. b.tween 1840–61 a series of Acts gave the court practically full power over almost all cases connected with shipping. The Supreme Court of Judicature Acts 1873–75 (*see* 7(*c*)(*i*)) passed Admiralty jurisdiction to the Probate, Divorce and Admiralty Division of the High Court, and the Administration of Justice Act 1970 transferred it to the Admiralty Court of the Queen's Bench Division.

(*e*) *The development of ecclesiastical jurisdiction*. One of the effects of the Norman Conquest was the establishment of *canon law* in England, by the creation of ecclesiastical courts administering law based on that of Rome. In 1533–34, following the Reformation, the system was radically altered; canon law was subordinated to the law of the State and the jurisdiction of the ecclesiastical courts was threefold:

(*i*) *penal* (dealing with clerical offences and acts contrary to religion and morals);

(*ii*) *civil* (matrimonial causes and testamentary matters); and

(*iii*) *ecclesiastical* (concerning the real and personal property of the Church).

As religious toleration grew, the jurisdiction in matters of morals and religious faith declined, while divorce and probate passed respectively to the *Divorce and Matrimonial Causes Court* and the *Probate Court*, under the Matrimonial Causes Act 1857 and the Court of Probate Act 1857. Subsequently, the Supreme Court of Judicature Acts 1873–75 transferred their jurisdiction to the Probate, Divorce and Admiralty Division of the High Court (the Family Division, under the Administration of Justice Act 1970).

(*f*) *The development of law reporting.* The growth of case law and the significance of precedent depended to a great extent on the availability of recorded judicial decisions. The earliest reports were found in the *Year Books* (*c.* 1270–1560), which comprised a series of unofficially reported cases, thought to be notes by law students or pamphlets issued by barristers for the use of their students. Digests of Year Book cases appeared in the *Abridgments* (*c.* 1480–1670) and from 1560–1780 there was a proliferation of *Private Reports*, published for profit and varying in quality. The *Term Reports* (1785–1800) began the practice of issuing regular and contemporary reports, but the multiplicity of private publications led to the establishment in 1866 of the *Incorporated Council of Law Reporting*, which currently issues the *Law Reports* (LR) and *Weekly Law Reports* (WLR). In addition, there still exist other publications, such as the *All England Reports* (All ER) and a significant feature of the English legal system is the fact that law reports are published by independent organisations.

7. The development of equity. After the Norman Conquest a party was sometimes unable to obtain redress for a wrong from the common law courts—possibly owing to the narrow confines of the forms of action, or the inadequacy of the remedy provided (damages). In such cases, petitions were presented to the King, as the "fountain of justice" and, as time went on, they were passed to the Chancellor for a report. This became increasingly formal and by 1377 petitioners were addressing themselves to the Chancellor alone. In 1474 the first decree made by the Chancellor's own authority was issued and herein lies the commencement of the jurisdiction of the *Court of Chancery*.

Chancellors were, in most cases, ecclesiastics and remedies were sought in the name of reason, right and conscience. Hence the Chancellor would examine the principles and moral standards of any act complained of and, if he considered that the workings of a law had proved contrary to the Law of God, he would assume the right to prevent its operation, if the plaintiff's hardship could be attributed to that law. In practice, he issued a decree, in the form of a declaration of rights, or of an order to the defendant—and, if the latter failed to comply, he was sent to prison until he decided to "purge" his conscience. This type of justice came to be known as *equity* and it merits examination in regard to its relationship with the common law.

(*a*) *The comparison*. Comparison between the common law and equity is best effected by considering:

(*i*) *The scope*. The common law is a complete system, whereas equity consists of certain rules devised to meet peculiar difficulties. It is a valuable supplement to the common law but it is not a completely separate system, and is intended merely to fill in gaps in the legal system. As Sir Henry Maitland has said: "Equity is a gloss on the Common Law".

(*ii*) *The procedure*. Equity was not bound by complicated forms of action, cases were heard in English (instead of Latin) and it developed new procedures unknown to the common law, e.g. the use of the *subpoena* (*see* III, 1(*b*)(*i*)), *discovery of documents* and *interrogatories* (*see* V, 2(*c*), (*d*)).

(*iii*) *The rights*. Equity introduced the whole area of the law of trusts, enforcing the obligation of trustees to beneficiaries. In connection with mortgages, it developed the *equity of redemption*, enabling borrowers to retain the security for their debts after the due date for payment.

(*iv*) *The remedies*. Whereas the only common law remedy was damages, awarded to a successful party *as of right*, equity introduced new remedies which were all *discretionary* (it being up to the court's discretion whether or not the remedy should be awarded). These included the injunction, the *decree of specific performance* and the *declaratory judgment* (*see* VI, 2(*b*)–(*d*)) also the right of *rescission* (withdrawing from a contract) and the appointment of *receivers*. All of these were unknown to the common law but, conversely, the Chancery Court could not award damages until 1858.

To emphasise the comparison between the common law and equity, the jurisdiction of the latter has been described as "exclusive, concurrent and auxiliary". In its *exclusive* sense it has recognised actions unknown to the common law (e.g. concerning trusts and mortgages); in a *concurrent* way it has added to existing common law remedies (e.g. by introducing the injunction and decree of specific performance); in an *auxiliary* sense it has employed a more flexible procedure.

(*b*) *The conflict*. In view of its advantages, the Court of Chancery became very popular, so that Vice-Chancellors were appointed and additional courts were established in various parts of the country. This led to strong opposition from the common lawyers, on account of loss of business and conflicting verdicts. The dispute reached its peak in the *Earl of Oxford's Case (1616)* and James I forced Lord Chancellor Ellesmere and Lord Chief Justice Coke to present the matter to the Attorney-General, Sir Francis Bacon, for arbitration. On Bacon's recommendation, the King then ordered that, in cases of conflict with common law, equity should prevail. This ruling was never completely accepted by the common law courts and some competition continued until the systems were finally co-ordinated.

(c) *The co-ordination.* Originally equity had no binding rules and each Chancellor gave judgment in a way that satisfied his own conscience. This led to considerable criticism concerning the possible outcome of cases and in the seventeenth century John Selden, an eminent jurist, summed up the situation by saying that "Equity varies with the length of the Chancellor's foot". In order to stifle such criticism, Lord Nottingham (Lord Chancellor 1673–82) commenced a systematisation of rules based on precedent and, by the nineteenth century, equity had become as rigid as the common law itself. Endless delays in reaching decisions were caused by scandalous patronage, a multiplicity of useless officials and an inadequate number of judges.

Reforms were effected by the Court of Chancery Act 1851 (which created a *Court of Appeal in Chancery*, as an intermediate appellate tribunal between the Chancery Court and the House of Lords), the Common Law Procedure Acts 1852–54 and the Chancery Amendment Act 1858, all of which tended to bring in line the procedures of common law and equity. Finally, concurrent administration was effected by the Supreme Court of Judicature Acts 1873–75 which brought about:

(i) *The establishment of the unified Supreme Court of Judicature.* This absorbed the following courts: Queen's Bench, Common Pleas, Exchequer, Chancery, Divorce and Matrimonial Causes, Probate, Appeal in Chancery and Exchequer Chamber. The Supreme Court was to consist of the *Court of Appeal* (exercising the jurisdiction of the former courts of Exchequer Chamber and Appeal in Chancery), also the *High Court*, originally comprising five Divisions but reduced in 1980 to three—Queen's Bench Division, Chancery Division, Probate, Divorce and Admiralty Division; the last-named was replaced (under the Administration of Justice Act 1970) by the Family Division.

(ii) *The fusion of the administration of common law and equity.* Law and equity were to be administered by all judges in all courts—thus complete relief could be obtained in one court. In this way matters of administration *but not principles* were fused by their being vested in one tribunal. The Acts have *not* abolished the distinction between equitable and legal rights; furthermore, equitable remedies have remained discretionary.

(*iii*) *The establishment of common procedures in the Supreme Court.* The Acts abolished the forms of action and introduced new rules of procedure—whereby, in particular, that relating to the issue of writs and other stages of litigation was much simplified.

PROGRESS TEST 1

1. Trace the development of law in a primitive society. **(1)**

2. Contrast and compare law and morality. **(2)**

3. Examine the arguments concerning the enforcement of morality by law. **(2)**

4. Distinguish between law and justice. **(3)**

5. Examine the nature and balancing of interests. **(4)**

6. How does the law control activities defined as "harmful"? **(5)**

7. What is meant by "absolute" and "relative" freedom? **(5)**

8. Trace the development of the common law courts prior to 1873. **(6)**

9. Why is equity considered to be a "gloss" upon the common law? **(7)**

10. "The Judicature Acts 1873–75 fused the administration but not the principles of Common Law and Equity." Examine this statement. **(7)**

CHAPTER II

The Sources of Law

THE EMERGENCE OF LAW

1. The origination of law. In relation to law, it can be said that there are in fact four possible meanings of the word *source*.

(*a*) There is the *literary source*, i.e. the records in which the law is to be found (e.g. statutes and law reports).

(*b*) There is the *formal source*, i.e. the authority which gives force to the rules of law (Parliament).

(*c*) There is the *historical source*, i.e. the causes which induced the creation of law (e.g. religious beliefs, moral standards, the reports of Royal Commissions, etc.).

(*d*) There is the *legal source*, i.e. the means by which the law is brought into existence.

English courts will recognise and apply only law that has originated from the following legal sources:

(*a*) *The recognition of custom.* Anglo-Saxon customs constitute the oldest source of English law and a distinction can be drawn between those which were general and those which were local in nature. *General custom* implies the body of rules which were obeyed throughout the realm but, by the fourteenth century, most of them had been absorbed into case law by court decisions (*see* (*c*)). *Local custom* implies rules and traditions obeyed by the inhabitants of a particular locality and for the requirements for recognition today *see* 2(*a*)–(*i*).

(*b*) *The enactment of legislation.* In some countries which have "written" constitutions (e.g. the USA) the courts have the power of *judicial review,* in that they can declare invalid the provisions of any enacted legislation which are inconsistent with the constitution. There are no such limitations on the law-making ability of the British Parliament, which enjoys *legal sovereignty* as, theoretically, it can make or repeal legislation on any topic—thereby creating what is termed *statute law.* To sustain future sovereignty, Parliament has always been subject to one legal restriction—in that technically it cannot enact any unrepealable provision which would bind its successors. Nevertheless, many treaty obligations impose restraints on passing legislation which is inconsistent with them.

Acts (or statutes) are initiated as *bills*, which are of three main types:

    (*i*) *The public bills.* These relate to the public as a whole and they are introduced by the Government in either the House of Commons or the House of Lords. For the procedure for their enactment *see* 3(*a*)–(*h*).

    (*ii*) *The private members' bills.* These are simply public bills which are introduced by back-bench MPs or peers (instead of by the Government).

    (*iii*) *The private bills.* These relate to particular localities, bodies or persons. Public bills which affect private interests in some way are termed *hybrid*.

A second attribute of sovereignty is that Parliament alone enjoys the power to make all law but, through pressure of business and lack of time, it cannot adequately discharge this function and thus it statutorily delegates law-making authority, (*see* 4(*a*)–(*c*)).

(*c*) *The decisions of courts.* By the doctrine of *stare decisis* ("the standing of decisions"), courts must follow rules and principles enunciated in the decisions of superior courts (and sometimes their own previous decisions). For a full explanation of this system of *judicial precedent, see* VII, 2. Case law originating in all courts may be called *common law, see* I, 6.

(*d*) *The law of the European Community.* In April 1951 France, West Germany, Italy, Belgium, the Netherlands and Luxembourg signed a treaty in Paris establishing (in July 1952) the *European Coal and Steel Community* (*ECSC*). In March 1957 the same six countries signed two further treaties in Rome creating (in January 1958) the *European Atomic Energy Community* (*Euratom*) and the *European Economic Community* (*EEC* or *"Common Market"*). Originally each Community was headed by a separate Council and a Commission but, under the Merger Treaty of 1965, these were amalgamated (in 1967) into one Council and one Commission. Under the Treaty of Accession, signed in Brussels in January 1972 (and ratified in Britain by the European Communities Act 1972), the United Kingdom, Denmark and the Republic of Ireland joined the Community on 1st January 1973. The Hellenic Republic was admitted to membership on 1st January 1981.

Within the Community there are four main institutions.

    (*i*) *The Council of Ministers.* This is the supreme decision-making body; it comprises ministers from each member-country and it meets in Brussels or Luxembourg.

    (*ii*) *The Commission.* This consists of fourteen commissioners representing (but totally independent of) the member-countries (with two each from France, West Germany, Italy and the United Kingdom). Its functions are to formulate recommendations, deliver opinions, take decisions, exercise powers conferred by the Council and supervise the application of community legislation.

(*iii*) *The European Parliament.* This was originally nominated by and from the national legislatures but it became subject to direct elections in the member-countries in June 1979. The 434 members serve for fixed terms of five years, meet for about a week each month in Luxembourg or Strasbourg and sit not as national delegations but as European political groups. Under the European Assembly Elections Act 1978, the eighty-one United Kingdom members represent specially created constituencies.

The Parliament has a purely advisory role and no legislative powers. However, it has the right to address questions to the Council and the Commission about all aspects of community business and, in extreme circumstances, it could dismiss the entire Commission (by passing a motion of censure with a two-thirds majority and more than half of the total members voting in favour).

Under the Budgetry Treaty of 1970, a "preliminary draft budget" is drawn up by the Commission with the Council controlling 75 per cent of the expenditure and the Parliament is empowered to amend only the remainder (termed "non-obligatory" items); nevertheless, if there are overwhelming reasons, it can reject the entire budget.

(*iv*) *The European Court of Justice.* This comprises ten judges and four advocates-general. It is situated in Luxembourg.

The main elements of community law are described at 5(*a*)–(*c*).

2. The recognition of custom. There are divergent opinions as to whether custom is actually law until it is recognised by the courts and, in order to gain recognition and enforcement, a local custom must fulfil the following requirements:

(*a*) *It must apply to a definite locality*, e.g. a shire, borough, parish or manor.

(*b*) *It must have been exercised from "time immemorial".* This became fixed at 1189 but, in practice, it is merely necessary to prove that a custom goes back as far as living memory, as in—

Mercer v. *Denne* (*1905*): The plaintiff claimed a customary right for the fishermen of Walmer to dry their nets on the defendant's land, proving user for seventy years—and, by reputation, even longer. The defendant pleaded that, at times since 1189, such land has been under the sea. Judgment was given for the plaintiff.

(*c*) *It must have been continuously exercisable*, without lawful interruption. It need not have been continuously *exercised* but at all times it must have been possible to exercise it lawfully, as in—

Wyld v. *Silver* (*1963*): A private Enclosure Act of 1799 entitled the inhabitants of a parish to hold an annual "fair or wake" on certain land but they had not exercised the right within living memory and the owner wished to build upon it. It was held that an injunction should be granted to restrain him from doing so.

(*d*) *It must have been exercised peaceably, openly and as of right*, i.e.—*nec vi, nec clam, nec precario* (not by violence, stealth or entreaty). The need for permission to be granted would invalidate an alleged custom, as in—

Mills v. *Corporation of Colchester* (*1867*): The defendants owned an oyster fishery and had, since the time of Elizabeth I, held courts at which, on payment of a fee, they granted fishing licences to inhabitants of certain parishes who had been apprenticed to licensed fishermen. The plaintiff had the qualifications and was willing to pay the fee but the defendants refused to grant him a licence. It was held that the inhabitants had never had such enjoyment *as of right* and there was merely a practice of granting licences in certain cases; therefore judgment must be given for the defendants.

(*e*) *It must be reasonable*. The test is "whether it is in accordance with the fundamental principles of right and wrong", as illustrated in—

Wolstanton Ltd. v. *Newcastle-under-Lyme Borough Council* (*1940*): The lord of a manor claimed the right to take minerals from under a tenant's land in accordance with an alleged manorial custom, and without paying compensation for resulting damage. It was held that this was unreasonable.

(*f*) *It must be definite in nature and scope*, as illustrated in—

Wilson v. *Willes* (*1806*): The tenants of a manor claimed an alleged custom entitling them to take from the manorial common as much turf as they required for their lawns. It was held that this was too uncertain.

(*g*) *It must be recognised as binding* on those affected by it.

(*h*) *It must not contravene statute law or the common law.*

(*i*) *It must not be inconsistent with other customs,* otherwise they cannot all be good.

THE CREATION OF LAW

3. The enactment of statutes. A public bill introduced in the House of Commons is subject to the following procedure:

(*a*) *The First Reading.* This is purely formal, with the Speaker calling the name of the sponsoring minister who bows from a seated position. The Clerk of the House reads out the short title of the bill, which can then be printed and published.

(*b*) *The Second Reading.* On the day appointed the sponsoring minister moves "that the bill be now read a second time" and he makes his main speech in favour of it. An Opposition spokesman then speaks and thereafter the House debates the *main principles* of the bill. Alternative methods of achieving its purpose may be discussed but changes in its detailed provisions are not permitted. Finally, the sponsoring minister (or another from the same department) sums up and the motion is normally carried.

(*c*) *The Committee Stage.* The bill is now automatically committed to a Standing Committee, unless a specific motion is passed to commit it to a Committee of the Whole House. The committee debates amendments to individual clauses but they must be *in detail* and cannot affect the general principles of the bill (which were agreed at the Second Reading). Sometimes voluntary timetable agreements are reached between the Government and Opposition Chief Whips to impose time-limits on the Committee and remaining stages of certain bills. If such an agreement cannot be reached, the Government may invoke the *guillotine* (a formal allocation of time).

(*d*) *The Report Stage.* On completion of the above stage, the chairman of the committee reports the bill to the House, so that amendments can be considered, other members can put down amendments (subject to the Speaker's discretion), the Government can propose amendments or new clauses, and the bill can also be sent back to committee. Where a bill authorises any expenditure, a financial resolution is taken by the House at this stage.

(*e*) *The Third Reading.* The amended bill is now finally reviewed by the House often formally and without debate at the end of the Report Stage, unless there is a motion on the Order Paper in the name of six members that the question "be not put forthwith". In such circumstances there is a brief debate and only minor verbal amendments may be made.

(*f*) *The Readings in the House of Lords*. The Clerk of the House takes the bill to the House of Lords, where it goes through the same stages as in the Commons. However, the Committee Stage takes place in a Committee of the Whole House, as there are no standing committees—though sometimes suitable bills are sent to a Public Bill Committee. Even when no amendments have been made in committee, there may be a Report Stage and amendments can be moved then (also on the Third Reading). When the Lords make no amendment to a bill, it is presented for the Royal Assent but, if amended, it is returned to the Commons.

(*g*) *The consideration of the Lords' amendments*. The House of Commons considers the Lords' amendments and, if it disagrees with them, a committee is set up to show the reasons for the disagreement and there is an exchange of messages between the two Houses. Should it prove impossible to resolve differences, the Commons can invoke the provisions of the Parliament Acts 1911–49, which limit the Lords' delaying power to one year.

(*h*) *The Royal Assent*. This is signified by letters patent under the great seal and signed by the monarch. Under the Royal Assent Act 1967, a bill is duly enacted if the assent is notified to each House separately by its Speaker or Acting Speaker. This has replaced a traditional ceremony which is normally used only at the end of a session.

The judicial interpretation of statutes is described at VII, 1.

4. The delegation of legislative authority. Those to whom Parliament statutorily delegates law-making authority include local authorities (which issue by-laws), public corporations (e.g. British Railways Board Regulations) and professional bodies (e.g. the Law Society), but by far the greatest delegation relates to ministers and government departments. This is because statutes nowadays tend to express general principles and to empower appropriate departments to regulate administrative details—generally by means of what are termed *statutory instruments* (SIs). The widespread use of these can be appreciated from the fact that in 1983 the numbers of Acts passed and SIs made were respectively 60 and 1,969.

Significant aspects of delegated legislation are:

(*a*) *The merits*. As well as effecting economy in parliamentary time, delegated legislative powers can be speedily exercised, also easily amended or annulled; thus unforeseen difficulties can be overcome and the lessons of experience may be quickly utilised (e.g. in road traffic regulations). Parliament often does not possess adequate knowledge to deal with technical subject-matter and many regulations (e.g. relating to building, health, etc.) are best framed by experts. Furthermore, Parliament is not always in session and its legislative procedures are cumbrous; consequently emergencies and urgent problems can be more easily overcome by delegating law-making functions.

(*b*) *The defects.* Loose definition in delegating legislative authority can enable ministers and departments to assume wide powers which may not be fully understood by the public, as subordinate legislation is subject to far less publicity than statutes. A much criticised practice is that of delegating the power to amend a statute (often the parent Act itself); this is known as the *Henry VIII Clause* and it usurps the prime function of Parliament. Such authority may be acceptable when it is necessary to amend local Acts, consequent on the passing of a major statute, or for the purpose of bringing an Act into operation effectively. Otherwise, however, it is undesirable to place such extensive legislative powers in unfettered ministerial hands.

(*c*) *The supervision.* This can take two forms:

(*i*) *The parliamentary control.* The Statutory Instruments Act 1946 prescribed procedures for the parliamentary supervision and the publication of statutory instruments. Most parent Acts provide that SIs made under them shall not come into force until "laid before Parliament" (which in the Commons entails the delivery of a copy to the Votes and Proceedings Office)—though it is sometimes possible for them to take effect beforehand, provided that the Speaker and Lord Chancellor are notified. Subsequent parliamentary action depends on the provisions concerning them. Some may have to be laid for information only (and no further action is taken); others may take effect unless a *negative resolution* is carried within forty days of their being laid; finally, there are those which need the closest scrutiny—and these are not permitted to become effective until they have been approved with an *affirmative resolution*. Every SI laid before each House is examined by a Joint Committee on Statutory Instruments, with a chairman from the Commons and a quorum of two. It can require written or oral explanations from the department concerned and, after receiving these, it determines whether an SI should be drawn to the attention of Parliament for any reason (other than its merits or policy) and particularly in certain specified circumstances.

(*ii*) *The judicial control.* Though the courts cannot question the provisions of a statute, they can overrule delegated legislation on the ground that it is *ultra vires* (beyond the powers of) the issuing authority, as in—

> *Daymond* v. *South West Water Authority* (*1975*): The Water Authorities (Collection of Charges) Order 1974 authorised water authorities to demand charges in respect of sewage disposal from ratepayers who were not connected to sewers, but the House of Lords held that this provision exceeded the powers conferred by the Water Act 1973, and was consequently invalid.

5. The law of the European Community. Community law must be applied in the courts of member-countries and prevails over national law. Basically it comprises:

(*a*) *The primary legislation.* This consists of all the treaties mentioned at 1(*d*) and also, in the United Kingdom, the European Communities Act 1972, and European Assembly Elections Act 1978, the European Assembly (Pay and Pensions) Act 1979 and the European Communities (Greek Accession) Act 1979.

(*b*) *The secondary legislation.* The Council or the Commission enacts community legislation by way of:

(*i*) *The regulations.* These have general application, are binding in their entirety and are directly applicable in all member-countries (without reference to their legislatures).

(*ii*) *The directives.* These are binding on the member-countries to which they are addressed in respect of the results to be achieved—but the method of implementation is left to the national authorities. They are appropriate measures where there is a need to modify existing national legislation.

(*iii*) *The decisions.* These are binding in their entirety on those to whom they are addressed (i.e. not only member-countries but also corporate bodies and natural persons). They are generally appropriate for implementing community law, granting authorisations or exceptions, imposing fines or obligations, etc.

In the House of Commons there is a Select Committee on European Secondary Legislation (comprising sixteen members with a quorum of five), which draws the attention of the House to any legal or political implications, also any possible effects on United Kingdom law. In the House of Lords a Select Committee on the European Community exercises somewhat wider powers, in that it can report on the merits of community proposals and it works through six sub-committees.

(*c*) *The decisions of the European Court of Justice.* The decisions of this court have the binding force of law in member-countries but it has no means of enforcing its judgments. Its jurisdiction relates principally to:

(*i*) *The proceedings against member-countries.* These may be brought by the Commission for alleged violation of treaty obligations, also by other member-countries, provided that they first "refer the matter to the Commission".

(*ii*) *The proceedings against community institutions.* These may be brought by member-countries, other community institutions and, in certain circumstances, by corporations or private persons. The procedure may be used to "appeal for annulment" of a regulation, directive or decision; to obtain a judgment to the effect that the Council or Commission has failed to act, when required to do so by a treaty; also to obtain compensation for damage caused by the illegal act of an institution.

(*iii*) *The preliminary rulings.* When a case involving the validity and interpretation of the treaties (or acts of the institutions) reaches a national court from which there is no appeal (e.g. the House of Lords), it *must* first be referred to the European Court for a *preliminary ruling*, unless the matter has previously been decided by the court. When this interpretation has been given, it is applied by the national court in deciding the case. Lower courts *may* (but do not have to) follow this procedure.

PROGRESS TEST 2

1. What are the principal sources of English law? **(1)**

2. What is the significance of the sovereignty of Parliament? **(1)**

3. Outline the requirements for the recognition of a local custom. **(2)**

4. Describe the procedure for the enactment of a public bill. **(3)**

5. Why and to whom does Parliament delegate legislative powers? Assess the advantages and disadvantages of the system. **(4)**

6. How effective do you consider the safeguards for delegated legislation to be? **(4)**

7. What is the importance of the European Communities Act 1972? **(5)**

8. Outline the nature of the European Community law which must be recognised in United Kingdom courts. **(5)**

CHAPTER III

The Institutions of the Law

THE COURTS OF FIRST INSTANCE

1. The structure of the courts. The word *court* can, in fact, have two possible connotations—as, in addition to being a place where justice is administered, it can also mean the judge(s) officiating there. Every court exercises *jurisdiction*, a term that can also have two meanings as it can signify either the power of the court to hear particular proceedings or, alternatively, the geographical area within which its judgments can be enforced. The jurisdiction exercised by a court may be *original* (or *first instance*, i.e. the hearing of cases for the first time) or *appellate* (i.e. the hearing of appeals from lower courts).

Basically, the courts of England and Wales fall into two categories:

(*a*) *The courts of criminal jurisdiction.* These deal with infringements of the criminal law of the state (ranging from minor parking offences to murder, etc.). First instance jurisdiction is exercised in the magistrates' courts (*see* **2(*a*)**) and Crown Court (*see* **2(*c*)**), wherein:

(*i*) *The proceedings are initiated with a summons or warrant.* A *summons* is a document from a court office requiring a person to attend before the court. A *warrant* is issued by a magistrate, after a written information upon oath, and it is addressed to a police officer, ordering him to bring the person named before the court. Warrants are used for serious offences or where a summons is ignored. Witnesses can be compelled to attend a magistrates' court by means of a summons or warrant but, in the Crown Court, a *witness summons* or *witness order* is used.

(*ii*) *The Crown prosecutes the accused*, with a view to *punishment*. Thus the form of citing cases is, for example, *R. v. Smith (1982)*—where R. stands for *Rex* (King) or *Regina* (Queen) and Smith is the accused. In practice, most prosecutions are initiated by the police but certain more serious offences necessitate prosecution by the *Director of Public Prosecutions* (*see* **IV, 1(*e*)**).

Prosecutions may be instituted by government departments (e.g. the Board of Inland Revenue, the Commissioners of Customs and Excise, etc.) and by private persons—though, in this case, it may be necessary to obtain the consent of the Attorney General (*see* IV 1(*b*)), the Director of Public Prosecutions or a judge.

(*iii*) *The accused is presumed to be innocent until proved guilty.*

(*iv*) *The case cannot be discontinued*, without the leave of the court or a *nolle prosequi* (*see* IV, 1(*b*)) entered by the Attorney-General.

(*v*) *The Crown may pardon a crime.*

(*b*) *The courts of civil jurisdiction.* These are concerned mainly with *litigation*—i.e. *actions* (legal disputes) between private parties, mostly in respect of breaches of contract and torts (civil wrongs such as negligence, trespass, nuisance, defamation, etc.). First instance jurisdiction is exercised primarily in the county court (*see* 3(*b*)) and High Court (*see* 3(*c*)), wherein:

(*i*) *The proceedings are initiated with a summons or writ.* County court proceedings are commenced with a *default summons* or *ordinary summons* (*see* V, 4(*a*)) and the attendance of witnesses can be compelled with a *witness summons*. High Court proceedings are initiated with a *writ* (*see* V. 2(*a*)) and witnesses can be compelled to attend by the issue of a *subpoena* (a writ requiring attendance *under a penalty*).

(*ii*) *The plaintiff sues the defendant*, seeking *redress*. Thus the form of citing cases is *Smith* v. *Brown* (*1980*)—where Smith is the plaintiff and Brown the defendant.

(*iii*) *There is generally no presumption favouring either party.*

(*iv*) *The action may be withdrawn by the plaintiff*, at any time.

(*v*) *The Crown cannot pardon a tort.*

Certain acts (e.g. causing injury by dangerous driving) may give rise to both a criminal prosecution and also a civil action.

2. The courts of criminal jurisdiction. In England and Wales criminal jurisdiction is exercised by:

(*a*) *The magistrates' courts.* In London and certain other places, courts are presided over by *stipendiary magistrates*, who are salaried barristers or solicitors of at least seven years' standing. In other magistrates' courts, however, there are *justices of the peace* (JPs), who have no essential legal qualifications but who are nowadays simply required to undergo a course of basic training. Furthermore, they are advised on matters of law and procedures by the *clerk of the court*, generally a barrister or solicitor of at least five years' standing. JPs are appointed on behalf of the Queen by the Lord Chancellor (*see* IV, **1**(*a*)), to whom recommendations are made by local advisory committees. Any person or organisation may suggest candidates to an advisory committee which, in its turn, must ensure that each bench of magistrates is broadly representative of all sections of the community. JPs are paid only travelling, subsistence and financial loss allowances and, except in certain circumstances, they are transferred to a supplemental list at the age of seventy. This administration of justice by laymen has been criticised on several grounds—notably the lack of uniformity in sentences (though this is partially overcome by circulating lists of suggested and average penalties), the absence of legal knowledge—with possibly a corresponding excess of influence by the clerks—the tendency to accept police evidence as indisputable, and the lack of suitable persons who can devote the necessary time. The merits, on the other hand, derive from the close contact of the JPs with everyday life and local conditions, the democratic value of associating laymen with the administration of criminal law, the resultant speedy provision of justice and the ensuing economic benefits to the state. Magistrates' courts exercise criminal jurisdiction in respect of offences committed by persons who have attained the age of seventeen and, under the Magistrates' Courts Act 1980, these fall into three categories:

(*i*) *The offences triable only summarily*. There are many relatively minor offences which are tried, without a jury, by "benches" of not less than three (nor more than seven) JPs, who decide whether the accused is guilty and, if so, award appropriate punishment. Often offences have stipulated punishments and, in general, the maximum is a fine of £2,000 and/or six months' imprisonment.

(*ii*) *The offences triable only on indictment*. More serious offences are tried by a jury in the Crown Court (*see* **2**(*c*)) where, as shown at V, **1**(*a*), the proceedings commence with a reading of the *indictment*. This is a formal document specifying the offence(s) which the accused is alleged to have committed and, in the event of there being more than *one*, each is set out in a separate paragraph called a *count*.

Before an indictable offence reaches the Crown Court, however, a magistrates' court must first carry out a preliminary investigation in what are called *committal proceedings*. The procedure differs from that of a summary trial in that there is no plea of "guilty" or "not guilty" and, if discharged, the accused may subsequently be charged again (*see* V, **1**(*b*)(*iii*)); furthermore, *depositions* (signed transcripts of evidence) must be taken down in writing. If all the evidence consists of written statements, also if all the accused are legally represented and do not plead that there is no case to answer, then the Magistrates' Courts Act 1980, s. 6 permits the court to commit the accused for trial without itself considering the evidence. This procedure saves a great deal of time and is often used.

To avoid prejudicing any subsequent trial, s. 8 of the same Act (as amended by the Criminal Justice (Amendment) Act 1981) makes it an offence to publish or broadcast in Great Britain details of committal proceedings, other than certain bare facts (e.g. the court, offence, names, decision, bail, legal aid, etc.), unless the accused requests that the restriction be lifted (e.g. to publicise the need for further witnesses), or is not committed for trial.

If the magistrates decide that a *prima facie* case (i.e. a case in which, at *first appearance*, there is some evidence in support of the charge) has been made out, they commit the accused (on bail or in custody) to the Crown Court for trial. At the same time they must make a *witness order* (requiring necessary witnesses to attend the trial) and warn the accused that, if he wishes to plead an alibi, he must give notice of it to the magistrates or police within eight days of committal.

(*iii*) *The offences triable either way*. Certain offences (listed in the Magistrates' Courts Act 1980, Sched. 1) may be tried either summarily or on indictment. Before deciding which is the more suitable method, a magistrates' court must first allow the prosecutor and the accused to make representations concerning the mode of trial. It must then consider the nature and circumstances of the alleged offence, whether the punishment which it could inflict would be adequate and any other relevant matters.

Where it appears that summary trial is the more suitable alternative, the court must explain to the accused that either he can consent to be so tried, or he can elect trial by jury. It must also point out to him that, if he is tried summarily and convicted, he may be committed to the Crown Court for sentence, if his past record merits greater punishment than the magistrates can inflict.

Certain offences (listed in the Magistrates' Courts Act 1980 Sched. 2) must be tried summarily if the value does not exceed £200. Conversely, summary trial is not possible if the Attorney-General, Solicitor-General or Director of Public Prosecutions is prosecuting and applies for the offence to be tried on indictment.

(*b*) *The juvenile courts*. These are composed of not more than three JPs (at least one of whom must be a woman) selected from a special panel to hear charges against children (under fourteen) and young persons (fourteen to seventeen), though homicide or offences for which long imprisonment is likely necessitate committal for trial. The parent or guardian of the juvenile must attend and may be required to pay any fine. The public are excluded, the police do not wear uniform and the words "conviction" or "sentence" must not be used. Press reports must not identify a juvenile unless the court or Home Secretary directs otherwise.

(*c*) *The Crown Court.* Under the Courts Act 1971 the former courts of Quarter Sessions and Assize were replaced by the Crown Court. Jurisdiction is exercised by High Court judges, circuit judges and recorders (*see* IV, **2**) but, for appeals and proceedings on committal for sentence, they sit with two to four JPs.

The courts' service is divided into six circuits (Midland and Oxford, North-eastern, Northern, South-Eastern, Wales and Chester, Western), each of which has towns designated as first-, second-, and third-tier centres. First-tier centres deal with both civil and criminal cases and are served by High Court and circuit judges. Second-tier centres deal with criminal matters only, and the same applies to third-tier centres which are served by circuit judges and recorders.

For the purposes of trial, criminal cases can be classified as follows:

(*i*) *The class 1 offences.* These must be tried by a High Court judge and they comprise murder, genocide, misprision of treason and treason-felony, offences for which a person may be sentenced to death (*see* VI, **1**(*a*)), or offences under the Official Secrets Act 1911, s. 1. Incitement, attempt or conspiracy to commit any of these offences also fall within this classification.

(*ii*) *The class 2 offences.* These must be tried by a High Court judge, unless released by a presiding judge (the High Court judge assigned to have particular responsibility for a circuit). They comprise manslaughter, infanticide, child destruction, abortion, rape, sexual intercourse or incest with a girl under thirteen, offences under the Geneva Conventions Act 1957, s. 1, sedition, mutiny, piracy, and also incitement, attempt or conspiracy to commit any of these offences.

(*iii*) *The class 3 offences.* These may be tried by a High Court judge, circuit judge or recorder and they comprise all indictable offences other than those in classes 1, 2 and 4. They include also robbery or assault with intent to rob, wounding or causing grievous bodily harm with intent.

(*iv*) *The class 4 offences.* These may be tried by a High Court judge, circuit judge or recorder (but generally one of the last two) and they are mainly the offences which are triable either way (*see* **2**(*a*)(*iii*)). They comprise also causing death by reckless driving, burglary, offences under the Forgery and Counterfeiting Act 1981, and incitement, attempt or conspiracy to commit any of these offences.

3. The courts of civil jurisdiction. In England and Wales, civil jurisdiction is exercised by:

(*a*) *The magistrates' courts*. These enjoy limited civil jurisdiction, comprising mainly:

(*i*) *The hearing of domestic proceedings*. Under the Magistrates' Courts Act 1980, ss. 65–74, members of a special panel of justices form a domestic court, which is empowered to make orders for financial provision for parties to a marriage and children of the family; orders for the custody of children under the age of eighteen (also the supervision of, and access to, them); orders for the committal of children to the care of a local authority; and also orders for the protection of a party to a marriage or a child of the family (attaching, if necessary, a power of arrest). The public is excluded from domestic proceedings and there are restrictions on newspaper reports.

(*ii*) *The recovery of statutory debts*. Only certain creditors, authorised by statute, may pursue their debtors in the magistrates' courts and principal examples are the collectors of taxes and rates, also public utility undertakings such as water, gas and electricity, etc.

(*iii*) *The granting of licences*. These include public houses, betting shops, etc.

(*b*) *The County Courts*. Throughout England and Wales there is a network of small courts to try cases involving limited sums of money. They are divided into districts, each of which has one or more circuit judges assigned to it. The administrative staff is headed by a *registrar* (generally a solicitor) who may hear certain cases (with his decision subject to review by the judge) and who can also act as an arbitrator (*see* 7 below). Jurisdiction is limited to causes of action arising within a court's locality and, under the indicated sections of the County Courts Act 1984, it consists principally of:

(*i*) *The common law jurisdiction (s. 15)*. This comprises actions in contract and tort (excluding libel or slander), subject to a limit of £5,000.

(*ii*) *The real property jurisdiction (s. 21)*. This comprises actions for the recovery of possession of land, also disputes as to title (right to ownership), provided that the rateable value does not exceed £1,000.

(*iii*) *The equity jurisdiction (s. 23)*. This relates to the administration of estates; the execution, declaration and variation of trusts; the foreclosure and redemption of mortgages; the maintenance and advancement of minors; the dissolution of partnerships; also relief against fraud or mistake, subject to a limit of £30,000.

(*iv*) *The family provision proceedings* (*s. 25*). These mainly comprise applications for orders under the Inheritance (Provision for Family and Dependants) Act 1975, s.2.

(*v*) *The admirality jurisdiction (s. 27)*. Some county courts have jurisdiction (to a limit of £5,000 – or £15,000 in salvage) in respect of damage received (or done) by a ship; loss of life or personal injury sustained from defects or wrongful acts by personnel in a ship; loss of, or damage to, goods carried; salvage, towage and pilotage of ships, aircraft, etc.

(*vi*) *The probate jurisdiction* (*s. 32*). This comprises actions concerning the grant or revocation of *probate* (the judicial authentication of an effective will by someone who has died *testate*) or *letters of administration* (granted when a person has died *intestate*— not leaving a valid will), if the net value of the estate is less than £15,000.

(*c*) *The High Court*. This has its headquarters at the Royal Courts of Justice in London but, under the Courts Act 1971, s. 2, it may sit anywhere in England and Wales—normally at first-tier centres (*see* 2(*c*)). Under the Supreme Court Act 1981, the High Court comprises the following three Divisions.

(*i*) *The Queen's Bench Division*. Here judges, sitting singly, deal mainly with cases in contract and tort—generally if the amount claimed exceeds the county court limit of £5,000.

Included in the Division is an *Admiralty Court* (handling maritime matters, e.g. collisions at sea and salvage), and also a *Commercial Court* (dealing with mercantile documents, insurance, banking, etc.). Additionally, the Queen's Bench Division has a *Divisional Court* (comprising generally three judges, sitting together) which hears certain criminal appeals (*see* 4(*b*)), appeals from the Solicitors Disciplinary Tribunal (*see* IV,3(*b*)(*iii*)), applications for judicial review (*see* VI, 2(*e*)), applications for the writ of *habeas corpus* (*see* VI, 2(*f*)) and matters relating to arbitration. The administrative staff of the Division is headed by eight barristers, known as *Masters*.

(*ii*) *The Chancery Division*. This is headed by the *Vice-Chancellor* and its jurisdiction covers contentious probate cases, partnerships, mortgages, trusts, administration of deceased persons' estates, rectification and cancellation of deeds, land law, company law and revenue matters. Many of the cases are not disputes but rather proposed courses of action requiring judicial approval.

Included in the Division is the Patents Court, whilst the *Divisonal Court* hears appeals from county courts in bankruptcy matters. The administrative staff of the Division is headed by seven solicitors, known as *Chancery Masters*.

(*iii*) *The Family Division*. This replaced the former *Probate, Divorce and Admiralty Division*. Its jurisdiction covers matrimonial causes (notably defended and complex divorce cases), adoption, wardship, guardianship of minors, legitimacy, consent to the marriage of minors, title to property in dispute between spouses, validity of marriages, presumption of death and granting of probate or letters of administration.

The *Divisional Court* hears appeals from magistrates' courts and county courts in family law matters. The administrative staff of the Division is headed by *Registrars*.

(*d*) *The Restrictive Practices Court*. Established by the Restrictive Trade Practices Act 1956, this court is served by six judges and seven lay members. It may sit as a single court, or in two or more divisions, and it judicially examines:

(*i*) *Commercial conduct detrimental to the interests of consumers*. The Fair Trading Act 1973 created the Monopolies and Mergers Commission and also the office of Director General of Fair Trading. If it appears to the Director that a course of conduct in a business is unfair to consumers (or detrimental to their interest), he must endeavour to obtain an assurance that it will be discontinued. Should he not receive such an assurance (or should it be broken), he may bring proceedings in the Restrictive Practices Court.

(*ii*) *Resale price maintenance*. The Resale Prices Act 1976 declared void any contractual conditions by suppliers to establish a minimum resale price of goods, unless they were specifically exempted by the Restrictive Practices Court.

THE COURTS OF APPEAL

4. The courts of criminal appeal. Appeals may be made against the decisions of the above courts and, in such circumstances, the party appealing is known as the *appellant*, whereas the other is termed the *respondent*. From the criminal courts appeals lie as follows:

(*a*) *From the magistrates' court*. There is a general right of appeal to the Crown Court on a point of law or fact but, if the accused has pleaded guilty, appeal lies only against sentence. The Crown Court may confirm, vary or reverse the decision appealed against *or* may remit the matter with its opinion to the original court *or* may make such other order as it thinks fit. If either party to a proceeding before justices wishes to question *either* a conviction on a point of law *or* the Crown Court's decision on an appeal, he may apply to have the *case stated* in a Divisional Court of the Queen's Bench Division.

(*b*) *From the Crown Court.* Appeals by convicted persons lie to the Court of Appeal (Criminal Division) and, if they are against *conviction* on solely *a question of law*, they lie *as of right*. However, if an appeal is against conviction on a matter of *fact* (or *mixed law and fact*), the leave of the Court of Appeal, or a certificate from the trial judge, is necessary. An appeal against *sentence* (where the penalty is not one fixed by law) lies only by leave of the Court of Appeal.

Appeals are heard by not less than three judges and the Court of Appeal (Criminal Division), which is headed by the Lord Chief Justice, comprises *Lords Justices of Appeal*, also the judges of the Queen's Bench Division (who may sit at the request of the Lord Chief Justice, after consultation with the Master of the Rolls (*see* IV, 1(*c*) and (*d*)).

(*c*) *From the Queen's Bench Divisional Court or Court of Appeal.* Appeal lies to the House of Lords—but only with the leave of the court below or of the House of Lords, if the court below has certified that *a point of law of general public importance* is involved, and it appears, either to the court below or to the House of Lords, that the point is one that ought to be considered by the House of Lords.

Under the Appellate Jurisdiction Act 1876, appeals to the House are heard by the *Lords of Appeal*. These comprise the Lord Chancellor, ex-Lords Chancellor, *Lords of Appeal in Ordinary* (persons who have held high judicial office and who are appointed to assist in the appellate functions of the House), also any other peers who hold (or have held) high judicial office (e.g. the Lord Chief Justice and the Master of the Rolls). The quorum is three and each peer delivers a separate judgment, the verdict being by a majority.

5. The courts of civil appeal. From the civil courts appeals lie as follows:

(*a*) *From the magistrates' court.* There is no general right of appeal in civil matters and any right that does exist must originate in the Act that empowers the magistrates to make a particular order (e.g. a Divisional Court of the Family Division hears appeals in respect of separation, maintenance and adoption orders, etc.). However, either of the parties in civil proceedings may request to have a *case stated* to a Divisional Court of the Queen's Bench Division, on the grounds that the magistrates have acted in excess of their jurisdiction or erroneously on a point of law.

(*b*) *From the county court.* As shown at 3(*c*)(*ii*), appeals in bankruptcy are heard by a Divisional Court of the Chancery Division, whilst those concerning guardianship of minors lie to a Divisional Court of the Family Division. Otherwise, appeals from the county court lie to the Court of Appeal (Civil Division); this is headed by the Master of the Rolls and comprises the Lords Justices of Appeal also High Court judges (who may sit at the request of the Lord Chancellor).

(*c*) *From the High Court.* From any Division appeal lies to the Court of Appeal (Civil Division) but leave must be obtained if the appeal has already been determined by a Divisional Court. Under the Administration of Justice Act 1969, s. 12, a judge of the High Court may give a certificate for an appeal from his decision to go direct to the House of Lords (by-passing the Court of Appeal—a procedure known as "leap-frogging"), if it involves a point of law of general public importance. The certificate can be granted only if the point of law relates to the construction of an Act or statutory instrument, or if it is covered by a previous decision of the Court of Appeal or House of Lords, and provided that both parties consent.

(*d*) *From the Restrictive Practices Court.* Appeal on any question of law lies to the Court of Appeal (Civil Division) in England and Wales, the Court of Session in Scotland, or the Court of Appeal in Northern Ireland.

(*e*) *From the Court of Appeal* (*Civil Division*). Appeal lies to the House of Lords, by leave of the Court or of the House, and leave will be granted only if a point of law of general public importance is involved.

THE ALTERNATIVES TO THE COURTS

6. The system of administrative tribunals. Many claims and disputes are nowadays settled by special tribunals, which are quite separate from the ordinary courts of law. There are in fact over 2,000 of more than fifty different types and terminology is remarkably confusing, as not all are actually named as "tribunals" (e.g. the local valuation courts, the General and Special Commissioners of Income Tax). Furthermore, they are sometimes referred to as "statutory tribunals", despite the fact that a few (e.g. the Criminal Injuries Compensation Board) were not constituted by

Act of Parliament. More commonly, they are often termed "administrative tribunals" (implying that they handle disputes involving government departments or public authorities), nevertheless some are concerned only with problems between individuals (e.g. the rent tribunals and the industrial tribunals). It also cannot be assumed that all of them settle claims and disputes, as there are those which have instead a licensing role (e.g. the Traffic Commissioners).

The composition of tribunals varies greatly but many comprise a chairman, a clerk (usually a civil servant from the relevant government department) and a number of (normally) unpaid lay members. Sittings may be in public or private, legal representation is generally allowed, evidence is rarely taken on oath, but adjudication is impartial. Significant aspects of such tribunals are:

(a) *The merits.* Compared with courts of law, tribunals are advantageous in respect of:

(i) *The procedure.* This is speedy, cheap, flexible and informal. Decisions are achieved quickly and delays are minimised; no fees are usually payable and the wide discretionary powers of a tribunal frees it from the rigidity of judicial precedent (*see* VII, 2). Litigious procedure does not provide the right atmosphere for the implementation of social schemes and the greater informality of a tribunal is less intimidating to the individual. Tribunals are not limited to considering only the information provided by the parties, but they can themselves play an active part in ascertaining facts.

(ii) *The expertise.* Tribunals may include persons with relevant qualifications (e.g. doctors determining disabilities) and others who, from their experience, acquire expert knowledge of their particular subject-matter.

(iii) *The work-load.* The courts would be over-burdened if they had to decide all the constantly recurring and relatively trivial individual problems heard by tribunals. The resultant need to increase the judiciary might cause a lowering of standards.

(b) *The defects.* Most tribunals receive little publicity; the reasons for their decisions are not always made known and there are variations in rights of appeal. Wide discretionary power can cause decisions to be unpredictable and inconsistent, also technical experts do not always act with impartiality.

(c) *The supervision.* The Tribunals and Inquiries Act 1971 (consolidating similarly-named Acts of 1958 and 1966) has provided safeguards by way of:

(i) *The Council on Tribunals.* This consists of ten to fifteen members appointed by the Lord Chancellor and the

Secretary of State for Scotland, having also a Scottish Committee. The Parliamentary Commissioner ("Ombudsman"), is an *ex officio* member of both the Council and the Committee. The Council's jurisdiction covers England, Scotland and Wales, and its principal functions are to review and report on the constitution and working of *certain* tribunals specified in a Schedule to the Acts; to consider and report on matters referred to it concerning *any* tribunal; also to be consulted before procedural rules are made for any of the scheduled tribunals. However, it has no say in the issues to be decided and it cannot overrule the decisions which are made.

(*ii*) *The provision for appeals.* If requested to do so, tribunals must give reasons for their decisions and many have statutory provision for appellate procedure. However, if a party to proceedings before specified tribunals is dissatisfied in point of law, he may appeal to the High Court or require the tribunal to state a case for the opinion of the High Court. Notwithstanding the provisions of any previous Act, the High Court may supervise the proceedings of any tribunal by way of judicial review (*see* VI, 2(*e*)).

(*iii*) *The approval of appointments.* Chairmen of specified tribunals must be selected from a panel of persons appointed by the Lord Chancellor and no Minister, other than the Lord Chancellor, may remove a member of a specified tribunal from office, except with the consent of the Lord Chancellor or the Lord President of the Court of Session in Scotland.

(*d*) *The judicial standards.* The common law imposes on courts, tribunals and individuals who "act judicially" an obligation to apply the *rules of natural justice*, and these are:

(*i*) *Audi alteram partem* (*"Hear the other side"*). This means that nobody shall be penalised by a judicial decision unless given prior notice of all relevant information which will be used against him, adequate time to prepare his case and the opportunity (orally or in writing) to state his case. Application of the rule may sometimes be impracticable—if, for example, there are justifiable grounds for confidentiality (e.g. in respect of medical or other personal reports), but natural justice or fairness must be observed in the reaching of any decision which seriously affects individual interests (notably livelihood, office, status or right to property), as illustrated in *Re Godden* (*1971*) at VI, 2(*e*)(*iii*).

(*ii*) *Nemo iudex in causa sua* (*"No one a judge in his own cause"*). This means that no one may act judicially *if he has a pecuniary interest in the proceedings or is subject to a reasonable suspicion* (*or real likelihood*) *of bias.* Any pecuniary interest, however small, would disqualify an adjudicator unless the parties were made aware of it and waived their objection, or unless all available adjudicators were affected by a disqualifying interest. There is no need to prove *actual bias*, because only a "reasonable suspicion" or "real likelihood" is necessary—and this may accrue on numerous grounds—e.g. kinship, prejudice, a commercial or professional relationship, a personal friendship or animosity, membership of a particular organisation, etc. The rule is illustrated in *R*. v *Leicestershire Fire Authority, ex parte Thompson* (*1978*) at VI, **2**(*e*)(*ii*).

7. The process of arbitration. To provide an alternative to litigation, many commercial contracts contain an *arbitration agreement*, requiring any dispute between the parties to be referred, for determination, to one or more persons called *arbitrators*. The agreement may specify them by name or supply a method of selection (e.g. appointment by a relevant trade association). Under the Administration of Justice Act 1970, provision is made for judges of the Commercial Court to act as arbitrators in commercial disputes. The circuit judges and registrars in county courts may also so act. If one party to an arbitration agreement starts proceedings in the ordinary courts, before submitting to arbitration, the other party may, before delivering pleadings, apply to the court to stay the action. In addition to arbitration agreements, various statutes also provide for the settlement of specified kinds of dispute by arbitration—regardless of any objection by the parties.

Arbitrators are not judges or court officials but hearings must be conducted in a judicial manner, in accordance with the Arbitration Act 1950, which empowers arbitrators to administer oaths, and the parties to seek writs of subpoena. Where reference is made to two arbitrators, they may at any time appoint an *umpire* to settle differences between them (and they must do so immediately, if they cannot agree). Where reference is made to three arbitrators, the decision of any two is binding, unless a contrary intention was expressed in the arbitration agreement.

An arbitrator's decision is called an *award* and, if the unsuccessful party fails to comply with it, he can be sued on it—or the successful party can seek leave of the High Court for the award to become an order of the court. The Administration of Justice Act 1977 provides that, if the sum involved is within a county court's jurisdiction (*see* III, **3**(*b*)), it is recoverable as if payable under an order of that court. An application to the High Court would preclude one to the county court, and vice versa.

Under the Arbitration Act 1975, the United Kingdom ratified the New York Convention on the Recognition of Foreign Arbitral

Awards, whereby arbitral awards made in other countries party to the convention are recognised and enforced in the United Kingdom, also court proceedings are stayed concerning disputes which should be arbitrated.

In examining arbitration, consideration must be given to:

(a) *The merits.* The main advantages of arbitration lie in:

(i) *The economy.* Although arbitrators' fees can be high, there is no court fee and no expense need be incurred in preparing pleadings; often there is no necessity for legal representation.

(ii) *The convenience.* The time and place of the hearing can be arranged to suit the convenience of the parties. Proceedings are private and informal.

(iii) *The speed.* No delay is incurred in waiting for the case to be called. The fact that an arbitrator can have special expertise in the subject-matter of a dispute can obviate the time-consuming calling of witnesses to provide a judge with basic information. Furthermore, the decision is immediate.

(b) *The defects.* If the subject-matter of a dispute is complex, normal court procedure might provide a more satisfactory solution. Moreover, if the unsuccessful party challenges an arbitral award (*see* (c)(ii) below), litigation could then ensue and negate financial economy.

(c) *The supervision.* The Arbitration Act 1979 provides the High Court with the following jurisdiction:

(i) *The determination of preliminary points of law.* At any time during the proceedings a party may, with the consent of the arbitrator or of all the other parties, apply to the High Court for the determination of a question of law. However, such an application will be entertained only if it might produce substantial savings in costs to the parties and provided that the question of law is one on which leave to appeal (under (c)(ii) below) would be likely to be given. Appeal from the High Court's decision lies to the Court of Appeal only with the leave of the High Court which must certify that the point of law is one of general public importance, or one which should be considered by the Court of Appeal for some special reason.

(ii) *The judicial review of awards.* In general, an arbitral award is final (*res judicata, see* VII, 2(b)(iii)). However, with the consent of all the other parties or with leave of the court, any party may appeal to the High Court on a question of law. Leave of the court will be granted only if the determination of the question could substantially affect the rights of one or more of the parties and (with certain exceptions) provided that they had not entered into an "exclusion agreement", precluding a right of appeal. The High Court may confirm, vary or set aside an award, also remit it with an opinion to the arbitrator for his reconsideration within three months. Appeal from the High Court's decision lies to the Court of Appeal on the same conditions as in (c)(i) above.

PROGRESS TEST 3

1. Outline the organisation and jurisdiction of the Crown Court. (2)

2. Comment critically upon the role of magistrates in the administration of justice. (2)

3. Consider the functions and value of the county courts. (3)

4. Assess the importance of the Court of Appeal. (4, 5)

5. A purchased a motor-cycle from B and discovered it to be unroadworthy. Advise A as to the courts to which he may apply to pursue a claim against B. (3, 5)

6. C is charged with committing murder. Describe the courts before which C may appear, assuming he takes every opportunity of appealing against conviction. (2, 4)

7. Explain the role of tribunals in the English legal system. (6)

8. Assess the importance of the Tribunals and Inquiries Act 1971. (6)

9. Explain how arbitration can be an inexpensive and efficient alternative to judicial trial. (7)

10. Consider the extent to which the High Court exercises supervision over arbitration. (7)

CHAPTER IV

The Personnel of the Law

THE JUDICIAL AND LEGAL OFFICES

1. The principal offices of the law. The principal legal and judicial offices in England and Wales are described below and it should be appreciated that the Lord Chancellor and Law Officers are political appointees—i.e. leading lawyers who support the party in power, and who lose office if there is a change of government. However, the other appointments are not political and do not involve loss of office.

(*a*) *The Lord Chancellor*. The Lord Chancellor is appointed on the recommendation of the Prime Minister (who is not required to consult the House of Lords) and, in examining his role, it is of value to distinguish:

(*i*) *The executive functions*. As a member of the Cabinet, he is the government's chief legal and constitutional adviser. Ministerially, he is responsible for the Land Registry, the Public Trustee Office and the Public Record Office. He is the holder of the Great Seal, which authenticates documents such as letters patent.

(*ii*) *The legislative functions*. In the House of Lords he plays three roles: (1) He presides over the House (sitting on the woolsack) but he has far less power than the Speaker in the Commons, as the Lords are masters of their own procedure and themselves decide matters of order. (2) He may speak as a Minister of the Crown (standing at the despatch box). (3) He may participate in debates as an ordinary peer (standing unwigged beside the woolsack).

(*iii*) *The judicial functions*. As head of the Judiciary, he presides over the House of Lords as the final court of appeal, and also the Judicial Committee of the Privy Council. He is president of the Supreme Court of Judicature (*see* I, 7(*c*)(*i*)), the Court of Appeal and the Chancery Division. He nominates the *puisne* ("younger" i.e. ordinary) High Court judges, circuit judges, recorders, Queen's Counsel (3(*a*)(*ii*)) and stipendiary magistrates. On behalf of the Crown, he appoints JPs, county court registrars and the Official Solicitor (*see* (*f*)). He also appoints the Council on Tribunals (*see* III, **6**(*c*)(*i*)), selects the chairmen of specified tribunals and his approval is needed for removing members of certain tribunals. He is responsible for the reform of the civil law (*see* VII, **5**(*b*)(*ii*)) and the organisation of the courts system (including the summoning of juries); he is chairman of the committee that makes rules of procedure for the Supreme Court and of the Statute Law Committee.

(*b*) *The law officers of the Crown.* These are the *Attorney-General*, the *Solicitor-General* and their Scottish counterparts, the *Lord Advocate* and the *Solicitor-General for Scotland*. They are appointed by letters patent and are normally members of the House of Commons (but not in the Cabinet).

The principal law officer for England and Wales is the Attorney-General and his main functions can be summarised as follows:

(*i*) He advises the Government on points of law and scrutinises draft bills.

(*ii*) He is an *ex officio* member of the Senate of the Inns of Court and the Bar (*see* **3**(*a*)).

(*iii*) He sometimes prosecutes personally in important criminal cases. He supervises the work of the Director of Public Prosecutions (*see* (*e*)) and his consent is necessary before certain prosecutions (e.g. under the Official Secrets Acts 1911–39) can be initiated.

(*iv*) He can stop trials on indictment by entering a *nolle prosequi* (an undertaking to forbear from proceeding).

(*v*) He is empowered by the Criminal Justice Act 1972, s. 36 to seek the opinion of the Court of Appeal (Criminal Divison) on a point of law, after an acquittal on indictment. The matter can thence be referred to the House of Lords but the acquittal itself cannot be affected.

(*vi*) He can represent the Crown in civil proceedings and, in certain circumstances (e.g. the infringement of public rights), he may bring what is termed a *relator action* at the request and expense of a private person. This is a means of overcoming the problem of *locus standi*—the question as to whether or not a person has sufficient "interest" (i.e. practical involvement) in a matter to be allowed by the court to sue for a remedy. Consent to a relator action is within the Attorney-General's discretion, the exercise of which is not subject to control or supervision by the courts—as enunciated in:

Gouriet v. *Union of Post Office Workers* (*1977*). Two Post Office trade unions announced that they would be calling on their members to boycott mail to South Africa. As this appeared to constitute a criminal offence, G sought a relator action for an injunction and, when the Attorney-General refused his consent, G sued in his own name. Reversing the High Court decision of Stocker J., the Court of Appeal held that he was entitled to do so and granted interim injunctions. Reversing this decision, the House of Lords held that, as G did not have any special interest, he was not entitled to initiate proceedings in his own name.

The Solicitor-General (normally a barrister) is, in most respects, the deputy of the Attorney-General, all of whose functions he is empowered to perform, under the Law Officers Act 1944, if the Attorney-General is unable to act or give his authority.

(*c*) *The Lord Chief Justice* (*L.C.J.*). The holder of this office is appointed by the Crown (nowadays from among the Lords Justices of Appeal) on the Prime Minister's recommendation. He is granted a peerage and presides over the Court of Appeal (Criminal Division) also the Divisional Court of the Queen's Bench Division (wherein he is the senior judge).

(*d*) *The Master of the Rolls* (*M.R.*). The holder of this office is also appointed on the Prime Minister's recommendation and is granted a peerage. He presides over the Court of Appeal (Civil Division) and is a member of the Criminal Divison. Formally, he admits newly qualified solicitors to the rolls of the court, thus enabling them to practise, and he appoints the Solicitors' Disciplinary Tribunal (*see* 3(*b*)(*iii*)). Originally, his responsibilities included the custody of the records of the superior courts but, under the Public Records Act 1958, this function was transferred to the Lord Chancellor, and the Master of the Rolls became chairman of the Lord Chancellor's Advisory Council on Public Records.

(*e*) *The Director of Public Prosecutions* (*D.P.P.*). The holder of this office must be a barrister or solicitor of at least ten years' standing; he is appointed by the Home Secretary and aided by a number of Assistant Directors, also a civil service staff. As specified in the Prosecution of Offences Act 1979, his main functions are as follows:

(*i*) He institutes, undertakes or carries on criminal proceedings in any court, at the instigation of the Attorney-General, also in cases which appear to require his intervention through their importance or difficult nature, etc.

(*ii*) He gives advice to chief officers of police, justices' clerks and other persons concerned, with regard to the conduct of any criminal proceedings.

(*iii*) He appears for the Crown or the prosecutor in criminal appeals from the Crown Court, Divisional Court or Court of Appeal, when directed to do so by the Divisional Court or Court of Appeal.

(*iv*) He may take over the conduct of private prosecutions at any stage.

(*v*) He is the only authorised prosecutor for certain offences against public order or good government (e.g. bribery and corruption, contravention of the Official Secrets Acts 1911–39, etc.). His consent is necessary before certain prosecutions (e.g. under the Bankruptcy Acts) can be initiated.

(*vi*) He holds the office of *Official Petitioner*, with the task of deciding whether to institute bankruptcy proceedings, subsequent to a Criminal Bankruptcy Order (*see* VI, 1(*e*)(*ii*)).

(*f*) *The Official Solicitor*. The holder of this office protects the interests of minors, mental patients and persons committed to prison for contempt of court, especially if they are unrepresented in pending judicial proceedings, as illustrated in—

> *Churchman* v. *Joint Shop Stewards Committee* (*1972*): Three dockers were committed to prison for contempt of court but the Official Solicitor took the matter to the Court of Appeal, which set aside the committal orders.

2. The characteristics of the judiciary. High Court judges are appointed from barristers of at least ten years' standing; circuit judges must also have been barristers of ten years' standing (or recorders of three years' standing); recorders, who act as part-time judges, are appointed from barristers or solicitors of at least ten years' standing.

To ensure the impartial administration of the law, it is clearly desirable that the judiciary should enjoy a high degree of independence—notably in respect of:

(*a*) *The Government*. As shown above, judicial appointments are made on the recommendation of the Prime Minister or Lord Chancellor, but political considerations pay no real part in the nominations—except with that of the Lord Chancellor himself and, to a certain extent, lay JPs. With the exception of the Lord Chancellor (who changes with the government), all senior members of the judiciary retire at seventy-five and, up to that age, they hold office *quamdiu se bene gesserint* (during good behaviour), being removable only by the Monarch on an address by both Houses of Parliament. Circuit judges and recorders may be removed by the Lord Chancellor on the ground of misbehaviour or incapacity.

Once appointed, judges cannot be controlled by the Government, or even required to implement its wishes; conversely, they enforce the law against ministers and their departments—as illustrated in:

Congreve v. *Home Office* (*1976*): The Court of Appeal held that the minister's threat to revoke TV licences purchased early, to avoid a fee increase, was unfair, unjust and unlawful.

Laker Airways v. *Department of Trade* (*1976*): The Court of Appeal held that the minister's attempt to withdraw the licence granted to Laker, to operate their "skytrain" service, was unlawful.

Secretary of State for Education and Science v. *Tameside Metropolitan Borough Council* (*1976*): The House of Lords held that the minister could not interfere with a local education authority unless he could show that it was acting unreasonably.

(*b*) *The legislature.* Judges (but not JPs) are excluded from membership of the House of Commons. In order to preclude parliamentary criticism or control, judicial salaries are not subject to annual debate (unlike other forms of national expenditure) and they are sufficiently high to avoid any question of corruption. Parliament will not debate any matter which is *sub judice* (in course of trial) and, unless there is a substantive motion, "reflections must not be cast in debate upon the conduct of judges" (Erskine May).

(*c*) *The public.* Judges may be sued, under the Habeas Corpus Act 1679, for a penalty of £500 if they wrongfully refuse to issue a writ of *habeas corpus* (*see* VI, 2(*f*)) in vacation but, with this exception, they are completely immune from civil or criminal proceedings in respect of acts done by them in the exercise of their judicial functions, and within the limits of their jurisdiction, even if they have acted maliciously or mistakenly, as illustrated in—

Sirros v. *Moore* (*1974*): Being mistaken as to his jurisdiction, a circuit judge refused an appeal against a deportation order and required the appellant to be detained. *Habeas corpus* was granted and the appellant sued the judge, also the arresting police officer, for false imprisonment. The Court of Appeal held that the detention was invalid but that the judge and police officers acting on his instructions were immune from liability.

It is a common law criminal offence of *contempt of court* to "utter in court disparaging or offensive words to the judge, or to utter such disparaging remarks out of court, concerning judges of the superior courts in relation to their office or otherwise". Contempt of court also covers failure to comply with an order of the court and the Contempt of Court Act 1981 makes it a statutory offence:

(*i*) To publish anything (by way of speech, writing, broadcast, etc.) that tends to interfere with the course of justice in particular legal proceedings, regardless of intent to do so. This does not preclude fair and accurate reports of legal proceedings held in public, published contemporaneously and in good faith. Furthermore, it is a defence to show that, having taken all reasonable care, the publisher did not know (and had no reason to suspect) the relevant proceedings were active.

(*ii*) To obtain, disclose or solicit details of a jury's deliberations.

(*iii*) To bring into court for use (without leave) a tape recorder, or to publish recordings made.

(*iv*) To insult wilfully the justices, counsel, solicitors or witnesses in a magistrates' court; to interrupt the proceedings wilfully or otherwise to misbehave. In such circumstances the magistrates may impose a fine not exceeding £1,000 or custody for not more than sixty days.

THE PROFESSION OF THE LAW

3. The branches of the legal profession. It is an important characteristic of the English legal system that lawyers are controlled by autonomous bodies and are therefore not State officials. For over six centuries the legal profession in England and Wales has been divided into two distinct branches:

(*a*) *The barrister.* The training, call and professional practice of barristers are controlled by the Senate of the Inns of Court and the Bar. There are four Inns of Court (Lincoln's Inn, Inner Temple, Middle Temple, Gray's Inn) and the profession is regulated as follows:

(*i*) *The training.* This commences with an academic stage, which is completed by graduating with an approved law degree—though other graduates and certain mature students may qualify by passing the *Common Professional Examination* (in six core subjects) after a one-year course. Students must then be admitted to one of the Inns of Court and undertake a one year vocational stage of training, carried out by the *Council of Legal Education* (appointed by, and subject to the control of, the Senate), which sponsors the *Inns of Court School of Law*. Having completed both stages, also having "kept terms" (by dining at least twenty-four times over one or two years in the hall of their Inn), students may then be "called to the Bar" but, before they can practise, they must complete a year's *pupillage* in the chambers of an established barrister.

(*ii*) *The functions.* Barristers do not deal directly with their clients (but only through solicitors—by whom they are "briefed") and they may not enter into partnership or employ each other. They may plead in court at all levels, though some spend most of their time in chambers, drafting opinions. After a period of generally not less than fifteen years, a barrister may apply to the Lord Chancellor to "take silk" and become a Queen's Counsel (QC), who leads "juniors" (barristers who are not QCs) instructed to appear with him.

(*iii*) *The complaints.* Complaints against barristers are made to the *Professional Conduct Committee* which may take no action, admonish the barrister, report the matter to the Treasurer of his Inn or refer a *prima facie* case to a Senate *Disciplinary Tribunal*. This body makes the ultimate decision as to what action should be taken but the final pronouncement is made by the individual Inn. Appeal lies to the Visitors of the Inns (the Lord Chancellor and all puisne judges) whose decision is final.

A barrister is not liable to an action by his client for negligence in respect of work performed in court or intimately connected with it, but the fact that this immunity does not extend to all pre-trial work was illustrated in—

Saif Ali v. *Sydney Michell & Co.* (*1978*): Consulted by solicitors about a car accident, involving three possible defendants, a barrister advised an action against only one. When this had to be discontinued, the plaintiff sued the solicitors, who joined the barrister as third party, and the House of Lords held that the advice given was not covered by immunity.

(*b*) *The solicitor.* The training, admission and professional practice of solicitors are controlled by the Law Society and, under the Solicitors Act 1974, the profession is regulated as follows:

(*i*) *The training.* This commences with an *academic stage*, which is completed by acquiring an approved law degree—though other graduates may qualify by passing the Common Professional Examination. Students must then enrol with the Law Society and undertake a *professional stage* of training. This comprises a year's course for the Final Examination and service under *articles of clerkship* with a practising solicitor for two years (at least eighteen months of which must be served after passing the Final Examination). Currently non-graduates are accepted as students but they must attend a recognised course of legal education and serve under articles for four years. On fulfilling the requirements, candidates may apply to have their names placed on the roll (*see* 1(*d*)) but, in order to practise, they must also obtain from the Law Society a practising certificate, which has to be renewed annually.

(*ii*) *The functions.* Solicitors deal directly with their clients, from whom they receive "instructions", and their work includes the conveyancing (legal transfer) of property, the drawing up and probate of wills, the preliminary conduct of litigation, the giving of legal advice on a wide variety of subjects and the representation of clients in lower courts. They enjoy a right of audience in magistrates' and county courts whilst, under the Courts Act 1971, s. 12, they may appeal in the Crown Court on appeal or committal for sentence from magistrates' courts. Under the Supreme Court Act 1981, s. 83, the Lord Chancellor may at any time grant solicitors right of audience in the Crown Court, if it is in the public interest.

In their practices, solicitors generally employ clerks who can qualify for membership of the Institute of Legal Executives. Under the Administration of Justice Act 1977, s. 16, the Lord Chancellor may grant a right of audience in county courts to specified categories of person employed to assist solicitors in the conduct of litigation.

(*iii*) *The complaints.* Solicitors can be sued for negligence but the immunity of a barrister may extend to a solicitor doing litigation work which could have been done by counsel.

Under the Solicitors Act 1974, ss. 46–55, complaints against solicitors, relating to provisions of the Act, can be made to the *Solicitors' Disciplinary Tribunal* (comprising two solicitor members and one lay member, who must not be a solicitor or barrister) appointed by the Master of the Rolls. The tribunal may make orders to strike a solicitor's name from the roll, to suspend him, to fine him, to restore his name to the roll, to effect payment of costs. Appeal lies to the Divisional Court of the Queen's Bench Division. Section 45 of the 1974 Act empowers the Lord Chancellor to appoint one or more "lay observers" to examine allegations concerning the Law Society's treatment of complaints about solicitors.

Lord Goodman has said that "The system which at present divides the legal profession in its two separate branches is thoroughly antediluvian". Nevertheless in most continental countries there are at least two types of lawyers—notaries and advocates. In the USA there is a fused profession of "Attorney and Counsellor at Law" but, within the larger American firms, a distinction often arises between the "court" and "office" lawyers—and the American Association of Trial Lawyers has become a form of Bar. The main arguments for preserving the present system in England and Wales are: (1) It allows freedom of choice in obtaining the services of a specialist, on the advice of a general practitioner—as in medicine. In America the client of one firm of attorneys cannot have the services of a particular expert if he does not belong to the firm. (2) It gives a solicitor access to a specialist without any fear of appearing inadequate or of losing his client to the other lawyer. (3) It supports the continued existence of small firms of solicitors. At present the average firm has only two to four partners and fusion would necessitate the creation of very much larger units. The present-day solicitor could not pursue his general work and simultaneously attend long cases in court, moreover, advocacy is a specialist skill, developed solely by long, frequent and varied experience. (4) It enables a relatively small Bar to become known to, and to develop a mutual confidence with, the Bench. (5) It provides the necessary detachment when the person who meets the client and prepares the evidence can become too personally involved.

THE ADJUDICATION OF FACT

4. The functions of juries. There are three main types of juries and these are found in:

(*a*) *The criminal courts.* All criminal cases in the Crown Court are heard before a jury of twelve persons, who may receive allowances for subsistence travel, loss of earnings, etc. Under the Juries Act 1974 anyone between the ages of eighteen and sixty-five who is registered as an elector and who has resided in the United Kingdom, Channel Islands or Isle of Man for at least five years since the age of thirteen is liable for jury service, unless he or she is:

(*i*) *Ineligible.* This category includes judges, magistrates, barristers, solicitors, court officers, coroners, police, prison and probation officers, priests of any religion, vowed members of religious communities and certain sufferers from mental illness.

(*ii*) *Disqualified.* This category includes anyone who has, in the preceding ten years, served any part of a sentence of imprisonment, youth custody or detention (including borstal) *or* received a suspended prison sentence, detention order or community service order *or* who has been placed on probation in the preceding five years. (Juries (Disqualification) Act 1984.)

(*iii*) *Excusable as of right.* This category includes members and officers of the Houses of Parliament, full-time serving

IV. THE PERSONNEL OF THE LAW

members of H.M. Forces, registered and practising members of the medical, dental, nursing, veterinary and pharmaceutical professions, also anyone who has served on a jury within the preceding two years.

The challenging of jurors is outlined at V, 1(c). If, through death, illness or discharge, the number of jurors is reduced, the Juries Act 1974, s. 16 permits the trial to continue, provided that the number is not reduced below nine. This does not apply in cases of murder or offences punishable with death, unless both prosecution and defence assent. The verdict of a jury is explained at V, 1(h). In criminal trials, the jury system provides disinterested adjudication, embodying the views of the man-in-the-street, at a time when judges are sometimes criticised for representing a limited social background. Juries are also free from the kind of prejudice which a judge may acquire from constant contact with the courts, but there are several valid criticisms of the system. In the first place, jurors can become confused and prejudiced in trials involving more than one accused and/or several charges. In some circumstances they appear too ready to acquit (i.e. find not guilty)—conceivably through misplaced sympathy, bigoted obtuseness, a wish to express disapproval of the law or the influence of eloquent counsel. The average juror is quite unsuitable for trials involving complex financial or commercial transactions—where special panels of professionally qualified jurors might be advantageous. Alternatively, it has been suggested that trial by jury should be replaced by trial by one single judge (as in most civil cases), by a number of judges (e.g. three) or by judges sitting with lay experts. All of these possibilities nevertheless have their disadvantages.

(b) *The civil courts.* High Court juries comprise twelve persons, selected as for criminal cases and with similar provisions for majority verdicts. The Supreme Court Act 1981, s. 69 provides that jury trial could be ordered, on the application of any party to the action, in cases of fraud, defamation, malicious prosecution and false imprisonment. In other case the court has a discretion to order that an action be tried by a jury—though, in practice, this is seldom done and generally cases are heard by a judge alone. There are no juries in the Chancery Division or in the Admiralty Court but either party may apply for a jury in probate or defended divorce cases. In county courts juries consist of eight members but are rarely encountered.

(c) *The coroners' courts.* Coroners are Crown officers who are required to hold inquests in respect of certain deaths and also in respect of treasure trove (money, gold, silver, plate or bullion found in the earth or other private place). A coroner may summon a jury of seven to eleven members for any inquest if he so wishes but, under the Coroners Amendment Act 1926, s. 13 (as amended by the Criminal Law Act 1977, s. 56), he is required to summon a jury when a death has occurred in prison or where there is reason to suspect that it has resulted from an accident, poisoning or a disease which is required to be notified to a government department, or circumstances which would be prejudicial to public safety or health if they continued or recurred. Under the Coroners Juries Act 1983 they must meet the qualifications required of criminal or civil juries; however, the jury of an inquest on a prisoner who dies in prison may not include any member of the prison staff or prisoners or anyone engaged in trade with the prison.

THE ENFORCEMENT OF THE LAW

5. The role of the police. The police forces in England and Wales comprise the Metropolitan Police, the City of London Police and also forces of counties and combined areas. Each has the following characteristics:

(*a*) *The control of the police.* Under the Police Act 1964, control is effected by:

(*i*) *The Home Secretary.* The Home Secretary is empowered (1) to make regulations concerning the government, administration and conditions of service throughout the various forces; (2) to approve voluntary, or initiate compulsory, schemes for amalgamation of forces, (3) to appoint an inspectorate and to withhold the whole or part of the annual government grant to police authorities (50 per cent of their expenditure); (4) to approve the appointment (or require the retirement) of Chief Constables, Deputy and Assistant Chief Constables, (5) to adjudicate on appeals in disciplinary matters (*see* (*ii*)); (6) to require co-operation (including supply of officers) between forces; (7) also to order inquiries into police matters and to obtain any required report from a Chief Constable.

(*ii*) *The Police Authority.* Each force must have a *Police Authority* and in London this is the Home Secretary (for the Metropolitan Police) and the Court of Common Council (for the City of London Police); elsewhere it is a *Police Committee*, comprising two-thirds councillors and one-third JPs. Its duties are (1) to maintain an adequate and efficient force for the area; (2) to appoint or retire the Chief Constable, Deputy and Assistant Chief Constables (with the Home Secretary's approval); (3) to determine the establishment of the force; (4) to provide premises and equipment; (5) to require an annual or other report from the Chief Constable (though he can decline to report on persons under arrest and other matters contrary to the public interest); (6) also to act as the disciplinary authority in respect of the Chief Constable and other very senior ranks.

(*iii*) *The Chief Constable*. Each force is headed by a Chief Constable (Commissioner in the Metropolitan Police) and his duties are (1) to control the force and ensure its efficiency; (2) to appoint, promote and discipline all but the most senior ranks; (3) also to record and investigate complaints against the police (*see* (*c*)).

(*b*) *The practices of the police*. Police powers of arrest and search are outlined at VIII, 6(*a*) and (*d*) but, in respect of prosecution and detection, three potential sources of controversy are:

(*i*) *The exercise of discretion*. Police discretion is exercised in deciding whether or not to prosecute a particular wrong-doer. This can be advantageous in the acquisition of evidence from informers, in preserving good public relations by merely issuing cautions in minor motoring offences, etc., also in experimenting with new techniques (e.g. the use of juvenile bureaux which caution young offenders). Nevertheless, it could lead to victimisation and in Scotland the Lord Advocate appoints *procurators fiscal*, i.e. lawyers independent of the police who initiate and conduct prosecutions in all but the most trivial cases. In 1981 the *Report of the Royal Commission on Criminal Procedure* recommended for England and Wales a statutory service with local prosecution departments headed by "Crown Prosecutors" who would conduct prosecutions, advising the police with regard to them and providing advocates. This recommendation is being adopted.

(*ii*) *The methods of detection*. In the investigation of crime, the police have to resort to a variety of tactics, some of which occasionally arouse criticism—and one example is the use of the *agent provocateur*. It is vital that such a person (be it an informer or a police officer) should not incite the commission of an offence which would not otherwise have been committed. If, however, it has already been planned, the police are under a duty to mitigate the consequences and it is perfectly proper for them to encourage an agent provocateur to participate in it, as stated in—

R. v. *Birtles* (*1969*): Having pleaded guilty to two separate charges, B was sentenced to consecutive terms of three and two years' imprisonment. The Court of Appeal held that, as there was a possibility that an informer and a police officer had both encouraged the commission of the offence, the sentence should be made concurrent.

R. v *Willis* (*1978*): Having infiltrated an existing drug "ring", a police officer encouraged the conspirators to supply him with cocaine. They were then arrested. Dismissing their appeal, the Court of Appeal held that the trial judge had been bound to admit the Crown's evidence, even though it may have been unfairly obtained. If, which was queried, he had the discretion to exclude it, it nevertheless fell on the right side of the line drawn in the case above, since the conspirators had clearly not been encouraged to commit a crime which they would not otherwise have committed.

(*iii*) *The methods of interrogation*. To protect the liberty of the individual, constraints must be imposed upon the powers of the police in investigating suspected crimes and a notable example is the *Judges' Rules*, which relate to interrogation procedures. Originally formulated by the King's Bench Division judges in 1912 and 1918, these were revised by the Queen's Bench judges in 1964 and are published in Home Office Circular 89/1978 (*Judges' Rules and Administrative Directions to the Police*). There are in fact six rules:

  I This states that a police officer investigating an offence is entitled to question anyone, provided that the person has not been charged with the offence or informed that he may be prosecuted for it.

  II This requires that, as soon as there is evidence which would afford reasonable grounds for suspecting that a person has committed an offence, he must be cautioned in a prescribed form before further questions are put. He is not obliged to say anything but, if he does, a written record must be kept, showing the place, time (of beginning and ending) and persons present.

  III This requires anyone charged with (or informed that he may be prosecuted for) an offence to be cautioned in a prescribed form. After he has been so charged (or informed), questions concerning the offence should be put to him only in exceptional circumstances (e.g. if necessary to minimise harm or loss to others, or to clarify a previous ambiguity) but a further caution must be given and a written record kept.

  IV This prescribes the form for written statements.

  V This requires that, if a police officer wishes to show to a person charged a written statement by another person charged with the same offence, he must give him a true copy and nothing must be said or done to invite reply or comment. If he should wish (or start) to make a reply, a further caution must be given.

VI This requires persons other than police officers to comply with the rules if it is their duty to investigate offences or charge offenders.

Non-compliance with these rules may render answers and statements inadmissible as evidence. Furthermore, they do not affect the principle that (other than by arrest) police officers cannot compel anyone against his will to visit or remain at a police station; also, at any stage, he should always be able to consult privately with a solicitor. The fundamental rule of evidence concerning the admissibility of confessions (*see* VII, **4**(*c*)) is applicable in all cases.

(*c*) *The complaints procedure of the police.* Complaints in respect of a police officer are initially investigated by an officer of a different division of the same force and he submits a report to (generally) the Deputy Chief Constable. Unless it is clear that no criminal offence has been committed, the matter must then be referred to the Director of Public Prosecutions, who decides whether a prosecution is merited. Subject to this, the Deputy Chief Constable decides whether any disciplinary charges should be instituted (but these must not be similar to any criminal charges which the DPP has decided not to bring). When this procedure has been completed and if it is decided that there shall be no disciplinary proceedings, the Deputy Chief Constable is required under the Police Act 1976, to send a copy of the complaint, the investigating officer's report, supporting documents and the reasons for his conclusion to the *Police Complaints Board* (comprising not less than nine members appointed by the Prime Minister). If the Board considers that disciplinary proceedings should have been instituted, it recommends charges to the Deputy Chief Constable and, in the event of disagreement, it can direct that proceedings be brought. In cases where the Deputy Chief Constable decides at the outset to institute disciplinary proceedings, an officer who admits the charge will be dealt with by the Chief Constable. If, however, he denies the charge, the matter is submitted to the Board for a decision as to whether the case should be heard by the Chief Constable alone, or by a *tribunal* comprising the Chief Constable and two members of the Board. Appeal against a finding of guilt or a punishment lies to the Home Secretary.

PROGRESS TEST 4

1. Consider the role of the Lord Chancellor in the English legal system. **(1)**

2. Explain the functions of the Attorney-General and the Director of Public Prosecutions in the administration of justice. **(1)**

3. Describe the system of appointment of High Court judges and circuit judges. How can they be removed? **(2)**

4. Explain the extent of judicial immunity. **(2)**

5. Consider the different functions of barristers and solicitors. **(3)**

6. What would be the advantages and disadvantages of having a unified legal profession? **(3)**

7. What are the advantages of the British system of trial by jury? **(4)**

8. Outline the system of jury trial in criminal cases. What criticisms might be made of it? **(4)**

9. Examine criticisms which are sometimes made about police methods of crime detection. **(5)**

10. Describe the method of dealing with complaints against the police. Do you consider that it is adequate? **(5)**

CHAPTER V

The Procedures of the Law

THE PROCEDURE OF THE CROWN COURT

1. The trial procedure of a criminal prosecution. As shown at III, 2(*a*)(*ii*), anyone accused of an indictable offence is first brought before a magistrates' court for committal proceedings and, if there is found to be a *prima facie* case, he or she is remanded (on bail or in custody) to the Crown Court, where the procedure is as follows:

(*a*) *The arraignment.* The accused is "put up to plead" at the bar of the court (i.e. called by name to the front of the dock); the clerk reads out the indictment and asks; "How say you, are you guilty or not guilty?" To this the accused must reply personally and not through counsel.

(*b*) *The pleas.* The following courses of action are now open to the accused:

(*i*) *He may plead guilty.* The court will then hear the facts of the case from the prosecution also evidence of character and pleas in mitigation, after which it passes sentence. In serious cases the accused is often advised to withdraw a guilty plea. If there are several charges and possibly a long hearing, there may be a question of *plea-bargaining*, whereby the prosecution has agreed to withdraw the most serious charges in return for the defence pleading guilty to one or more of the less serious. This practice does not exist to the same extent as in America but it is open to abuse and has been criticised by the Court of Appeal.

(*ii*) *He may "stand mute"* (*i.e. say nothing*). In this case a jury may be empanelled to try whether he is "mute of malice" (deliberately silent) or "by visitation of God" (e.g. deaf and dumb). If he is found to be mute of malice, a plea of not guilty is entered for him but, if he is found to be mute by visitation, the question of his fitness to plead must then be considered.

(*iii*) *He may plead autrefois acquit or autrefois convict*, i.e. that he cannot be tried for a crime in respect of which he has previously been acquitted or convicted.

(*iv*) *He may plead not guilty*. The procedure outlined at (*c*)—(*i*) then ensues.

(*c*) *The swearing of the jury*. Before the oath is administered, an opportunity to challenge each member separately must be given to the prosecution and defence. Without having to give any reason, the defence (but not the prosecution) may make a *peremptory* challenge (by merely calling out "Challenge") in respect of not more than three jurors. In addition to this, the defence and prosecution may also challenge any number of jurors *for cause* (e.g. on the ground that they are not impartial). After the jury has been sworn, the accused is "put in charge of the jury" and the clerk addresses them, stating the nature of the charge.

(*d*) *The case for the prosecution*. The indictment is then "opened", i.e. counsel for the prosecution addresses the jury and tells them what evidence he proposes to adduce—but he should regard himself as assisting the jury in arriving at the truth, rather than as an advocate pressing for a conviction. On concluding his address, he calls his witnesses, who are "examined in chief" (by the prosecuting counsel), cross-examined (by defending counsel) and possibly re-examined (by prosecuting counsel). At the end of the prosecution case, defending counsel may submit that there is no case to answer.

(*e*) *The case for the defence*. If the submission that there is no case to answer is either refused or not made, defending counsel then "opens" his case and calls his witnesses for examination-in-chief, cross-examination and re-examination. The accused may give evidence on oath, in which case he would be subject to cross-examination. At this stage the prosecution can not call further evidence unless the judge exercises his discretion to permit it, in order to rebut defence evidence which could not have been foreseen by the prosecution.

(*f*) *The closing speeches*. Counsel for the prosecution and defence then sum up their cases, with the defence having the right to the last word.

(*g*) *The summing up*. The judge then sums up the case to the jury, pointing out that the burden of proof is always on the prosecution (to prove that, first an offence was committed and, secondly, that it was committed by the accused), directing them on points of law, possibly advising them on the weight of evidence, asking them definite questions of fact and drawing their attention to any evidence that establishes a defence (even though defending counsel may not have done this).

(*h*) *The verdict*. The jury may then retire to consider their verdict and thereafter they must not separate (though an individual may withdraw for urgent reasons). During their retirement, they may have further assistance from the judge—in open court or by written note (which must be read out in open court). The first delivery of the verdict is not final, as the judge may direct the jury to reconsider it. If they are unable to agree, he may discharge them, so that the case could be retried before another jury. Formerly the verdict of the jury had to be unanimous but the Criminal Justice Act 1967, s. 13 now provides for majority verdicts of at least ten to two, where there are the normal twelve jurors. If the jury is reduced to eleven or ten, there may be one dissentient but, if there are only nine, the verdict must be unanimous. The court may not accept a majority verdict unless the jury has deliberated for at least two hours.

(i) *The judgment.* In order to decide upon the appropriate sentence for anyone found guilty, the court may hear evidence of previous convictions (limited by the Rehabilitation of Offenders Act 1974), pleas in mitigation, evidence of character, etc. The convicted person may also request the court to take into consideration other offences. Common sentences are described at VI, 1.

THE PROCEDURES OF THE HIGH COURT

2. The pre-trial procedure of a High Court action. In order to bring a civil action in the Queen's Bench Division, the following procedure must first take place:

(a) *The plaintiff serves the writ.* The necessary form may be obtained from the Central Office of the Supreme Court in London, or from a District Registry. The plaintiff's claim is outlined in the most general terms but the remedy sought must be stated. After the writ has been completed, the next step is to *issue* it (i.e. make it an official document emanating from the court). For this purpose, the plaintiff or his solicitor must take two copies to the Central Office or District Registry, sign one and pay a fee. The signed copy is stamped and filed, whilst the other is sealed and returned, it then becomes *the writ in the action.* It is next necessary to *serve* the writ on the defendant, by giving him a sealed copy—though often his solicitor agrees to accept service. A writ may be served at any time of the day or night, excluding Sundays.

(b) *The defendant acknowledges service.* This entails returning a form of acknowledgment to the court office from which the writ was issued. Thus the defendant submits to the jurisdiction of the court.

(c) *The parties deliver the pleadings to each other.* The pleadings, which are generally drafted by counsel, must state facts and not law, cover material facts only and not include the evidence by which the facts are to be proved. They comprise.

(*i*) *The statement of claim*. This is delivered by the plaintiff to the defendant and it sets out his cause of action, giving all necessary details concerning his injuries and losses. At the trial the plaintiff will not be permitted to make any allegation of which the defendant has not been given notice.

(*ii*) *The defence*. This is delivered by the defendant to the plaintiff and it must deal with each of the allegations in the statement of claim. A general denial is inadmissible and any allegation not denied will be deemed by the court to be admitted.

(*iii*) *The reply*. This is not essential but it enables the plaintiff to deal with any new facts raised by the defence.

If a party has worded his pleading so vaguely that the line of attack or defence cannot be determined, his opponent should apply for *further and better particulars*. Furthermore, if a party refers to any document in his pleadings, his opponent can give notice that he wishes to see and copy it. This is known as discovery of documents—and it must be emphasised that "discovery" relates to evidence, whereas "particulars" concern allegations.

(*d*) *The plaintiff takes out a summons for directions*. This causes the parties' solicitors to appear before a Queen's Bench Master, to whom any party may apply for directions concerning the future conduct of the action. The Master has power to decide whether there shall be further pleadings, whether there is to be a jury, whether to order *general discovery of documents* (requiring a party to swear an affidavit (written statement on oath) disclosing all relevant documents in his possession), and whether to administer *interrogatories* (whereby a party is required to answer certain questions on oath before the trial), etc. Should the plaintiff fail to take out a summons for directions, the defendant may apply to have the action dismissed "for want of prosecution".

(*e*) *The plaintiff sets down the action for trial*. If the plaintiff fails to *set down* the action at the Central Office, the defendant may do it himself or apply to have the action dismissed. Eventually the case appears in the *Day's List* and the parties must attend in court.

3. The trial procedures of a High Court action. The trial procedure for a civil action in the Queen's Bench Division is as follows:

(*a*) *The swearing of the jury* (*if there is one*). The plaintiff's junior counsel then "opens the pleadings", briefly outlining their nature but not stating the amount of damages claimed. In trials before a judge alone, this is omitted.

(b) *The case for the plaintiff.* The plaintiff's leading counsel "opens his case", explaining the matter in dispute, reading the pleadings, outlining the plaintiff's argument, indicating the supporting evidence and possibly discounting defences, in anticipation. He calls his witnesses, who are examined-in-chief (and possibly cross-examined by the defendant's counsel) and puts in all material documents.

(c) *The case for the defendant.* If the defendant's counsel states that he does not intend to call witnesses or put in documents, the plaintiff's counsel then addresses the court. If, however, there are witnesses or documents, the defendant's counsel addresses the court; he then calls any witnesses, who are examined-in-chief (and may be cross-examined by the plaintiff's counsel), he also puts in any documents upon which he relies. Sometimes at the close of the defendant's case, the plaintiff may call "rebutting" evidence, in answer to any affirmative case raised by the defendant.

(d) *The addresses to the jury (if there is one) or the judge.* Counsel for the defendant makes his speech, followed by counsel for the plaintiff. During these speeches, the judge may indicate to each counsel the weak points of his case.

(e) *The summing up by the judge to the jury (if there is one).* The judge directs the jury on points of law, outlines the questions of fact that they must decide and reminds them of the evidence. When the jury returns its verdict, the judge *enters judgment.* In non-jury cases, he delivers judgment at the conclusion of counsels' speeches, stating his reasons. If, however, important legal questions are raised, the judge may *reserve judgment,* for "further consideration". The counsel for the successful party then asks for costs (*see* VI, 4) and, if he thinks of appealing, the counsel for the unsuccessful party should ask for a *stay of execution* (suspension of the operation of the judgment). Common civil remedies are outlined at VI, 2(a)–(c).

THE PROCEDURE OF THE COUNTY COURT

4. The procedure of a county court action. The jurisdiction of a county court has been outlined at III, 3(b) and one of its functions is to serve as a "small claims" court wherein, without the aid of solicitors, parties can personally bring and defend actions (not exceeding £500), which are generally heard by the registrars. The procedure of a county court action is as follows:

(a) *The request for a summons.* The plaintiff must first complete a *request* form, obtainable from the county court office. To recover a debt or a specific sum of money (e.g. the price of goods sold or cost of repairs to a damaged vehicle), it is necessary to request a *default summons*, but other claims necessitate an *ordinary summons*. The request is delivered to the county court office, together with two copies of a written *particulars of claim* (outlining the facts in support of the claim) and a small fee. The court prepares a summons and the plaintiff is given a *plaint note* (showing the plaint number of the action). A copy of the summons, particulars of claim and a *form of admission, defence and counter-claim* are then served on the defendant (generally by the court bailiff).

(*b*) *The filing of a defence.* If the defendant wishes to contest the action, he must complete the defence section of the form of admission, defence and counterclaim, and return it to the court office within fourteen days. A simple denial of liability is not sufficient. At the same time, the defendant can file a counterclaim, which is a separate claim against the plaintiff.

(*c*) *The pre-trial review.* On a fixed date, both parties appear before the registrar, who gives all necessary directions for securing the just, expeditious and economical disposal of the action. He endeavours to obtain all reasonable admissions and agreements, and fixes a date for the trial.

(*d*) *The trial.* The normal sequence of events is: plaintiff's opening speech, plaintiff's witnesses, defendant's witnesses, defendant's speech, plaintiff's speech in reply, judgment.

From this chapter it can be seen that, in both criminal and civil cases, the procedure is *accusatorial*, i.e. the courts are neutral and hear arguments by both sides. Some other countries, however, follow *inquisitorial* procedure, whereby the court produces the evidence.

PROGRESS TEST 5

1. Describe the various stages of a criminal trial in the Crown Court. **(1)**

2. Outline the steps necessary before a civil action is tried in the High Court. **(2)**

3. Explain the trial procedure of a civil action in the High Court. **(3)**

4. Without the aid of a solicitor, how would you personally pursue a "small claim" in the county court? **(4)**

CHAPTER VI

The Decisions of the Law

THE JUDGMENTS OF THE LAW

1. The sentences of the criminal courts. As explained at I, **5,** the purpose of criminal sanctions may be deterrent, reformative or preventative and this needs to be considered when examining the principal examples, which are:

(*a*) *The death penalty.* Sentence of death can (but is unlikely to) be imposed on persons of eighteen or over who are found guilty of treason, piracy with violence and arson in H.M. ships, marine stores or dockyards. The death penalty for murder was abolished by the Murder (Abolition of Death Penalty) Act 1965, which made life imprisonment the punishment for murder and empowered judges to recommend a minimum period of confinement.

(*b*) *The custodial sentence.* Loss of freedom may be effected by:

(*i*) *The committal to prison.* Sentence of imprisonment (varying from one day to life) may be imposed on persons aged twenty-one or over. Under the Powers of Criminal Courts Act 1973, s. 18−21, anyone convicted on indictment of a statutory offence, where the sentence is not limited to a specified term (or extended to life) cannot be imprisoned for more than two years.

Sections 22−7 of the same Act provide that any court passing a sentence of up to two years may order that it be suspended—so as not to take effect unless, from one to two years later, the offender commits in Great Britain another offence punishable with imprisonment, and a court orders that the original sentence should take effect. The Criminal Law Act 1977, s. 47 provides that, if a sentence of imprisonment for six months to two years is passed on an adult, the court may order that, after part has been served, the remainder (not less than a quarter and not more than three-quarters) may be suspended. Where maximum terms of imprisonment are stipulated for offences, sections 28−9 of the 1973 Act provides for these to be exceeded in the case of persistent offenders.

The Criminal Justice Act 1967, s. 59 constituted a *parole board* to advise the Home Secretary concerning the release on licence of prisoners whose cases have been referred to the Board by him. Under the Criminal Justice Act 1972, s. 35, prisoners in certain classes (in practice those serving shorter sentences where there has been no violence) can be released on the recommendation of a local review committee, without the involvement of the parole board.

(*ii*) *The detention centre order*. Male offenders aged fourteen to twenty convicted of an offence punishable with imprisonment if they had been twenty-one or over may be committed to a detention centre for not more than four months, provided that they have not already a period of imprisonment, borstal training (now discontinued), detention or youth custody (Criminal Justice Act 1982, s. 4).

(*iii*) *The youth custody sentence*. Offenders aged fifteen to twenty convicted of offences punishable with imprisonment if they had been twenty-one or over may be sentenced to youth custody, provided that reasons are given for the appropriateness of a sentence exceeding four months. The period is normally greater than four months and the maximum is the same as for imprisonment in respect of the same offence—though an offender under seventeen is not sentenced to youth custody for more than twelve months at a time. Anyone under twenty-one convicted of murder or an offence resulting in life imprisonment can be sentenced to *custody for life* (Criminal Justice Act 1982, ss. 6–8).

(*iv*) *The hospital order*. On summary conviction by magistrates of an offence punishable with imprisonment, or on conviction in the Crown Court of an offence punishable by imprisonment where the sentence is not fixed by law, an offender may be ordered to be admitted to (or detained in) a special hospital, on the evidence of two medical practitioners that he is suffering from a mental illness which makes it appropriate. If it is considered necessary for the protection of the public, the Crown Court may make a *restriction order* (or magistrates may commit the offender to the Crown Court for such an order), whereby the person becomes subject only to powers exercisable by the Secretary of State, and no application may be made to a Mental Health Review Tribunal (*see* VIII, 2(*b*) below). By warrant, the Secretary of State may direct that any person may be detained in a specified hospital "during Her Majesty's pleasure"; this has the effect of a hospital order, together with a restriction order, without limitation of time (Mental Health Act 1983, ss. 35–46).

(*c*) *The supervisory measures*. The use of the following orders is dependent upon the age of the offender:

(*i*) *The probation order*. Where anyone of over seventeen is convicted of an offence for which the sentence is not fixed by law, the Powers of Criminal Courts Act 1973, ss. 2–13 empowers a court, where appropriate, to make a probation order. This requires the person to be under the supervision of a probation officer for one to three years (though the Secretary of State may vary these periods under the Criminal Law Act 1977, s. 57) and it may include specific conditions (e.g. regarding residence, medical treatment, attendance at a day training centre, etc.). If an offender fails to comply with such an order (or commits a further offence), he can be brought back to the court.

(*ii*) *The supervision order.* If juveniles under the age of seventeen are found guilty of offences, or considered to be in need of care or control, a juvenile court does not make a probation order but, under the Children and Young Persons Act 1969, s. 1(3)(*b*) and 7(7)(*b*), it may make a supervision order. This lasts from one to three years and the magistrates declare whether the supervision shall be carried out by the local social services department or by the probation and after-care service.

A supervision order can prescribe *intermediate treatment*, by requiring the person concerned to comply with any directions given to him by his supervisor, to live in a specified place, to report to a specified person or to take part in a specified activity.

Should the person fail to respond to the supervision order, he or she can be brought back to the juvenile court by the supervising officer and, if the court so wishes, it can make a *care order*, so that the social services department then takes the person into its care and places him in a family-group home, hostel or community home until eighteen years of age. When it is felt desirable for the juvenile court to make a care order, it is important that the person concerned should be legally represented.

(*d*) *The fine.* This is an order that a convicted person must forfeit a certain sum of money to the Crown. Except for certain offences for which there are fixed penalties, the Powers of Criminal Courts Act 1973, s. 30 empowers any court to fine an offender in lieu of, or in addition to, other sanctions (except a probation order). Default of payment of fines may result in imprisonment according to a table in the Criminal Justice Act 1982, s. 69.

(*e*) *The ancillary orders.* The indicated sections of the Powers of Criminal Courts Act 1973 empower courts to make the following orders:

(*i*) *The compensation order* (*ss. 35–8*). A court may order a convicted offender to pay compensation in respect of any personal injury, loss or damage which appears to have resulted from the offence. A magistrates' court can order up to a maximum of £1,000 compensation in respect of each offence proved, but there is no limit to the amount of compensation that the higher courts may order. In a similar way, a court may make a *restitution order*, in respect of stolen property.

(*ii*) *The criminal bankruptcy order* (*ss. 39–41*). The Crown Court may make this order against a convicted offender whose offences have led to large-scale loss (initially £15,000). The order sets out the amount each victim lost as a result of each offence and it constitutes an *act of bankruptcy*, thus exposing the offender to the possible institution of bankruptcy proceedings. While any creditor, or any victim named in the order, could then take bankruptcy proceedings against the offender, the office of *Official Petitioner* has been created; this is held by the Director of Public Prosecutions, who has the task of considering whether to institute bankruptcy proceedings in the public interest.

(*iii*) *The community service order* (*ss. 14–17*, as amended by the Criminal Justice Act 1982, s. 68 and Sched. 12). Courts may make this order against offenders of sixteen or over, if they have been convicted of an offence punishable with imprisonment. It requires them to carry out unpaid work of service to the community during their spare time, for a minimum of forty hours and a maximum of 240 hours (120 hours for those under seventeen) within twelve months of the date of the order. The nature of the work and the time when it is to be done are matters for a probation officer or local authority social worker. A community service order cannot be combined with a fine or probation order for the same offence—but it can be combined with other orders, such as a compensation order or disqualification from driving.

(*iv*) *The forfeiture order* (*s. 43*). A court which convicts an offender of an offence punishable on indictment with two or more years' imprisonment can order the forfeiture of property in the offender's possession, if it is satisfied that it was used, or intended for use, for criminal purposes. The property would then be taken into the possession of the police and disposed of under the Police (Property) Act 1897. Section 44 of the 1973 Act empowers the Crown Court to disqualify an offender from driving, if a motor vehicle was used in committing the offence, even if the offender was not the actual driver.

(*v*) *The attendance centre order*. Offenders under the age of twenty-one may be ordered to attend at an attendance centre for a specified number of hours, not less than twelve (except for those under the age of fourteen) nor more than twelve (if under fourteen), twenty-four (if aged fourteen to seventeen) or thirty-six (if aged seventeen to twenty-one). Such an order may not be made if the offender has already served a period of imprisonment, borstal training, detention or youth custody (Criminal Justice Act 1982, s. 17).

(*f*) *The miscellaneous sanctions*. Other sanctions include endorsement of driving licences, disqualification from driving, etc. When a court thinks that it is inexpedient to inflict punishment and that a probation order is inappropriate, it may grant an *absolute* or *conditional discharge* (i.e.conditional upon the person not committing any offence during a period not exceeding three years—or such period as may be ordered by the Secretary of State under the Criminal Law Act 1977, s. 57). There is also a procedure (often termed *binding over*) whereby a person *enters into recognisances* to pay a sum of money if he fails to carry out stipulated conditions (e.g. to keep the peace).

2. The remedies of the civil courts. In general, the purpose of civil remedies is to redress harm and to restore injured parties to their former position; the principal examples are:

(*a*) *The award of damages*. Damages may first be classified as *general* (automatically awarded by a court in respect of loss or injury which it presumes to have arisen) and *special* (which have to be specially pleaded in respect of any loss or injury which the court does not presume to have arisen—e.g. medical expenses).

When awarded, damages may be of six main types: (1) *contemptuous* (e.g. one penny, awarded as a sign of the court's displeasure to unmeritorious plaintiffs, who are nevertheless entitled to succeed); (2) *nominal* (a small token award when there has been a minor tort or breach of contract, involving no actual loss); (3) *substantial* (pecuniary compensation intended to put the plaintiff in the position that he would have enjoyed before the tort, or if a contract had been performed; (4) *aggravated* (in excess of the actual pecuniary loss, where an injury has been aggravated (made worse) by the motives or conduct of the defendant); (5) *exemplary* (similar to aggravated damages but containing a punitive or deterrent element); and (6) *liquidated* (actually expressed in a contract).

(*b*) *The granting of an injunction*. This is an equitable remedy (*see* I, 7(*a*)(*iv*)), in the form of an order, granted *at the court's discretion*, provided that it can be effectively enforced by the court, that pecuniary damages would not be adequate compensation and that, in the case of a contract, the defendant is doing something that he agreed *not* to do.

Injunctions are of four main types: (1) *perpetual* (unlimited in time); (2) *prohibitory* (granted to prevent the doing of an act, e.g. closing a right of way); (3) *mandatory* (granted to compel the defendant to perform some act, e.g. to abate a nuisance); and (4) *interlocutory* (granted to prohibit the commission or continuance of some activity by the defendant, pending the hearing of the action).

Sometimes an application can be made for an interlocutory injunction *ex parte* (i.e. in the absence of the defendant) but this will be granted only to protect the plaintiff for a short time, until another application can be made in the presence of the defendant.

(*c*) *The decree of specific performance.* This is an equitable (and therefore discretionary) remedy for breach of contract, more fully explained at XVII, 5(*d*).

(*d*) *The declaratory judgment.* Without awarding any of the above remedies, a court (generally of the Queen's Bench Division) may, at its discretion, make a declaration on a question of law or rights. The scope for such judgments is very wide and three examples, in respect of ministerial actions, have been given at IV, 2(*a*).

(*e*) *The application for judicial review.* Under Order 53 of the Rules of the Supreme Court (and the Supreme Court Act 1981, s. 31), this procedure is used to obtain any of the *prerogative orders* described at (*i*)–(*iii*) below and it may also be used to seek an injunction or declaration. All five remedies may be sought singly or in the alternative and damages may be awarded if such a claim is maintainable in law. Except in vacation, the application is made to the Divisional Court of the Queen's Bench Division and it is first necessary to apply *ex parte* (i.e. direct to the court and not by writ, etc., to the other party—although all interested parties must be informed) for *leave to apply.* This will not be granted if the court considers that the applicant lacks *locus standi* (*see* IV, 1(*b*)(*vi*)) or if there has been undue delay. If leave is given, the court later hears the case and decides whether or not to grant the relief sought. Appeal lies to the Court of Appeal and the House of Lords. The prerogative orders are:

(*i*) *The order of mandamus.* This is used to command a person or body to perform a mandatory (but not discretionary) public duty, which must be specific and enforceable by law; furthermore, the applicant must have called for its fulfilment and have met with a refusal or non-compliance. It will not be granted if a satisfactory alternative remedy exists and is illustrated in *Re Godden* (1971)(*see* (*iii*) below).

(*ii*) *The order of certiorari.* This is used to bring before the Divisional Court any decision of an "inferior court", on the grounds that it has acted *ultra vires*, in contravention of the rules of natural justice or erroneously in law. The term "inferior court" includes not only courts of law but also any public body or person exercising judicial or quasi-judicial functions. On granting *certiorari*, the Divisional Court may itself vary a sentence passed by a magistrates' or Crown Court; alternatively, it may remit the matter to the inferior court for reconsideration in accordance with the finding. Illustrative cases include:

R. v. *Leicestershire Fire Authority, ex parte Thompson* (*1978*): The Chief Fire Officer had intended personally to hear a charge against T, a station officer, for disobeying an order but referred the matter to the Fire Authority, after being accused by T of victimisation. The committee found the charge proved and cleared the room to consider sentence but called in the CFO, to advise on the practical implications of the various possible sentences. The Divisional Court granted *certiorari* to quash the award, as there had been a breach of the principle that justice must manifestly be seen to have been done—even though the Chief Fire Officer had not participated in the committee's deliberations.

R. v. *Huntingdon District Council, ex parte Cowan* (*1984*): In connection with an application for an entertainments licence for a proposed discotheque, the Council had received observations from the police and fire authority, also a petition from certain objectors. Without informing the applicants of the objections (or giving them the opportunity to make representations in reply), it refused the application and *certiorari* was accordingly granted.

(*iii*) *The order of prohibition.* This is used to prevent an "inferior court" from *beginning or continuing* a case where it is acting *ultra vires* or contrary to the rules of natural justice, also to control ministers or public authorities in the exercise of their judicial or quasi-judicial functions. It will not lie against a non-statutory body (e.g. a sports club) nor if a final decision has been reached (in which case there is recourse to *certiorari*). It has been illustrated in—

Re Godden (*1971*): Accusations against his superior made by G, a chief inspector of the Kent police force, were not upheld in a report by a Chief Constable of another force. Erotic documents had also been found in G's desk and, having seen the report, Dr Crosbie Brown, chief medical officer of the Kent force, certified him unfit for duty on account of mental disorder. G's own consultant psychiatrist was not allowed to see the report and certified him "completely normal". In order compulsorily to retire G, the police authority nominated Dr Brown to determine whether he was "permanently disabled", under the Police Pensions Regulations 1971. Reversing the decision of the Divisional Court, the Court of Appeal held that an order of prohibition should issue to disqualify Dr Brown from determining the matter as, having already committed himself to a view, he could not bring an impartial judgment to bear in performing a quasi-judicial function. An order of *mandamus* was also granted to compel the police authority to disclose the report to G's medical advisers.

(*f*) *The prerogative writ of habeas corpus.* If any person (except a prisoner of war or interned enemy alien) is confined without legal justification, he may secure his release by the prerogative writ of *habeas corpus.* This necessitates the submission of an affidavit to a Divisional Court of the Queen's Bench Division (or, in vacation, to a judge in chambers) by the prisoner or by any person acting on his behalf. If the need is urgent and a case is made out, the court may make an *order absolute* for the issue of the writ, which affords immediate release. Alternatively, an *order nisi* may be granted, to give the other side a chance to oppose. Where there is opposition, the case is argued and, if good cause for detention is not shown, the order is made absolute. The writ must be issued unconditionally or not at all, and appeal by either side lies to the House of Lords, by leave of the Divisional Court or of the House, but it is not necessary to show that a point of law of general public importance is involved. The use of the writ has been illustrated in *Sirros* v. *Moore* (*1975*) IV, **2**(*c*).

THE RELIEFS OF THE LAW

3. The granting of bail. Bail is the process in criminal proceedings whereby a person is released from pre-trial detention by the police (after arrest without a warrant) or by the magistrates' court, Crown Court, High Court or Court of Appeal, on condition that he presents himself at an appointed time and place for a court hearing. He is required to enter into a recognisance, undertaking to forfeit a sum of money if he fails to appear and recognisances may also be demanded of one or more other persons, known as *sureties*; technically, he is then not set free but instead released from the custody of the law to that of the sureties—who may, if they wish, return him before the appointed time. Any contract to indemnify a surety is void, as contravening public policy and is an offence. Where it appears necessary, further conditions may be imposed (e.g. the surrendering of passports, regular reporting to the police, etc.).

On an appeal from the Crown Court to the Court of Appeal, bail will be granted only in exceptional circumstances (e.g. a *prima facie* likelihood of success or the risk that the sentence will have been served by the time the appeal is heard). In the magistrates' courts, with the exceptions outlined in (*a*) and (*b*) below, there is a general right to bail and, if it is refused, reasons must be given (in writing to those not legally represented). Furthermore, there is a right to apply to a High Court judge in chambers or to the Crown Court for release from custody or for review of unduly onerous bail conditions. The Bail Act 1976, Sched. 1 draws a distinction between:

(*a*) *The persons accused or convicted of imprisonable offences.* These may (but must not) be refused bail (1) if there are substantial grounds for believing that they would fail to surrender, commit an offence, interfere with witnesses or otherwise obstruct the course of justice; (2) if the court is satisfied that they should be kept in custody for their own protection (or welfare, if juveniles); (3) if they are in custody as a result of a court sentence or that of a Service authority; (4) if it has not been practicable to obtain sufficient information for the necessary decisions; (5) if, having been released on bail, they have been arrested for absconding or breaking conditions; (6) also if the case is adjourned for inquiries or a report which it would be impossible to complete without custody.

(*b*) *The persons accused or convicted of non-imprisonable offences.* These may (but must not) be refused bail (1) if they have previously failed to surrender to bail in criminal proceedings and the court believes that they would again do so; (2) if the court is satisfied that they should be kept in custody for their own protection (or welfare, if juveniles); (3) if they are in custody as a result of a court sentence or that of a Service authority; (4) also if, having been released on bail, they have been arrested for absconding or breaking conditions.

In 1979 approximately 20,000 of the 500,000 persons bailed by the police (and 9,000 of the 228,000 bailed by magistrates) failed to surrender. In America absconding is deterred by requiring the deposit of money or a bond at the time of granting bail. This practice has given birth to a race of professional "bondsmen", acting as sureties for a fee, but often refusing to accept people as good risks. In the 1960s several promising experiments (notably by the Vera Institute of Justice in New York City) were conducted in providing assurances in lieu of bail for indigent accused persons (e.g. a points system, awarding two for living with one's family, three for keeping a job for a year, etc.); alternatively, some states have made failure to surrender a criminal offence.

4. The ordering of costs. The term *costs* means the sum of money which a court may, at its discretion, order one party to pay to the other in compensation for expenses incurred in the case (e.g. fees of solicitor, counsel, expert witnesses, etc.). Costs may be awarded in:

(*a*) *The courts of civil jurisdiction.* In general the unsuccessful party has to pay the other's costs but procedures vary in the different courts:

(*i*) *The High Court.* In the Queen's Bench Division the court may award a lump sum or accept a bill of costs claimed, drawn up by the successful party's solicitor. If the opposing solicitor disputes the bill, it becomes subject to *taxation* (i.e. examination and possible reduction) by taxing officers (sometimes called Taxing Masters). Both sides attend and there is a right of review by a judge in chambers; from there appeal may lie (generally with leave of the judge) to the Court of Appeal. Certain fixed charges are laid down (e.g. in respect of pre-trial procedures) but some items are discretionary. Generally costs are awarded *as between party and party* (allowing only the expenditure necessary for conducting the litigation, and discounting charges incurred in conducting it more conveniently); however, a more generous method is the *common fund basis* (whereby all reasonable expenses are recoverable and the solicitor's bill to his client is generally paid by the opponent in full). No costs are normally recoverable if less than £600 is awarded and a plaintiff who fails to recover £3,000 receives costs only on the county court scale.

(*ii*) *The county court.* Here taxation is carried out by the registrar, with a right of appeal to the circuit judge, and there is a scheme of five scales of itemised costs, varying with the amount of the judgment (if the plaintiff wins) or claim (if he loses). In admitted or undefended cases, counsel's fees are not allowed and the court must certify whether small defended cases are "fit for counsel".

(*iii*) *The magistrates' court.* This may order "just and reasonable" costs (Magistrates' Courts Act 1980, s. 64).

(*iv*) *The appellate courts.* A winning party in the Court of Appeal is generally awarded the costs of the trial and the appeal; however, if permitted to adduce new evidence or fresh arguments, a successful appellant may be refused costs. If a new trial is ordered, the cost of all hearings are based on its result. A successful respondent may be awarded costs in all courts.

Taxed costs rarely cover the amount that a successful party has to pay to his own solicitor and the difference, which he must contribute himself, is known as *extra costs*; these can constitute an appreciable deterrent to litigation. As an unsuccessful party is seldom totally in the wrong, the "loser pays all" principle is also open to criticism—particularly when a decision (notably relating to a point of law) is reversed on appeal and the loser has to meet the expenses of both the trial and the appellate proceedings. There has consequently been argument in favour of paying from a public fund the costs of such appeals.

(*b*) *The courts of criminal jurisdiction.* Under the Costs of Criminal Cases Act 1973, the prosecution may apply for an order for costs out of central funds or against a convicted person. Likewise, an acquitted person may apply for an order for costs against the prosecution or out of central funds.

5. The provision of legal aid. Lord Justice Darling's comment that "The Law, like the Ritz Hotel, is open to all", with its implication that recourse to the courts is a prerogative of the wealthy, is to a certain extent no longer pertinent, since the introduction of legal aid. The system is regulated by the Legal Aid Acts 1974–82 which provide for legal *advice, assistance* and *aid* to persons of small or moderate means. Eligibility is dependent upon the applicant's *disposable capital* (gross capital less the value of his house, furniture and household possessions) and *disposable income* (gross income less deductions for dependants, interest on loans, income tax, rates, rent, National Insurance contributions, etc.). Except where they are separated or have conflicting interests, the means of husband and wife are aggregated. The figures are assessed and certified by the Social Security Advisory Committee.

(*a*) *The provision of advice and assistance.* This covers oral or written advice concerning the application of English law to any particular circumstance and the appropriate steps to be taken in connection with it, also representation in any proceedings before a court, tribunal or statutory inquiry. The scheme covers the costs of a "duty" solicitor who is present within the precincts of a magistrates' court or county court and who is requested by the court to represent a person who is in need of help. Advice and assistance from a solicitor (and, if necessary, a barrister) may be obtained by anyone whose disposable capital and income do not exceed a certain figure.

Under what is called the "green form scheme" any solicitor can give advice and assistance provided that his costs and expenses do not exceed £40 but, for any figure in excess of this, the leave of the area legal aid committee must be obtained. The solicitor's costs and expenses are paid out of the client's contribution, any moneys recovered from another party and from the legal aid fund.

Notably in under-privileged areas, *legal centres* have been established, often in the form of ordinary shops, to assist those living in the neighbourhood. Some are set up by the Law Society and operate within the framework of the above system, with means tests, etc. Others are funded by charitable organisations and provide a free service. Citizens' Advice Bureaux can give information about local solicitors and many have honorary legal advisers.

(*b*) *The provision of aid in civil proceedings.* Legal aid, involving representation in court, can be granted for civil proceedings, including matrimonial causes, but applications will not be approved for actions in defamation, election petitions or where it appears that the applicant would gain only a trivial advantage. Applications for *civil aid certificates* must be made to local legal aid committees (or *area* committees, in the case of appellate proceedings) of the Law Society. Appeal from the refusal of a local committee lies to an area committee. Where a certificate is granted, the applicant may select a solicitor (and, if necessary, counsel) from a panel and the expenses are paid out of the legal aid fund. A court may also order that the costs of a successful unassisted party be paid from the fund.

(*c*) *The provision of aid in criminal proceedings.* Courts of criminal jurisdiction may make a *legal aid order* if it appears that a person's means are such that he requires assistance in meeting the expenses which he may incur. A single order may be made to cover legal aid before magistrates, at the Crown Court (if the accused is committed for trial) also advice on (and preparation of) appeal thereafter. In magistrates' courts the aid does not include representation by counsel, except in the case of indictable offences where the court is of the opinion that it is desirable, on account of the gravity or difficulty of the circumstances. Legal aid to a person who is ultimately convicted includes advice on whether there are reasonable grounds for appeal and, if so, also assistance in applying for leave to appeal.

If a person's means are insufficient, the court *may* make a legal aid order if it is considered desirable to do so in the interests of justice, but it *must* make one if the accused is committed for trial on a charge of murder or if the prosecutor appeals to the House of Lords. Applicants for legal aid must furnish a written statement of means, and inquiries as to means are made by the Social Security Advisory Committee.

There is a liability on the part of legally assisted persons to contribute towards or repay the costs incurred and, after disposing of a case, a court is empowered to make such order as appears reasonable, having regard to the person's resources and commitments. Before granting legal aid, a court can also require an applicant to make a payment on account of any contribution that may be ordered at the end of the case.

If any doubt arises concerning whether a legal aid order should be made in respect of any person, the doubt must be resolved in that person's favour.

The Legal Aid Act 1982, s. 5 enables regulations to be made to transfer the grant and control of legal aid orders from the courts to the Law Society Legal Aid Committees. Moreover, s. 6 of the Act provides that, if a legal aid order is refused by a magistrates' court, appeal shall lie to such court or other body as may be specified in regulations.

PROGRESS TEST 6

1. Describe the powers available to magistrates to deal with young offenders. Do you consider that they are adequate? (1)

2. Examine the sentencing powers of the Crown Court over adult offenders, in the light of their deterrent or reformative effect. (1)

3. Discuss the awarding of damages and the granting of an injunction. (2)

4. Explain the use of the three prerogative orders. (2)

5. Describe the method of obtaining release from pre-trial detention. (3)

6. Consider any weaknesses in the bail system and possible ways of reforming it. (3)

7. Describe the system of costs. (4)

8. In what way do costs act as a deterrent to litigation? Do you consider that any reforms are necessary. (4)

9. Examine the roles of solicitors and legal centres in helping persons of limited means. (5)

10. Would it be possible to devise a simple unified system of dispensing legal aid and advice in civil and criminal matters? (5)

CHAPTER VII

The Application of the Law

ELEMENTS OF JUDGE-MADE LAW

1. The interpretation of statutes. It has been estimated that over 50 per cent of cases in the Court of Appeal (and over 75 per cent in the House of Lords) relate to the interpretation of statutes. In this connection, the first function of a judge is to decide whether a statute is ambiguous and, if he does reach this conclusion, he must then determine which (if any) of a number of (often conflicting) rules should be applied. Reference may not be made to the parliamentary debates preceding the passing of the Act, or to its marginal notes (which are not inserted by parliamentary authority). In general, interpretation is effected in accordance with the following principles.

(*a*) *The statutory provisions.* Consolidating previous legislation, the Interpretation Act 1978 prescribes the manner in which certain words or expressions are to be interpreted. *Unless the contrary intention appears in a particular statute*, words importing the masculine gender include the feminine (and vice versa); words in the singular include the plural (and vice versa); the measurement of any distance relates to a straight line on a horizontal plane, an expression of time connotes Greenwich Mean Time; a "month" means a calendar month; to "swear" includes to affirm and declare; a "person" can be a body of persons, corporate or incorporate (*see* VIII, 1(*a*)–(*b*)); "writing" covers typing, printing, lithography, photography and any other modes of representing or reproducing words in a visible form. Where one statute repeals another and is then itself repealed, the original one is not revived. Where an Act empowers the making of delegated legislation, expressions in it have the meaning that they bear in the enabling Act. All of these provisions may nevertheless be confuted by a contrary intention, as illustrated in—

Rolloswin Investments v. *Chromolit Portugal* (*1970*): It was held that a Limited Company was *not* a "person" within the meaning of the Sunday Observance Act 1677, as it was incapable of public worship and also a creature of law unknown in 1677.

(*b*) *The literal rule.* Initially the words of a statute must be applied according to their "ordinary, plain and natural meaning". Thus, if hardship results and there is no ambiguity, the only remedy is an amending statute (cf. **2(*f*)(*iii*)**). An illustrative case is—

Mesure v. *Mesure* (*1960*): Under the Matrimonial Causes Act 1950, as amended, five years' continuous treatment for mental illness was a ground for divorce, at the petition of the spouse. Mrs. M had been in a mental hospital from 1952–9 but, for eleven weeks in 1955, she was in a sanatorium being treated for tuberculosis. It was held that no divorce could be granted, as the mental treatment was not continuous.

(*c*) *The golden rule.* This implies that the literal application of words may be modified if it would lead to "an absurdity or repugnancy or inconsistency with the rest of the instrument". This has been illustrated in—

Maddox v. *Storer* (*1962*): The Road Traffic Act 1960 made it an offence to drive at over 30 mph a vehicle "adapted to carry more than seven passengers". The appellant had been convicted of driving a minibus, originally constructed to carry eleven passengers and not altered. The offence was held to be proved as "adapted" was taken to mean "suitable or apt" (rather than "altered so as to be apt").

(*d*) *The mischief rule.* If the literal or golden rules fail to assist the judge, he may seek the aid of the mischief rule, enunciated in *Heydon's Case* (*1584*). This entitles him to consider:

    (*i*) What was the common law before the passing of the Act?

    (*ii*) What was the mischief and defect for which the common law did not provide?

    (*iii*) What was the remedy resolved by Parliament for curing the defect?

An illustrative case is—

Elliott v. *Grey* (*1960*): Under the Road Traffic Act 1930, it was an offence for a car to be "used on the road" without a valid insurance policy and the Court of Appeal held that a jacked-up car with its battery removed was being "used on the road", as it could create a hazard.

(*e*) *The ejusdem generis Rule.* This means that, where particular words are followed by general words, the general words must be limited to the same kind as the particular; for example—

> *Gregory* v. *Fearn* (*1953*): The Sunday Observance Act 1677 provided that "no tradesman, artificer, workman, labourer *or other person whatsoever* shall do or exercise any worldly labour, business or work of their ordinary callings upon the Lord's Day". The Court of Appeal held that the words "or other person whatsoever" must be construed *ejusdem generis* with those that precede them; thus the provision did not apply to an estate agent (who was not a tradesman because he did not buy and sell things).

(*f*) *The presumptions of interpretation.* Unless a statute contains express provision to the contrary, it may be presumed that

    (*i*) It applies to the United Kingdom as a whole.

    (*ii*) It does not bind the Crown.

    (*iii*) It does not restrict individual liberty or deprive anyone of property.

    (*iv*) It does not have retrospective effect.

    (*v*) It does not infringe international law.

    (*vi*) It does not make any major constitutional change.

    (*vii*) It does not impliedly repeal another Act.

2. The doctrine of judicial precedent. In examining the doctrine of judicial precedent, the following points are of particular importance:

(*a*) *The binding precedent.* When a judgment is delivered in court, the *ratio decidendi* (reason for the decision) is given and it is this which creates a *binding precedent*, which *must* be followed as shown below:

    (*i*) *The House of Lords.* Like all English courts, this is bound by the decisions of the European Court of Justice. Formerly the House regarded itself as being bound by its own previous decisions but, under the *Practice Statement* (*Judicial Precedent*) (*1966*), it can depart from previous decisions where it appears right to do so.

    (*ii*) *The Court of Appeal* (*Civil Division*). This is bound by decisions of the House of Lords and also by *its own previous decisions*. However, it was ruled in *Young* v. *Bristol Aeroplane Co.* (*1944*) that the court would not be so bound if there were conflictions in its previous decisions, or if a previous decision was made *per incuriam* (in error).

    (*iii*) *The Court of Appeal* (*Criminal Division*). This is bound by decisions of the House of Lords and basically by *its own*

previous decisions. However, in *R.* v. *Newsome* (*1970*), Widgery
L. J. said that a court of five judges might depart from an earlier
view expressed by a court of three. The two Divisions of the Court
of Appeal do not bind each other.

(*iv*) *The Divisional Courts of the High Court.* These are
bound by decisions of the House of Lords, Court of Appeal and
their own previous decisions.

(*v*) *The Ordinary Courts of the High Court.* These are
bound by decisions of the House of Lords, Court of Appeal and
Divisional Courts of the same Division.

(*vi*) *The county courts.* These are bound by decisions of the
House of Lords, Court of Appeal and High Court.

(*vii*) *The Crown Court and magistrates' courts.* These are
bound by decisions of the House of Lords, Court of Appeal, High
Court (in civil matters) and Divisional Court of the Queen's Bench
Division (in criminal matters).

(*b*) *The terminology.* In the practical application of judicial
precedent, the significance of the following terms needs to be
appreciated:

(*i*) *Distinguishing.* The binding precedent of a higher
court may sometimes be evaded by distinguishing, i.e. by finding
some material differences between the facts of the earlier case and
those of the one being decided.

(*ii*) *Reversing.* A precedent may be reversed when a higher
court allows an appeal *in the same litigation*, disagreeing with a
point of law which decided the matter in the court below. This has
been illustrated at IV, 1(*b*)(*vi*) in *Gouriet* v. *Union of Post Office
Workers* (*1977*).

(*iii*) *Overruling.* A precedent may be overruled when, *in a
later case*, a higher court decides a similar matter differently. This
does not, however, affect the decision in the earlier case because,
under the maxim of *res judicata* (in full—*res judicata pro veritate
accipitur*—"a thing adjudicated is received as the truth"), once an
issue between parties has been litigated and decided, it cannot be
raised again between the same parties. *See*:

Re Waring, Westminster Bank v. *Burton Butler* (*1948*): Under
a will, annuities (yearly payments of a certain sum of money)
were left to A and B. In 1942 A was a party in an appeal to the
Court of Appeal, which ruled that income tax must be deducted
from the annuity. In 1946, in a similar case involving different
parties, the House of Lords overruled the 1942 decision. Consequently both A and B applied to the High Court, to determine
whether tax should be deducted from their annuities. It was held

that only A was liable to deduction, on account of the 1942 case, which could not be re-opened.

(c) *The persuasive precedent*. In addition to the binding form described above, there is also the persuasive precedent, which need not be followed but which is worthy of the court's consideration. It generally originates from:

(i) *The decisions of English courts not binding the one concerned*, also those of the Judicial Committee of the Privy Council, Scottish, Commonwealth and United States courts, as in—

Westward Television Ltd. v. *Hart* (1968): In this tax case the Court of Appeal held that the decision of the Scottish Court of Session in another case should be followed.

(ii) *The obiter dicta of English judges*. The term *obiter dicta* covers explanations, illustrations, etc., said "by the way" and not necessary to the decision of the case that was being tried.

(iii) *The writings of leading authorities*. These have no binding authority in themselves but they sometimes influence the decisions of judges. Theoretically, no living writer should be cited in an English court as an authority but, in practice, judges accord due weight to the opinions of eminent contemporaries, as in—

R. v. *Local Commissioner for Administration for the North & East Area of England, ex parte Bradford Metropolitan City Council* (1979) Local commissioners are empowered by statute to investigate complaints of *maladministration* by local authorities and it was necessary for the Court of Appeal to determine the meaning of this word. Lord Denning M.R. adopted the definition suggested by Mr. R. H. W. Crossman, Lord President of the Council, when the legislation was being considered by the House of Commons. Being prohibited from referring to the official reports of parliamentary debates (*see* 1), the Master of the Rolls acquired the quotation from the writings of a leading constitutional lawyer.

(iv) *The rules of Roman law*. Persuasive authority has been accorded to Roman law, notably Justinian's Digest, as in—

Tucker v. *Farm & General Investment Trust* (1966): In this case relating to animals acquired on hire-purchase terms, the Court of Appeal followed the Roman rule as to the ownership of the progeny.

(d) *The creation of a precedent*. If a case to be decided is one without precedent (i.e. unlike any previous case), the judge must decide it according to general principles of law. By so doing, it can be said that he lays down an *original precedent*, which later judges will follow if they encounter a similar case. Some authorities consider that judges merely *declare* the law (*jus dicere*), while others hold that they actually *make it* (*jus dare*). This, of course, implies that the facts of a case were previously governed by no law, and it is like arguing that a piece of land is valueless until it has been sold.

The two opinions may be resolved by saying that, in any proceedings, it can be assumed that there is somewhere a rule of law which will cover the facts in dispute but, once the judgment has been rendered, it may be admitted that the new decision has modified the law. It should also be emphasised that the judges' role in interpreting statutes (*see* 1 above) has given rise to a large body of case law.

(*e*) *The advantages of the system.* The advantages of the system of judicial precedent are that:

(*i*) It provides greater detail than is possible with a purely enacted system of law. Statutes assume the existence of the common law and are addenda and errata to it; they would be meaningless if it were swept away. On the other hand, when statute and common law conflict, it is the former that prevails—on account of the sovereignty of Parliament.

(*ii*) It creates precision and consistency in the application and development of the law. It thus provides some degree of certainty, upon which people can base their conduct. Many continental systems have only persuasive precedent.

(*iii*) It is based on factual situations of a practical nature and it creates flexibility—as a general *ratio decidendi* can be applied to numerous circumstances. It also has aptitude for growth as the needs of society alter.

(*f*) *The disadvantages of the system.* Critics of the system argue that:

(*i*) It restricts the discretion of judges and "distinguishing" can lead to over-subtlety and artificiality.

(*ii*) It makes the law difficult to find—because of the volume of cases. Not all decisions are reported but this does not affect their validity as precedent.

(*iii*) It lacks ability to correct its own defects. Bad decisions are binding until reversed or overruled; sometimes, therefore, the common law must be amended by statute, as in—

Bowles v. *Bank of England* (*1913*): The plaintiff claimed from the Bank the sum of £52, which had been deducted as income tax, in accordance with a budget resolution in a committee of the House of Commons, prior to the passing of the Finance Bill. It was held that there could be no taxation without the authority of a statute, so the deduction was illegal. Parliament then passed the Provisional Collection of Taxes Act 1913, which gave temporary effect to House of Commons taxation resolutions.

THE LAW OF EVIDENCE

3. The classification of evidence. The word *evidence* can be defined as "all the legal means, exclusive of mere argument, which tend to prove or disprove any matter of fact, the truth of which is submitted to judicial investigation". Crucial to any evidence is the question as to whether it is *admissible*, i.e. acceptable to a court. In any jury trial, matters of *law* (including the admissibility of evidence) are determined by the *judge*, and matters of *fact* (including the credibility and weight of evidence) by the *jury*. In both criminal and civil cases, all relevant facts must be proved, except where the court may take *judicial notice* of matters which are so notorious or clearly established that formal evidence is unnecessary (e.g. British jurisdiction, parliamentary procedure, local government boundaries, weights and measures, etc.). In general, there are three types of evidence—oral, documentary and real. *Oral* evidence comprises statements made by witnesses in court. *Documentary* evidence covers public and private documents, also written statements of relevant facts; oral evidence given in connection with documents is termed *extrinsic* evidence. *Real* evidence is that of material objects ("exhibits") produced for inspection by the court. Although there is no official classification, the three types of evidence can be categorised as follows:

(*a*) *Direct and circumstantial. Direct* evidence is that which relates to a fact actually in issue, e.g. the testimony of a witness concerning what he had perceived with his own senses, or an original document or material object. *Circumstantial* evidence is evidence of facts not directly in issue (e.g. motive, preparation, subsequent conduct) from which a fact actually in issue (e.g. a criminal offence) may be inferred. It is admissible, as it can make the facts in issue probable and it can sometimes be of higher probative value than direct evidence (which can be subject to mistake or perjury). An illustrative case is—

McGreevy v. *DPP* (*1973*): M was charged with murder on entirely circumstantial evidence. Ten times during the summing-up, the judge had told the jury that they must be satisfied of M's guilt beyond reasonable doubt. M was convicted and appealed, contending that the jury should have been warned not to convict unless the evidence was inconsistent with any other explanations. Dismissing the appeal, the House of Lords held that no such direction was necessary.

(b) *Primary and secondary. Primary* evidence is the best and highest kind of oral, documentary and real evidence, which the law regards as affording the greatest certainty of a fact in question, e.g. an original document, a witness who saw an incident, etc. *Secondary* evidence is an inferior or substitutionary form which indicates the existence of a more original source of information, but which is *not* admissible if primary evidence is available—

R. v. Nowaz (1976): N was charged with making a false declaration for registration as a citizen of the United Kingdom and Colonies. The Pakistani consul, who had shown the documents to the police, claimed diplomatic immunity from attending the trial and a police officer gave oral evidence of what he had seen. The Court of Appeal held that the secondary evidence was rightly admitted.

(c) *Original and hearsay. Original* evidence may be oral, documentary or real and a witness gives original evidence when he testifies from his own knowledge. If, however, his information is derived from other persons and he himself has no personal knowledge of the facts in question, then his evidence is said to be *hearsay*. It should nevertheless be emphasised that what may be hearsay for one purpose may be original for another. Thus evidence that a witness had been told by a servant that his master was abroad is hearsay and inadmissible for proving that the master really was abroad—but it would be original and admissible evidence of an unsuccessful search for the master. The admissibility of hearsay evidence is considered below.

4. The principles of evidence. In general, the principles of the law of evidence are common to both criminal and civil cases, but the following distinctions must be drawn:

(a) *The burden of proof.* Criminal prosecutions must be proved *beyond reasonable doubt* (which does not mean "beyond the shadow of a doubt") and the onus normally rests on the prosecution throughout the trial. In the relatively few circumstances when the burden of proving a fact rests on the defence, the standard of proof is "on a balance of probabilities". The elements necessary for conviction of a criminal offence are described at XVIII, 1.

Civil cases are proved by *preponderance of evidence* and, at the beginning of a trial, the onus normally rests on the plaintiff. Nevertheless, as the case proceeds, the burden may shift and, even at the outset it may sometimes rest on the defendant, e.g. where the maxim *res ipsa loquitur* ("the facts speak for themselves") applies in negligence, as in—

> *Lloyde* v. *West Midlands Gas Board* (*1971*): L was severely injured by an explosion resulting from an escape of gas, where the supply system had disintegrated. It was held that he could invoke *res ipsa loquitur* and the burden of disproving negligence was thrown on to the defendants.

(*b*) *The admissibility of hearsay.* In criminal cases, hearsay evidence is generally inadmissible, apart from certain dying declarations (e.g. in cases of murder and manslaughter) and also certain statements contained in public documents and documents forming part of a record of a trade or business; this has been illustrated in—

> *R.* v. *Marshall* (*1977*): M admitted buying goods from a man who told him that they were stolen. As there was no evidence to support the fact that the goods were stolen—other than M's statement (which was hearsay and consequently inadmissible), it was held that there was no case to answer. (*See* XXII, 7(*a*) below.)

In civil cases, hearsay is admissible in accordance with the Civil Evidence Act 1968, Part I or any other statutory provision or by agreement of the parties. Under the Civil Evidence Act 1972, hearsay evidence of opinion is similarly admissible.

(*c*) *The admissibility of confessions and admissions.* In criminal cases, confessions are admissible only if they are free and voluntary, i.e. *not* induced by the promise or threat of a person in authority, by hope of reward (other than spiritual) or by fear of punishment. The onus of proving that a confession was voluntary rests on the prosecution, as in—

> *R.* v. *Bamford* (*1978*): Appellants claimed that they had made certain confessions after being told "If you make a statement admitting it, I can get bail sorted out". The trial judge had said that this was not an inducement but a statement of fact; however the Court of Appeal quashed the conviction on the ground that he had not applied the proper test.

Under the Criminal Justice Act 1967, the defence can make formal admissions to the court, to obviate the need for proving the facts but apart from this, every factor relevant to the guilt of the accused must be proved.

With regard to civil proceedings, it has been shown at V, 2(*c*)(*ii*) that the defendant must answer every allegation in the plaintiff's statement of claim and anything not denied is assumed to be admitted.

(*d*) *The evidence of character.* In criminal cases, evidence as to the good character of the accused is always admissible but the prosecution cannot adduce evidence as to his bad character unless the accused puts his character in evidence or attacks the character of a prosecution witness, as in—

R. v. *Lamb* (*1981*): By a majority verdict, the appellant had been convicted of wounding with intent, having been identified by two witnesses from amongst 900 Criminal Record Office photographs. The prosecution had produced an album of these in court and, as they indicated a previous criminal record, the Court of Appeal quashed the conviction.

In civil cases, evidence as to the good character of either party is inadmissible but in certain circumstances (e.g. the defence of justification in an action for defamation) evidence of character may be adduced for attacking credit.

(*e*) *The necessity for corroboration.* In criminal cases, evidence must be corroborated (though not necessarily by a second witness) in charges of perjury, certain sexual offences, personation at elections and exceeding the speed limit. The unsworn evidence of children of tender years must be corroborated and it is the duty of judges to warn juries that it is unsafe (though not prohibited) to convict anyone on the uncorroborated evidence of an accomplice. Illustrative cases are—

R. v. *Buck* (*1981*): The appellant had been convicted of theft, the only independent direct evidence of which had been given on oath by a nine-year-old girl. The Court of Appeal quashed the conviction, as the trial judge should have warned the jury of acting on the uncorroborated sworn evidence of a child, and should have indicated what evidence, if any, amounted to corroboration.

R. v. *Timmins* (*1981*): The appellant had been convicted of handling stolen goods, the main prosecution witness having been the thief. The judge had warned the jury that it was dangerous to act on such uncorroborated evidence but, although there was powerful corroboration, he had failed to identify it and the Court of Appeal quashed the conviction.

In civil cases corroboration is not normally required.

THE INSTIGATION OF REFORM

5. The reform of the law. The reform of the law is initiated principally by:

(*a*) *The Government.* Proposed legislation is agreed by the Cabinet, drafted by the relevant government department and considered by the following Cabinet committees:

(*i*) *The Legislation Committee.* This considers draft bills (to ensure that they comply with Cabinet decisions) and watches their progress through Parliament. The chairman is the Lord President of the Council and meetings are generally attended by the Leader of the House of Commons and the departmental minister concerned.

(*ii*) *The Future Legislation Committee.* This considers projected bills and prepares the programme for each parliamentary session.

In addition to the *public bills* introduced by the Government, there are also *private members' bills*, introduced by individual MPs and these can reform the law if they become statutes (e.g. Mr David Steel's bill which became the Abortion Act 1967).

(*b*) *The advisory committees.* These are part-time bodies which advise the Lord Chancellor or Home Secretary and principal examples are:

(*i*) *The Statute Law Committee.* This is presided over by the Lord Chancellor; the vice-chairman of the Law Commission (*see* (*c*)) and the twenty-four members include the Attorney-General and Lord Advocate. It is concerned primarily with the form (rather than the content) of statutes and it therefore deals with *consolidation* (the amalgamation of existing Acts), rather than *codification* (the amalgamation of statute and case law). One example of its work is the Taxes Management Act 1970.

(*ii*) *The Law Reform Committee.* This reports to the Lord Chancellor on civil law and it comprises five judges, four practising barristers, two solicitors and three academic lawyers. One example of its work is the Occupiers' Liability Act 1957.

(*iii*) *The Criminal Law Revision Committee.* This reports to the Home Secretary on criminal law. Like the Law Reform

Committee, it does not contribute a great deal but one example of its work is the Theft Act 1968.

(c) *The Law Commission*. Constituted under the Law Commissions Act 1965, this comprises five full-time legally qualified members, headed by a High Court judge as chairman, with a research staff and parliamentary draftsmen. Its duties comprise a continuous review of the law, codification of the law, also recommendations for the repeal of obsolete enactments and the elimination of anomalies. It issues annual reports, which are laid before Parliament, and one example of its work is the Family Law Reform Act 1969.

PROGRESS TEST 7

1. Outline the rules governing the interpretation of statutes. **(1)**
2. Consider any ways of improving the interpretation of statutes. **(1)**
3. Explain how the doctrine of judicial precedent operates. **(2)**
4. Do judges make the law—or merely declare it? **(2)**
5. Explain what evidence is admissible in a criminal trial. **(3)**
6. Should the rules of evidence be more stringent in criminal cases than in civil matters? **(4)**
7. Examine the composition and functions of the Law Commission. **(5)**
8. Do you consider that existing arrangements for law reform are adequate? **(5)**

CHAPTER VIII

The Law of Persons

THE RECOGNITION OF LEGAL RELATIONSHIPS

1. The categories of persons. In law the term "person" means any
entity which is capable of having rights and obligations (notably the
ability to sue, to be sued and to own property) and there are two
classes—*natural persons* (human beings) and *artificial* (or *juristic*)
persons (corporations). A clear distinction must therefore be drawn
between:

(*a*) *The corporation.* A corporation comprises a body of persons with an existence, a name, rights and duties distinct from
those of the individuals who form it from time to time. A relatively
rare type consists of only one human being (e.g. a bishop) and it
is then termed a *corporation sole*, which can own property and
which (unlike the human officer-holder) cannot die; new corporations sole must be created by statute. Much more common are
corporations comprising more than one member and these are of
three main kinds—chartered, statutory and registered.

(*i*) *Chartered corporations* are created by the grant of a
royal charter (e.g. the BBC, the Law Society, the universities).

(*ii*) *Statutory corporations* are constituted by Act of
Parliament (e.g. the nationalised industries).

(*iii*) *Registered corporations* are formed by registration in
accordance with the Companies Acts (e.g. public and private
companies). Public companies have a minimum of seven members
(shareholders) and their shares are freely transferable on The Stock
Exchange. Private companies have between two and fifty members,
and their shares cannot be made available to the general public.

Companies may also be described according to the liability of the
members, they can therefore be *limited by shares* (*see* (*i*) below) or
limited by guarantee (where the liability of the members is limited
to a sum of money (often £1) in the event of a winding-up).

Significant aspects of corporations are:

(*i*) *The personality.* The constitution of a limited company
is defined in two main documents (the *Articles of Association* and

Memorandum of Association) which, together with the accounts, etc., are open to public inspection.

Management is vested in a Board of Directors and dissolution may be effected by a *compulsory winding-up by the court* (e.g. if there is inability to pay debts), a *voluntary winding-up* (at the instigation of the members or creditors) or a *winding-up under the supervision of the court*; in each case a *liquidator* (or liquidators) would be appointed to administer the property of the company. In the event of liquidation, the liability of a member is limited, to the value of his shares (thus, if these have been paid for, he has no further obligation); the fact that a company is a separate person from the shareholders has been illustrated in—

Salomon v. *Salomon & Co. Ltd.* (*1897*): S converted his boot business into a seven-member limited company, which purchased the firm from him partially in the form of £10,000 in debentures (documents in evidence of the debt, giving him right of repayment before other creditors). Owing to a strike in the trade, the company was wound up with assets of £6,000 and debts to S; also £7,000 due to other creditors. These claimed that, as S & Co. was really the same person as S, he could not owe money to himself and that they should be paid first. Reversing the decision of the Court of Appeal, the House of Lords held that, as the company had a separate identity in law, S was entitled to the £6,000

   (*ii*) *The criminal liability.* This is considered at XVIII, 4(*b*) below.

   (*iii*) *The tortious liability.* In general, a corporation has full liability for torts except those (e.g. assault) which it could not possibly commit. Furthermore, as shown at 5(*c*)(*i*), a *master* (employer) is liable for all torts committed by his *servants* (employees with contracts of service) *in the course of their employment*, i.e. when they do improperly what they are employed to do properly.

   (*iv*) *The contractual capacity.* For ability of a corporation to make a contract, see X, 3.

(*b*) *The unincorporated association.* This may be a club, society, partnership, trade union, etc., and none of these is a juristic person. They therefore differ from corporations in the following ways:

   (*i*) *The personality.* A club or partnership does not require any formal method of creation but the latter is limited from two to twenty members (though the maximum may be exceeded in the case of solicitors, accountants or members of a stock exchange). The rights of partners among themselves are generally governed by a partnership agreement or deed of partnership (which is private to the members). Unless otherwise agreed, every partner participates in the conduct of the business and is liable for its debts to the whole extent of his property. Dissolution may be effected by bankruptcy, the decision or death of a partner, or an order made by a court.

(*ii*) *The criminal liability*. One partner is not liable for the criminal acts of another unless it can be shown that they acted in concert, as in—

> *Parsons* v. *Barnes* (*1973*); B was convicted of an offence under the Trade Descriptions Act 1968 as his partner had signed B's name upon an invoice, on partnership notepaper, for the repair of a roof by "turnerising" despite the fact that this process had not been used. Although not present when the work was done, B had attended an initial inspection of the roof when turnerising was discussed. Dismissing B's appeal, the Divisional Court held that it was justifiable to conclude that the partners had acted in concert throughout.

(*iii*) *The tortious liability*. All members of a partnership are liable for any tort committed *in the ordinary course of the firm's business* or *with the authority of all the partners*, as in—

> *Hamlyn* v. *Houston & Co.* (*1903*): A partner bribed a rival's clerk to betray his employer's secrets and all the partners were held liable, as the act—though wrongful—was performed in the ordinary course of the business, part of which was to obtain information concerning competitors.

As a club or society has no legal personality, theoretically all members should be joined as co-plaintiffs or co-defendants in any action for tort. Where, however, all the members have an *identical interest* in defending an action, application can be made to a court for a *representation order* against certain members, who are sued as representing the members as a whole. Where such an action succeeds, judgment can be enforced against the association property and also that of any individual member, as in—

> *Campbell* v. *Thompson* (*1953*): C sought to sue a members' club (which employed her as a cleaner) for injury sustained on the stairs of its premises. As all the 2,500 members had a common interest in resisting her claim, an order was made that the Honorary Secretary and Chairman of the House Committee be appointed to represent all the persons who were members on the relevant date.

In a like manner, members of an unincorporated association can themselves bring a representative action in tort.

(*iv*) *The contractual capacity*. If any member of a partnership enters into a contract concerning the firm's usual business (even if he had no authority to do so), all the partners will be liable, unless the other party was aware of a lack of authority or did not think that he was contracting with a partnership. Should the contract be apparently unconnected with the firm's usual business, only the partner who entered into it would be liable (unless his action was authorised by the other partners).

A trade union can sue and be sued in contract but a club or society is not a competent contracting party and, if a contract is made on its behalf, recourse lies only against the person who actually made it (and any other members who authorised him to do so), as in—

Rowntrees of London (*Builders*) v. *Screen Writers Club* (*1953*): Three members of the committee of a club had been held personally liable in the county court for payment for work done on the club premises. Dismissing their appeal, the Court of Appeal held that in the absence of any other evidence, the judge was entitled to infer that the work had been ordered by the committee and that the members before him were liable.

2. The forms of status. Each class of person may have several forms of *status* (depending on such factors as age, nationality, etc.) and this will often determine rights and duties, powers and disabilities. In the main, it can be assumed that the common law was developed to apply to the sane, sober, British, male, adult human being. This being the norm, special conditions exist for persons differing from the norm:

(*a*) *The minor*. Under the Family Law Reform Act 1969, a minor (formerly termed "infant") is a person under eighteen years of age and, at common law, he is *legitimate* if the parents were validly married at the time of conception (even though they might be divorced before the birth) or birth (even though they might have been unmarried at the time of conception). Under the Legitimacy Acts 1926–76, an illegitimate child can be legitimated by the subsequent marriage of its parents.

Under the Adoption Acts 1950–76 an adoption order made by the High Court (Family Division), a county court or magistrates' court, vests in the adopter(s) the parental rights and duties relating to a child, who ranks in law as the legitimate offspring of the adopter (and not that of any person other than the adopter). An adopted person over the age of eighteen may apply to the Registrar-General for information to enable him to obtain a full certificate of his birth. An adopter and an adopted child are within the prohibited degrees for the purposes of marriage to one another.

Under the Guardianship of Minors Act 1971, as amended by the Guardianship Act 1973, the appointment of a guardian may be made by either parent of a child, by deed or will, to take effect after his or her death. In certain circumstances, it may also be made by the High Court (Family Division), county courts and magistrates' courts. This is particularly the case in wardship proceedings in the Family Division. Applications for a minor to become a *ward of court* (whereby the court is given extensive powers of control over the minor's person and upbringing) may be made by either parent or any other "interested person" (e.g. grandparent or foster-parent); alternatively, in divorce proceedings, a judge may direct that a wardship summons should issue.

The legal position of a minor can be considered in respect of:

(*i*) *The criminal liability.* Under the Children and Young Persons Act 1963, there is a conclusive presumption that a child under the age of ten cannot be guilty of any criminal offence. From ten to fourteen there is a presumption that a child is *doli incapax* (incapable of evil) but this may be rebutted by strong evidence that the child knew that his or her conduct was criminal. A boy under fourteen cannot be convicted of rape, assault with intent to commit rape, or other offences involving sexual intercourse; however, he can be convicted of abetting another to commit such offences and of indecent assault. Over the age of fourteen a minor is fully open to prosecution but is still subject to special treatment (*see* VI, 1(*b*)(*iii*) and (*c*)(*ii*)).

(*ii*) *The tortious liability.* This is considered at 5(*c*)(*iv*).

(*iii*) *The contractual capacity.* This is considered at X, 1.

(*iv*) *The miscellaneous disabilities.* A minor cannot vote or sit in Parliament (or on the council of a local authority), marry under the age of sixteen, make a will (except for soldiers, sailors and airmen—and then only in exceptional circumstances) or legally own land (though he may own movable property).

(*b*) *The mentally-disordered person.* The Mental Health Act 1983 defines "mental disorder" as meaning "mental illness, arrested or incomplete development of mind, psychopathic disorder, and any other disorder or disability of mind". In the majority of such cases admission to hospital is on a voluntary basis but a patient may be admitted and detained for not more than twenty-eight days, if suffering from a mental disorder which warrants the detention, on a written application for admission for assessment of two registered medical practitioners. Further detention is not permissible in the absence of a subsequent application, order or admission for treatment. Within fourteen days of admission for assessment (or within six months of admission for treatment) a patient or his nearest relative may make an application for discharge to the appropriate *Mental Health Review Tribunal* (comprising a lawyer (president), a doctor and a lay member).

The legal position of persons suffering from mental disorder can be examined in respect of:

(*i*) *The criminal liability.* This is considered at XIX, 1 below.

(*ii*) *The tortious liability.* Insanity is, in itself, no defence in tort, unless it is so extreme as to make the defendant's act involuntary or to prevent the defendant from evincing malice or intention (where this is a necessary element, as shown at 5(*b*)), or to preclude the defendant from possessing the necessary knowledge (in negligence). An illustrative case is—

Morriss v. *Marsden* (*1952*): The defendant to all appearances a normal person, violently attacked the plaintiff, was charged with criminal assault, found unfit to plead and detained at Broadmoor; nevertheless the plaintiff's action against him succeeded.

(*iii*) *The contractual capacity.* This is considered at X, 2.

(*c*) *The married woman.* Unless personally involved, the husband of a married woman cannot be held liable in respect of her crimes, torts or contracts, but these require separate consideration.

(*i*) *The criminal liability.* Under the Criminal Justice Act 1925, s. 47, "on a charge against a wife for any offence other than treason or murder, it shall be a good defence to prove that the offence was committed in the presence of, and under the coercion of, the husband", the burden of proving such "marital coercion" rests on the accused. Under the Theft Act 1968, s. 30, one spouse may be prosecuted for stealing or damaging the other's property, but normally the leave of the Director of Public Prosecutions is necessary.

(*ii*) *The tortious liability.* Under the Law Reform (Husband and Wife) Act 1962, both parties to a marriage have a right of action in tort against each other, subject to the court's discretion to stay proceedings, if no substantial benefit would accrue.

(*iii*) *The contractual capacity.* A married woman can, in her own right, acquire, hold or dispose of property; she is capable of suing and being sued in contract and is also subject to the law relating to bankruptcy. Marriage does not empower a wife to bind her husband in contract with third parties but there is a presumption (of agency) whereby she is entitled to pledge his credit for all necessaries suitable to his station in life. The onus of proving that goods are necessaries lies on the supplier—otherwise he can bring an action only against the wife, unless he can prove the husband's express or implied assent to the contract. The presumption does not extend to the borrowing of money.

3. The status of nationality. Anyone who is not a British subject, a British protected person or a citizen of the Republic of Ireland is termed an *alien* and he or she may not own (or have a share in) a British ship or aircraft, sit in either House of Parliament or vote in an election (parliamentary or local). Such persons are also liable to immigration legislation and deportation; otherwise they are in the same position as British subjects in so far as crime, contract and tort are concerned. Formerly everyone born within the British Empire owed allegiance to the Monarch and enjoyed the status of *British subject* but, with the advent of the Commonwealth (a voluntary association of totally independent states, all equal in status), subservience to Britain disappeared and individual countries sought to acquire the allegiance of their own nationals. To attain this end, *citizenship* became the primary status in each state (which legislated accordingly) and the British Nationality Acts 1948–65 recognised "Citizenship of the United Kingdom and Colonies". The British Nationality Act 1981 provided for this to be replaced by three new categories—British citizenship, citizenship of British dependent territories and British overseas citizenship, in connection with which it is necessary to consider:

(*a*) *The acquisition of British citizenship.* British citizenship shall be acquired automatically by all those citizens of the United Kingdom and Colonies with a right of abode here at the commencement of the Act; thereafter, acquisition shall be by:

(*i*) *Birth.* British citizenship shall be acquired (1) by those born in the United Kingdom (including the Channel Islands and Isle of Man) to a parent who is a British citizen or who is settled here; (2) by foundlings; (3) by persons born in the United Kingdom, one of whose parents subsequently becomes settled here or a British citizen; and (4) by children adopted by order of a court in the United Kingdom.

(*ii*) *Descent.* British citizenship shall be acquired by those born overseas if one of their parents is a British citizen by virtue of birth in the United Kingdom or a British citizen in Crown service, or in service designated as closely associated with the overseas activities of the British Government.

(*iii*) *Registration*. The Home Secretary shall be empowered to register any minors as British citizens. Minors born abroad shall be entitled to be registered if one of their parents is employed overseas by a United Kingdom based company or organisation; or where either of their parents is a British citizen and they or their families return to live in the United Kingdom. Provision is made for the preservation of the rights of certain other categories of persons entitled to registration under the previous legislation.

(*iv*) *Naturalisation*. The Home Secretary may grant a certificate of naturalisation to anyone of full age and capacity who is of good character, has sufficient knowledge of the English or Welsh language and intends to make his principal home in the United Kingdom or to serve in a United Kingdom organisation. He must not have been absent from the United Kingdom for more than 450 days in the preceding five years or ninety days in the preceding twelve months.

(*b*) *The loss of British citizenship*. British citizenship may be lost by:

(*i*) *Renunciation*. Any British citizen of full age and capacity shall be able to make a declaration of renunciation of British citizenship and this will be registered if he has (or will acquire) another nationality or citizenship. Registration of such declarations can be withheld in wartime. A person who has renounced British citizenship shall be entitled to resume it at any time—but only once.

(*ii*) *Deprivation*. A registered or naturalised British citizen can be deprived of his citizenship by the Home Secretary if: (1) he shows himself disloyal to the Monarch; or (2) he trades with the enemy in time of war; or (3) he is sentenced to twelve months' imprisonment in any country within five years of acquiring his citizenship.

The Home Secretary must be satisfied that deprivation of citizenship is conducive to the public good and the person concerned may apply for the case to be referred to a committee of inquiry.

(*c*) *The acquisition of domicile*. Totally independent of nationality and citizenship is the question of domicile, i.e. the country in which a person has (or is presumed to have) his permanent residence. Everyone (even a stateless person) must have a domicile, which connects him with a system of law and may thus determine his legitimacy, the validity of his marriage, divorce or will and the distribution of his property on intestacy. There are three types of domicile:

(*i*) *The domicile of origin.* This is acquired at birth by a child and the law presumes that a person retains his domicile of origin throughout his life, until the contrary is proved.

(*ii*) *The domicile of choice.* This is acquired when a person possessing the necessary capacity takes up residence in another country with *animus manendi* (intention of remaining). There must be a definite determination to abandon the old domicile, coupled with an intention to establish a permanent residence (and actually take it up) in a new domicile. If a domicile of choice is abandoned, the domicile of origin revives until a new domicile of choice is acquired and the burden of proof lies on the person asserting that he has acquired a domicile of choice.

(*iii*) *The domicile by operation of law.* This is a domicile, other than one of origin, possessed by those who do not have the legal capacity to acquire a domicile of choice. Formerly a wife took the domicile of her husband but, under the Domicile and Matrimonial Proceedings Act 1973, her domicile is now ascertained as in the case of any other person. The domicile of a legitimate minor normally follows that of his father but, if the parents are living apart and the child lives with the mother, the child's domicile is that of the mother.

4. The status of public authorities. Private citizens who are aggrieved by the conduct of public authorities (i.e. Ministers, civil servants, local authorities or other bodies exercising statutory powers) can seek criminal prosecutions or the normal civil remedies in the ordinary courts. There are, however, two areas of litigation which deserve particular consideration:

(*a*) *The actions against Government departments.* Under the Crown Proceedings Act 1947, government departments can be sued for breaches of contract or torts committed by their civil servants in the course of their employment, subject to the following limitations:

(*i*) *The restriction of discovery.* Where discovery of documents (*see* V, 2(*c*)) is sought, the Crown can refuse disclosure (even though it may not be a party to the proceedings)—but only if it would be "contrary to the public interest". This is termed *Crown privilege* and formerly it was held that an objection to the production of documents made personally by the relevant minister should be accepted as conclusive; however, this was overruled in—

Conway v. *Rimmer* (*1968*): A dismissed police officer sued his former superintendent for malicious prosecution and the Home Secretary claimed Crown privilege for certain relevant reports.

The House of Lords held that the minister's statement was not conclusive and that a court should, where appropriate, inspect the documents and decide whether to accept the claim.

(*ii*) *The restriction of actions.* Actions will not lie in respect of the Queen in her personal capacity, the execution of judicial process, or the death of (or personal injury to) a member of H.M. Forces. In the last case, neither the Crown nor any member of the Forces is liable in tort, provided that the death or injury is attributable to service for the purposes of pension.

(*iii*) *The restriction of remedies.* No injunction, decree of specific performance or order for the recovery of land (or delivery of property) may be made against the Crown; also execution cannot be levied against Crown property.

(*b*) *The actions for misuse of powers.* In addition to the normal torts, an action will lie against a public authority for wrongful use of its powers because, if these are exercised in excess of what is authorised by statute or common law, the use is said to be *ultra vires* and resultantly invalid. Illustrations have been given at II, 4(*c*)(*ii*) and IV, 2(*a*) and the principle has been extended to cover *abuse* of powers, so that it can be invoked if a public authority is shown to have exercised its powers—

(*i*) *For an improper purpose.* This has been illustrated in—

Webb v. *Minister of Housing and Local Government* (*1965*): Bognor Urban District Council had made a compulsory purchase order, under the Coast Protection Act 1949, to acquire land mainly for promenade development. Although this was confirmed by the minister, the Court of Appeal held that it was not necessary for coast protection; consequently it was *ultra vires* and void.

(*ii*) *In an unreasonable manner.* This has been illustrated in—

Lee v. *Secretary of State for Education and Science* (*1967*): The Secretary of State proposed to alter the articles of government of Enfield Grammar School and allowed only four days for representations to be made to him under the Education Act 1944. Donaldson J. held that it was "wholly unreasonable", the period was increased to four weeks and the minister was ordered to pay the costs of the hearing.

(*iii*) *By delegated authority.* Sometimes a statute may expressly or impliedly authorise delegation of functions but, apart from this, *delegatus non potest delegare* (it is not possible to subdelegate) as illustrated in—

Vine v. *National Dock Labour Board* (*1957*): The Dock Workers (Regulation of Employment) Order 1947 empowered local Dock Labour Boards to give dock workers seven days' notice of termination of employment. After failing to report for work, the plaintiff was given notice by a Disciplinary Committee, appointed by the local Board. The House of Lords held that the Board could not delegate this function to a committee; therefore it was *ultra vires* and void.

(*iv*) *In an unbusinesslike or unfair manner.* This has been illustrated in—

Bromley London Borough Council v. *Greater London Council* (*1983*): Bromley LBC sought the quashing of a supplementary rate precept (requisition) by the GLC, to enable London Transport to reduce bus and underground fares by 25 per cent. The House of Lords held that the precept was *ultra vires* and void—as the GLC was in breach of its duty to manage the transport service on ordinary business principles and to balance fairly the interests of ratepayers and transport users.

THE NATURE OF TORTIOUS LIABILITY

5. The principles of tortious liability. As already explained, a tort is a breach of a civil duty imposed by the common law (e.g. negligence, trespass, nuisance, defamation, etc.), the principal remedies for which are damages and/or an injunction. In examining the nature of tortious liability, it is necessary to consider:

(*a*) *The relevance of harm.* In connection with any civil wrong, a distinction can be drawn between *injuria* (the violation of a legal right) and *damnum* (actual harm caused). In actions for tort the onus normally rests on the plaintiff to prove the former and sometimes the latter is not essential; hence it is necessary to differentiate between:

(*i*) *Injuria sine damno* (the violation of a legal right without any actual harm being caused). In most cases of tort (e.g. nuisance, negligence, etc.) an action will not succeed unless the plaintiff can show that some actual harm accrued. However, there are certain torts (e.g. libel and trespass) where the plaintiff enjoys an *absolute right* and, if the defendant infringes this, he is legally liable, even though he may not have caused any real harm. Such torts are said to be actionable *per se*.

(*ii*) *Damnum sine injuria* (harm caused without any legal right being violated). As stated above, an action for tort will succeed only if there has been a violation of a legal right; consequently not every form of harm suffered is actionable, as illustrated in—

> *Bradford Corporation* v. *Pickles* (*1895*): Water percolated in undefined channels beneath the defendant's land and flowed eventually to the plaintiffs' land where it was used for a city supply. In an endeavour to coerce the plaintiffs to buy his land at his own price, the defendant started to extract the water and the action against him failed because his conduct was lawful, even though the plaintiffs suffered harm.

(*b*) *The relevance of motive.* In most actions for tort the defendant's motive is entirely irrelevant, i.e. the absence of malicious intent will not make an unlawful act lawful, nor will the presence of malice make an otherwise lawful act unlawful (as illustrated in the case above). However, there are certain torts (e.g. deceit and malicious prosecution) wherein the plaintiff must prove the defendant's malice, in the sense of an improper motive. There are also others (e.g. nuisance, conspiracy and injurious falsehood) in which malice is not an essential element but where the plaintiff will succeed if he proves that the defendant acted maliciously, as in—

> *Christie* v. *Davey* (*1893*): Whenever his neighbour gave music lessons, the defendant created a din and it was held that an injunction to restrain the nuisance should be granted, because he had acted deliberately and maliciously to annoy the plaintiff.

(*c*) *The circumstances of vicarious liability.* In tort vicarious liability arises most commonly in respect of:

(*i*) *The servant.* A *master* (employer) is liable for all torts committed by his *servants* (employees with contracts of service) *in the course of their employment*, i.e. when they do improperly what they are employed to do properly, even if the master had expressly forbidden the wrongful act, as in—

> *Rose* v. *Plenty* (*1976*): Contrary to an express prohibition by his employers, a milkman arranged for a boy to help him with his round and gave him a lift on his vehicle. Due to the milkman's negligent driving, the boy was injured and the Court of Appeal held that the employers were vicariously liable for the tort.

> *Iqbal* v. *London Transport Executive* (*1973*): The defendants' bus conductor, who had been prohibited on many occasions

from driving buses, injured a fellow-employee when he attempted to drive a bus at the depot. He was assisting in getting his own bus on the road but the Court of Appeal held that he was not driving in the course of his employment and his employers were not liable.

(*ii*) *The independent contractor.* Basically an independent contractor is a person who is under the control of an employer as to what he must do but is free to select the method of doing it. Generally an employer is not liable for the torts of his independent contractors unless he completely supervised their work or employed them to do something unlawful, extra hazardous or likely to cause a nuisance.

(*iii*) *The agent.* A person's agent is one who does something at his request and for his purposes; this relationship can give rise to vicarious liability, as in—

Ormrod v. *Crosville Motor Services Ltd.* (*1953*): O was asked by his friend Murphie to drive M's car to Monte Carlo so that they could use it for a joint holiday. On the way he collided with C's bus and the Court of Appeal held that Murphie was liable as O was his agent, because the car was being used at the time partly for Murphie's purposes. Mere permission to drive would not have established such liability.

(*iv*) *The minor.* Minors are fully liable for their torts but, where it is necessary to prove malice or intention, a minor defendant may be held to be too young to have evinced it; also, where lack of reasonable care must be shown, the standard of care expected of a minor will be that commensurate with his age and understanding. As a plaintiff, a minor sues by his "next friend" (usually his parent) but generally a parent is not liable for any tort by his child unless he authorised it or was employing the child (thus being liable as a master) or was negligent in affording the opportunity for the tort, as in—

Newton v. *Edgerley* (*1959*): A farmer allowed his son, aged twelve, to buy a gun and showed him how to use it. He told him not to take the gun off the farm and not to use it when other children were present. Disobeying these instructions, the son went off shooting with four other boys and accidentally shot one of them in the heel. It was held that the farmer had been negligent because he could not ensure that his instructions were obeyed and had not taught his son how to handle the gun when other persons were present.

THE PROTECTION OF FREEDOM

6. The rights of the individual. Quite separate from the European Community is the *Council of Europe*, a body of twenty-one member-countries, founded in 1949 and based in Strasbourg. Its executive organ is the *Committee of Ministers*, in which the Foreign Ministers of the member-states meet twice yearly. Permanent representatives (who act as ministers' deputies) meet monthly and there is a *Parliamentary Assembly* (whose members are chosen by the national parliaments) which annually holds three week-long sessions. Of major significance are the numerous conventions and agreements concluded by the Council and probably the most important is the *European Convention for the Protection of Human Rights and Fundamental Freedoms*, originally signed by fifteen nations (including the United Kingdom) on 4th November 1950. By this the signatories agreed to secure to everyone within their jurisdiction certain specified rights and freedoms. Having exhausted all domestic remedies, any person, non-governmental organisation or group of individuals claiming to be the victim of a signatory's violation of the specified rights may petition the *European Commission of Human Rights* (comprising one member from each contracting country), which investigates and reports on the complaint. If there is shown to be a case against the signatory and a satisfactory settlement cannot be reached the matter is passed to the Committee of Ministers and thence it may be referred to the *European Court of Human Rights*, whose decisions are enforceable only by the good will of the signatories. In an endeavour to make the convention enforceable by action in United Kingdom courts, Lord Wade has, on more than one occasion, introduced a private member's *Bill of Rights Bill* in the House of Lords but it has invariably failed to pass through all its stages.

At the moment in Britain there are certain "freedoms" which are looked upon as fundamental rights but which are nevertheless negative in nature (as they are based on the tautologous principle that anything is lawful which is not unlawful). The foremost examples are:

(*a*) *The freedom of the person.* The use of the prerogative write of *habeas corpus* has been described at VI, 2(*f*) and another means of protecting personal freedom is a civil action for the tort of *false imprisonment*. This will lie if it can be shown that there has been a total restraint (either physical or by a mere show of authority) for some period, however short, upon the liberty of a person, without lawful justification.

As explained at III, **1**(*a*)(*i*), police officers can arrest persons under warrants issued by magistrates but each individual must be named and the nature of the charge must be stated. Of much greater significance are the various offences for which a person may be arrested without a warrant and common examples arise from:

(*i*) *The statute law*. Legislation authorising arrest without a warrant includes:

(1) *The Coinage Offences Act 1936, s. 11*. Anyone may arrest without a warrant any person committing an offence under the Act and take him or her before a magistrate; furthermore, anyone finding any counterfeit coin, counterfeiting instrument or counterfeiting material may seize it and take it before a magistrate.

(2) *The Public Order Act 1936, s. 5*. A constable may arrest without a warrant anyone who, in a public place or at a public meeting, uses threatening, abusive or insulting words or behaviour with intent to provoke a breach of the peace, or whereby a breach of the peace is likely to be occasioned.

(3) *The Prevention of Crime Act 1953, s. 1*. A constable may arrest without a warrant anyone who carries an offensive weapon in a public place without lawful authority or reasonable excuse. Depending on how they are used, many articles may constitute "offensive weapons" but whether they do so is a question of fact (for the jury in a Crown Court trial), as stated in—

> *R.* v. *Williamson* (*1978*): W had pleaded not guilty to possessing an offensive weapon, a sheath knife, in a public place but changed his plea to guilty when the judge ruled that the knife did constitute one. Allowing the appeal, the Court of Appeal held that the question was for the jury to decide.

(4) *The Sexual Offences Act 1956, s. 41*. Anyone may arrest without a warrant a man who persistently solicits or importunes in a public place for immoral purposes.

(5) *The Street Offences Act 1959, s. 1(3)*. A constable may arrest without a warrant anyone whom he finds in a street or public place and reasonably suspects of loitering or soliciting for purposes of prostitution.

(6) *The Police Act 1964, s. 51*. A constable may arrest without a warrant anyone who assaults, resists or obstructs him in the execution of his duty. However, "obstructing" must be likely to cause a breach of the peace or be calculated to prevent the lawful arrest of another, as stated in—

Wershof v. *Metropolitan Police Commissioner* (*1978*): W, a solicitor, refused to allow two police officers to take from a jeweller a ring (which they thought to be stolen), without giving a receipt. One officer then arrested W for obstructing him in the execution of his duty but, having been acquitted of the offence, W was awarded damages in a subsequent action for assault and false imprisonment.

(7) *The Criminal Law Act 1967.* This defined an *arrestable offence* as one for which the sentence is fixed by law (e.g. murder, treason or arson in H.M. ships and dockyards) or one for which (or for attempts at which) a first offender may be imprisoned for a minimum of five years.

Under the Act, a *private citizen* may arrest, without a warrant, anyone whom he reasonably suspects of committing such an offence or, if it has definitely been committed, he may arrest anyone whom he reasonably suspects of it.

A *police officer* may arrest, without a warrant, anyone whom he reasonably suspects of being about to commit an arrestable offence and, if he reasonably suspects that it has been committed, he may arrest anyone whom he reasonably suspects of it. On all of these occasions, the general nature of the charge must be made known to the person arrested and the reasonableness of a police officer's suspicion is a question of fact, as in—

King v. *Gardner* (*1980*): Receiving a radio message that two males, a female and a dog were loitering in the street, a constable found a man, a girl and a dog. The man refused to permit the examination of a bag he was carrying and hit the constable, when detained. The magistrate dismissed the charge of assaulting a police officer in the execution of his duty, holding that the radio message was not a reasonable ground for suspicion; therefore the constable had not been acting in the execution of his duty. The Divisional Court upheld this decision.

(8) *The Firearms Act 1968, s. 50.* A constable may arrest, without a warrant, anyone whom he reasonably suspects of having with him in a public place (without lawful authority or reasonable excuse) a loaded shotgun, a loaded air weapon or any other firearm (loaded or not) with suitable ammunition; also anyone who enters premises as a trespasser with a firearm and anyone who possesses a firearm if he has served three years' detention.

(9) *The Theft Act 1968, s. 25.* Any person may arrest, without a warrant, anyone who if, when not at his place of abode, has with him any article for use in the course of, or in connection with, any

burglary, theft or cheat. There must however be evidence of some such burglary, etc., to be committed in the future, as stated in—

> *R. V. Ellames* (*1964*): E was convicted of having an article that had been used for a burglary prior to his possession of it and the Court of Appeal allowed his appeal.

(10) *The Misuse of Drugs Act 1971, s. 24*. A constable may arrest without a warrant anyone reasonably suspected of committing a drug offence if he believes that the person will abscond if not arrested or cannot ascertain his name and address (or is not satisfied that these are genuine).

(11) *The Road Traffic Act 1972, s. 8*. A constable in uniform may arrest, without a warrant, a driver who shows an excess of alcohol over the prescribed limit, who refuses to take a breathalyser test or who is reasonably suspected of driving whilst disqualified.

(*ii*) *The common law*. A police officer or a private citizen has a common law right to arrest, without a warrant, anyone committing a breach of the peace in his presence or threatening to commit or renew such a breach, so that he reasonably and honestly believes that it will be committed in the immediate future. A breach of the peace occurs whenever harm or violence is threatened, so as to be likely, to a person or his property, or when a person is put in fear by reason of some assault, riot or affray, provide that the conduct concerned relates to violence. This was enunciated in—

> *R.* v. *Howell* (*1982*): At 4 a.m. H was one of a group causing a disturbance outside a house where a party was being held. He was warned by a constable to stop swearing, was subsequently arrested and struck the constable. The Court of Appeal upheld his conviction.

Where there has been an arrest without a warrant, an officer in charge of a police station may inquire into the case (and *must* do so if the accused cannot be brought before a court within twenty-four hours); as shown at VI, 3, he may also grant bail.

During the preparation of a case, remand in custody must be for not more than eight clear days without there being a further remand; however, with his consent, the accused can be remanded in his absence on three successive occasions, up to a limit of twenty-eight days.

(*b*) *The freedom of expression*. In general, anyone can say or write what he likes, subject to certain restrictions—imposed by:

(*i*) *The statute law*. Legislation restricting freedom of expression includes:

(1) *The Official Secrets Acts 1911, s. 2.* This makes it unlawful to retain, without permission, any information obtained in Crown employment, to communicate it to an unauthorised person, or for anyone to receive it.

(2) *The Incitement to Disaffection Act 1934, s. 1.* This makes it unlawful maliciously and advisedly to seduce any member of the Forces from his duty.

(3) *The Police Act 1964, s. 53.* This makes it unlawful to do any act calculated to cause disaffection in a police force or to induce a policeman to commit a breach of discipline.

(4) *The Sex Discrimination Act 1975, s. 38.* This makes it unlawful to publish an advertisement (e.g. for employment) which is discriminatory against either sex.

(5) *The Race Relations Act 1976, s. 70.* This makes it unlawful to publish or distribute written matter, or use in any public place or at a public meeting, language which is threatening, abusive or insulting and likely to stir up hatred against any racial group in Great Britain. Section 29 of the Act makes it unlawful to publish (or place for publication) an advertisement or notice which indicates (or might reasonably be taken to indicate) an intention to do an act of racial discrimination.

(*ii*) *The common law.* The *tort* of defamation comprises speech, writing, pictures, effigies, etc., made falsely and without lawful justification in respect of another person, so that he is exposed to "hatred, ridicule or contempt" or his reputation is lowered "in the eyes of right-thinking members of society". If the defamation is in a permanent form, it constitutes *libel* but, if it is merely transient, it is *slander* (in which case it is generally necessary to prove some pecuniary damage). Both may give rise to civil actions, provided that there has been publication—i.e. communication of the defamation to a person other than the plaintiff.

(*c*) *The freedom of association.* Persons may freely associate and demonstrate unless they are contravening the law and restrictions are imposed by:

(*i*) *The statute law.* Meetings and demonstrations may be subject to local Acts and by-laws, also prosecutions can be brought under the Highways Act 1980, s. 137 (whereby an offence is committed if a person, without lawful authority or excuse, in any way wilfully obstructs the free passage along a highway). The most important statute is, however, the Public Order Act 1936, which was passed at the time of the British Union of Fascists, but the adequacy of which was questioned forty-four years later in confrontations between the Anti-Nazi League and the National Front. The main provisions of the Act are: (1) *Section 1* It is an offence to wear a uniform signifying association with a political organisation (or with the promotion of a political object) in any public place or at any public meeting. (2) *Section 2* It is an offence to control or manage the training of persons in any organisation to enable them to usurp the functions of the police or armed forces, or to display physical force in promoting a political object. (3) *Section 3* It is within the power of a chief officer of police to prescribe routes for processions and prohibit entry into specified public places if he has reasonable grounds for believing that there might be serious disorder. (4) *Section 4* It is an offence to be in possession of an offensive weapon, without lawful authority, at any public meeting or public procession. (5) *Section 5* It is an offence to use threatening, abusive or insulting words or behaviour in any public place or at any public meeting, with intent to provoke a breach of the peace (or whereby a breach of the peace is likely to be occasioned).

(*ii*) *The common law.* If three or more persons meet together to carry out some purpose which is likely to involve violence (or to cause reasonable apprehension of violence in the minds of normally courageous bystanders), they are liable to prosecution for *unlawful assembly*, even though they may not implement the purpose. They cannot, however, be prosecuted for doing a lawful act, merely because it might lead to violence by others, unless this was really the purpose, as in—

Beatty v. *Gillbanks* (*1882*): Members of the Salvation Army, parading through Weston-super-Mare, were opposed by a rival organisation, called the Skeleton Army. The magistrates ordered the Salvationists to refrain from assembling but they did so and were convicted of holding an unlawful assembly; however their appeal was allowed.

Wise v. *Dunning* (*1902*): A "protestant crusader" held public meetings in Liverpool and used words highly insulting to Roman Catholics, a number of whom were present. He was bound over to keep the peace and his appeal was disallowed, as the natural consequence of his conduct was to produce unlawful acts by others.

An unlawful assembly becomes a *rout* if the persons involved make some advance towards implementing their common purpose, and it develops into a *riot* on the execution of that purpose, with an intent to help one another by force and a display of force.

(*d*) *The freedom of property*. In this context it is relevant to examine the following powers of search and seizure:

(*i*) *The search of the person*. Before an arrest the police have no right to search—except for drugs (under the Misuse of Drugs Act 1971) or firearms (under the Firearms Act 1968). After an arrest they may search for and remove objects which they reasonably suspect to be connected with a criminal offence committed by the accused *or* with which a prisoner might do injury *or* which might be used to effect escape, as stated in—

R. v. *Naylor* (*1979*): After being arrested for obstruction, N was placed in a detention room where her rings, a necklace and earrings were forcibly removed. N struggled and was charged with assaulting a police officer but it was held that there was no case to answer, as the jewellery did not comprise the objects listed above.

Brazil v. *Chief Constable of Surrey* (*1983*): For conduct likely to lead to a breach of the peace in a public house, B was arrested and taken to the police station where she emptied her handbag and pockets but refused to be further searched. The officer in charge said that everyone brought to the station had to be searched for their own safety and, though he suspected possession of prohibited drugs, he did not state this. The Divisional Court quashed B's conviction of assaulting officers in the execution of their duty, as the general search rule could not be upheld and she was not given the reason.

(*ii*) *The search of premises*. Entry on land possessed by another without lawful authority (or remaining on it after authority has been withdrawn) constitutes the tort of *trespass*, without any need to prove actual damage. Statutory right of entry is, however, enjoyed by numerous people (e.g. Customs and Excise Officers, Public Health officials, electricity and gas inspectors, etc.).

To enter or search private premises, the police generally need a warrant from a magistrate but, under the Theft Act 1968, s. 26, an officer of or above the rank of Superintendent may give written authority to a policeman to search any premises for stolen goods if the occupier has, within the previous five years, been convicted of handling stolen goods (or of any other offence involving dishonesty and punishable by imprisonment) *or* if anyone who has been convicted of handling stolen goods within the previous five years has occupied the premises within the preceding twelve months.

Under the Criminal Law Act 1967, s. 2(6), a police officer

supecting anyone of committing an arrestable offence may (forcibly if necessary) enter and search any place where the person is (or is reasonably suspected to be).

The police may also enter premises without a warrant to avert a breach of the peace, to prevent a serious crime or to recapture a prisoner. A police officer who enters (or remains on) premises without authority is a trespasser; consequently he is not acting in the course of his duty and it is therefore not an offence to obstruct him, as in—

> *McLorie* v. *Oxford* (*1982*): M's brother was arrested at his home and charged with attempted murder—it being alleged that he had used a certain car in connection with the crime. Later, police officers saw the vehicle at his home but his father refused to let them remove it without a warrant. They attempted to take it forcibly and M resisted them. He was charged and convicted of assaulting a constable in the execution of his duty, but the Divisional Court quashed his conviction.

(*iii*) *The seizure of property*. From the cases outlined below four conclusions can be drawn:

(1) If the police enter premises with a warrant, they may lawfully seize property unconnected with it but which is successfully used as evidence for another prosecution—

> *Elias* v. *Passmore* (*1934*): Executing a warrant for the arrest of one Hannington, for a seditious speech in Trafalgar Square, P (a police officer) entered premises and arrested him—but also seized letters written by E inciting sedition, for which E was sentenced to two year's imprisonment. Horridge J. ruled that the seizure was justified because the letters were capable of being, and were, used as evidence against E; however, he awarded damages for the taking of other documents which were not so used.

(2) If the police seize property without a valid warrant, it is nevertheless admissible in evidence—

> *R.* v. *Adams* (*1980*): Executing a search warrant obtained under the Obscene Publications Act 1959, s. 3(1), police seized certain items in A's bookshop and a summons was issued but subsequently withdrawn. Six days later, with the same warrant, further items were seized and a summons was issued. The Court of Appeal held that the warrant authorised only one entry, search and seizure but the evidence from the second visit was admissible.

(3) If the police enter premises with a search warrant, they may seize property unconnected with it but which they reasonably believer to have been stolen—

Chic Fashions (West Wales) Ltd. v. *Jones (1968)*: Executing a search warrant for stolen clothing made by a particular manufacturer, police entered the plaintiffs' shop and seized other garments which they reasonably believed to be stolen. The plaintiffs gave an explanation (which the police accepted) and were awarded damages for trespass but the Court of Appeal held that the police were not liable.

(4) If the police seize property on the suspicion that a serious crime has been committed, they may lawfully retain it only if they have reasonable grounds for believing that it is the fruit of the crime, the instrument of the crime or material evidence to prove the commission of the crime—

Ghani v. *Jones (1970)*: Suspecting that a Pakistani immigrant had been murdered, the police searched her father-in-law's house, without a warrant, and seized the family's passports. The Court of Appeal held that, as they did not fulfil the above three requirements, the plaintiffs were entitled to recover them.

PROGRESS TEST 8

1. "A corporation is an artificial legal person." Explain this statement. **(1)**

2. Give examples of unincorporated associations and examine their legal position. **(1)**

3. Consider the liability of a minor in crime and tort. **(2, 6)**

4. What is the significance of domicile and how is it acquired? **(3)**

5. Discuss the principles relating to a civil action against a government department. **(4)**

6. Explain the term *ultra vires*. **(4)**

7. Consider the liability of a master for the torts of his servants. **(5)**

8. Outline the powers of the police in respect of public demonstrations. **(6)**

9. What limitations are imposed upon the search and seizure of a person's property? **(6)**

10. In what circumstances may an arrest be effected without a warrant? **(6)**

PART TWO

CHAPTER IX

The Elements of a Simple Contract

THE OFFER

1. The requirements of an offer. A *contract* is a *legally binding agreement*, between two or more parties, which the law will enforce. One form is a *deed* (which must be signed, sealed and delivered) but the vast majority are *simple contracts*, which may be made in any manner but which require four essential elements—

(*a*) An offer;
(*b*) An acceptance;
(*c*) Consideration; and
(*d*) An intention to create legal relations.

An *offer* is an undertaking by the offeror (party making the offer) to be contractually bound in the event of a proper acceptance by the offeree (party to whom the offer is made). It is subject to the following rules:

(*a*) *It must be firm in form.* An offer is constituted when the offeror makes a firm promise to be bound, provided that certain conditions are fulfilled. An offer will *not* be constituted by a mere statement of price or an *invitation to treat* (i.e. an attempt to induce an offer) which exists, for example, when goods are advertised in a catalogue or exhibited in a shop-window, etc. However, certain advertisements (e.g. offering rewards for lost possessions) do constitute an effective offer, in what is sometimes called a "unilateral contract" (cf. *Carlill* v. *Carbolic Smoke Ball Co.* (*1893*), see 2(*c*)).

Harvey v. *Facy* (*1893*): Plaintiff sent telegram to defendant: "Will you sell Bumper Hall Pen? Telegraph lowest price".

Defendant replied: "Lowest cash price for Bumper Hall Pen £900", and plaintiff then telegraphed: "We agree to buy Bumper Hall Pen for £900 asked by you". There was no reply to the last message and plaintiff claimed that there was a contract. It was held that "Lowest price £900" was not an offer but merely a statement of the figure in the event of a decision to sell. The last message could therefore not be regarded as an acceptance and no contract existed.

Pharmaceutical Society of Great Britain v. *Boots Cash Chemists Ltd.* (*1953*): Defendants operated a self-service shop in which drugs were displayed with prices attached. Plaintiffs contended that sales took place when goods were taken from the shelves and placed in wire baskets; consequently sales were not "under the supervision of a registered pharmacist", as required by the Pharmacy and Poisons Act 1933. *Held*: the display of goods was an invitation to treat and an offer was made by the customer when he presented the goods at the cash desk—where transactions were supervised by a pharmacist.

Partridge v. *Crittenden* (*1968*): Having advertised bramble-finches at £1. 5s. 0d (£1.25p) each, appellant had been convicted of offering for sale wild birds, contrary to the Protection of Birds Act 1954. The Divisional Court quashed the conviction on the ground that he had made no offer for sale—but merely an invitation to treat.

(*b*) *It must be definite in substance.* The terms of an offer must be certain. Sometimes, however, an uncertainty may be cured by reference to the previous course of dealing between the parties, a special provision for resolving the uncertainty, a trade custom or a statute. Meaningless terms can be ignored and the contract will operate without them.

Scammell & Nephew Ltd. v. *Ouston* (*1941*): Defendant ordered a van from plaintiffs "on the understanding that the balance of the purchase price can be had on hire-purchase terms over a period of two years". *Held*: the order (i.e. offer) was so vague that it had no definite meaning and further negotiations were necessary; thus no contract existed.

Foley v. *Classique Coaches Ltd.* (*1934*): An agreement for the sale of petrol "at a price to be agreed by the parties in writing from time to time" contained a provision that, in the event of a dispute, reference should be made to arbitration under the

Arbitration Act 1889. *Held*: this provision resolved the uncertainty; thus a valid contract existed.

Nicolene Ltd. v. *Simmonds* (*1953*): An agreement for the sale of steel bars was perfectly clear except for a statement that the transaction was subject to "the usual conditions of acceptance". *Held*: the words were meaningless and should be ignored; thus there was a valid contract.

(*c*) *It must always be communicated to the offeree.* An offer may be made in any manner whatsoever (e.g. orally, in writing or by implication from conduct); furthermore, it may be made to a particular person (*see Duff's Executors' Case* (*1886*), 1(*e*)), a group of persons or to the world at large (*see Carlill* v. *Carbolic Smoke Ball Co.* (*1893*), 2(*c*)). However, it has no validity until it is communicated to the offeree (thus anyone returning a lost or stolen article cannot claim a reward unless he knew that it had been offered).

Taylor v. *Laird* (*1856*): During a voyage, plaintiff gave up command of defendant's ship but helped to work it home and claimed payment for this. *Held*: he had not communicated his offer to do the work, so there was no contract.

(*d*) *It may be revoked at any time before acceptance.* Revocation is not effective until communicated to the offeree, but the information may be given by words or conduct—and not necessarily by the offeror himself. A *letter of revocation* takes effect from the *time of receipt*, but a *letter of acceptance* is effective from the *time of being properly posted* in the normal manner (but not merely handed to a postman delivering letters). An *option* (i.e. an undertaking to keep an offer open for a stipulated period) is not binding unless embodied in a second (*collateral*) contract with its own consideration (*see* XV, 4(*a*)(*v*), XVI, 1(*d*) and (*e*)(*iii*)).

Payne v. *Cave* (*1789*): Defendant made the highest bid for plaintiff's goods at an auction, but withdrew his bid before the fall of the hammer. *Held*: there was effective revocation, therefore no contract. This now has statutory provision in the Sale of Goods Act 1979, s. 57.

Dickinson v. *Dodds* (*1876*): On 10th June defendant offered to sell plaintiff a house and it was agreed that the offer should remain open until 9 a.m. on 12th June. On 11th June plaintiff heard from one Berry that the defendant had agreed to sell the house to one Allen: he nevertheless handed over an acceptance of the offer just before 9 a.m. on 12th June. *Held*: the revocation was effective, although communicated by a third party; therefore no contract existed.

Henthorn v. *Frazer* (*1892*): On 7th July defendant offered plaintiff some houses for sale. At 12.30 p.m. on 8th July he wrote revoking the offer, at 3.30 p.m. plaintiff posted a letter of acceptance and at 5 p.m. he received the letter of revocation. *Held*: there was a valid contract from 3.30 p.m.

(*e*) *It remains open until accepted, rejected, revoked or lapsed*. An offer lapses on the death of either party or after a stipulated period (or a reasonable time if no period is stipulated)—

Duff's Executors' Case (*1886*): A company offered D shares in exchange for certain others. D died and his executors purported to accept the offer. *Held*: they could not do so.

Ramsgate Victoria Hotel v. *Montefiore* (*1866*): On 8th June defendant made an offer to take shares in the hotel and this was accepted on 23rd November. *Held*: the interval was unreasonable and the offer had lapsed.

(*f*) *It may be constituted by a tender*. If it relates to *a single transaction*, a tender constitutes a *definite offer* (which may be accepted to form a binding contract); however, if it is for the supply of goods or services *as and when demanded*, then it becomes a *standing offer*. In the latter case there is a separate acceptance (and contract) each time an order is placed and a standing offer can be revoked at any time (except in respect of goods or services actually ordered) unless there is a *binding* undertaking to keep it open for a stipulated period—

Great Northern Railway v. *Witham* (*1873*): Plaintiffs accepted defendant's tender to supply for twelve months goods "in such quantities as the Company may order from time to time". Several orders were carried out but, before the year had elapsed, defendant refused to execute one. *Held*: there was a standing offer to be converted into a series of contracts by the subsequent acts of the plaintiffs, who succeeded in their action for breach.

Percival Ltd. v. *London County Council* (*1918*): Plaintiffs submitted a tender for the supply of certain goods in such quantities and at such times as defendants should, from time to time, require. The tender was accepted but orders were placed elsewhere. *Held*: there was no contract and therefore no breach.

THE ACCEPTANCE

2. The validity of an acceptance. Many negotiations are so intricate that it is difficult to define easily the stages at which there was an offer and then an acceptance. One problem arises in the case of *cross-offers* (i.e. where two parties simultaneously communicate identical offers to each other); in such circumstances, and with no clear precedents, it would appear that there would be no acceptance, and consequently no contract. An acceptance of an offer is subject to the following rules:

(*a*) *It may be made only by the offeree.* This rule is relevant only if the offer was made to a particular person or group of persons (cf. *Duffs Executors' Case* (*1886*), 1(*e*) above).

(*b*) *It must be unqualified.* To be valid, an acceptance must correspond in every detail with the terms of the offer. A *counter-offer* operates as a rejection of the original offer (which therefore lapses). A *tentative assent* (e.g. an acceptance "subject to contract") is *not* binding, but this must be distinguished from a *provisional agreement* (e.g. "this is a provisional agreement until a legal document is drawn up") which *is* binding.

Hyde v. *Wrench* (*1840*): Defendant offered to sell plaintiff his farm for £1,000. Plaintiff offered £950 (which defendant refused) and then purported to accept the offer to sell for £1,000. It was held that this had been rejected and had ceased to exist.

Stevenson v. *McLean* (*1880*): Defendant offered a quantity of iron to plaintiff, who sent back a telegram asking what credit limit could be given. Defendant then sold the iron to a third party and plaintiff sent a second telegram accepting the offer. It was held that the first telegram was a mere request for information and not a counter-offer; there had been no revocation, therefore there was a valid contract.

Eccles v. *Bryant & Pollock* (*1948*): The parties agreed on the sale of certain property "subject to contract". The contract was drawn up and counterparts were provided for each party. The purchaser signed his counterpart and posted it to the vendor, who did not sign his counterpart. It was held that no contract existed.

Branca v. *Cobarro* (*1947*): Plaintiff agreed to purchase the lease and goodwill of defendant's mushroom farm and they both signed a document which ended with the words: "This is a provisional agreement until a fully legalised agreement, drawn up by a solicitor and embodying all the conditions herewith stated, is signed". It was held that the words showed that the parties intended the agreement to be binding and it would therefore remain in force until its provisions were embodied in a formally drawn-up document.

Butler Machine Tool Co. Ltd. v. *Ex-Cell-O Corporation* (*1979*): Plaintiffs offered machinery for sale on condition that orders would be accepted only on the terms set out in their quotation, which contained a price variation clause. The defendants placed an order on their own form (which did not include a price variation clause) with a tear-off slip, on which the plaintiffs acknowledged the order. Due to the defendants' delay in accepting delivery, the plaintiffs invoked the price variation clause and the Court of Appeal held that the defendants' reply was a counter-offer which the plaintiffs had accepted by their acknowledgment.

(*c*) *It must generally be communicated to the offeror*. Normally an acceptance is ineffective unless and until it is communicated to the offeror. The two main exceptions to this rule arise when acceptances are made by post (in which case they are effective as soon as posted—even if subsequently mislaid and not delivered) and also when the offeror expressly or impliedly waives communication (e.g. in a general offer, where performance constitutes acceptance), as in—

Carlill v. *Carbolic Smoke Ball Co.* (*1893*): Defendants offered £100 to anyone who contracted influenza after using their smoke-ball thrice daily for a fortnight. Plaintiff did so but caught influenza and claimed £100. It was held that the offer contained an intimation that performance was adequate acceptance and there was a valid contract.

(*d*) *It must involve positive conduct*. Mere mental acceptance is not sufficient nor may the offeror stipulate that he will take silence to be acceptance, and thus bind the offeree—

Felthouse v. *Bindley* (*1863*): Plaintiff was negotiating for the purchase of his nephew's horse for either £30 or thirty guineas and he wrote: "Split the difference—unless I hear from you to the contrary, the horse is mine for £30.15 (shillings)". The defendant, an auctioneer, later sold the nephew's stock, including the horse. *Held*: the plaintiff did not own the animal, even though there had not been any reply to his letter.

(*e*) *It may normally be communicated in any manner.* However, if the offeror expressly or impliedly prescribes a mandatory (but not merely directory) mode of acceptance, communication in any other manner would not suffice.

> *Holwell Securities* v. *Hughes* (*1974*): An option to purchase land was granted, subject to its being exercisable by notice in writing within six months. A notice was posted and never arrived but the Court of Appeal held that, in this case, the general rule of acceptance by post (cf. 2(*c*)) did not apply and the option was *not* validly exercised.

> *Yates Building Co.* v. *R. J. Pulleyn & Sons* (*1975*): An option to purchase land was granted subject to its being exercisable by notice in writing "sent by registered post or recorded delivery". The intending purchaser's solicitors sent a notice by ordinary post and the Court of Appeal held that the prescribed form of posting was directory and not mandatory; therefore the option had been validly exercised.

THE CONSIDERATION

3. The existence of consideration. For a simple contract to be valid it is necessary to prove the existence of *consideration*, i.e. an act or forbearance (or the promise therof) by the offeree, in return for the promise of the offeror. Consequently, a gratuitous offer to do something for another cannot be enforced with an action for breach of contract. Consideration is said to be either *executed* (if carried out at the time of the agreement) or *executory* (if merely promised for some future time). It is subject to the following rules:

(*a*) *It must be real.* Consideration must have some value, thus it cannot be constituted by an existing duty (e.g. a public duty or contractual liability); however, it may be sufficient if a party does more than he was already bound to do. It does not matter how small the value is, so long as it is worth something, therefore inadequacy of consideration is no ground for avoiding a contract unless it is "so gross as to amount to conclusive evidence of fraud" (*per* Lord Eldon). However, consideration will *not* be sufficient if it is vague, incapable of performance, illegal or merely "good" (e.g. natural love and affection)—

> *Stilk* v. *Myrick* (*1809*): A ship's captain promised his crew the wages of two deserters if they would share the work of the missing men. *Held*: there was no consideration by the crew, as they

were already contractually bound to do any extra work to complete the voyage.

Glasbrook Bros. Ltd. v. *Glamorgan County Council* (*1925*): To protect a coal-mine during a strike, the police authorities considered that a mobile force was sufficient; however, the colliery wanted a static guard and it was agreed to provide this for £2,200. Subsequently, the company refused to pay and pleaded that the police were already bound to provide such protection. *Held*: the agreement was binding, as the police had done more than they were bound to do under their public duty.

(*b*) *It must move from the promisee*. Anyone seeking to enforce a promise must prove that *he himself* (and not a third party) has given consideration for it—

Tweddle v. *Atkinson* (*1861*): T's father and prospective father-in-law, William Guy, agreed between themselves respectively to pay T £100 and £200 on his marriage. This took place but Guy failed to pay the £200 and later died. T sued Guy's executor for the sum. *Held*: his action must fail as he had not given any consideration.

The doctrine of privity of contract (*see* XVI) is merely an aspect of this rule.

(*c*) *It must not be past*. An act performed by one party prior to the other's promise cannot normally be consideration to support that promise. However, a previous act may constitute valid consideration if it was performed on the understanding that there should be some consideration and the subsequent promise simply fixed the amount—

Re McArdle (*1951*): A bungalow was left to a widow for her lifetime and thereafter ownership was to pass to her children. A daughter-in-law, who lived there, made extensive repairs to the building and all the children then wrote to her, promising to pay her £488 "in consideration of your carrying out certain alterations and improvements". However, the money was not paid. *Held*: as all the work had been finished before the promise was made, the repairs constituted past consideration; thus there was no contractual obligation to pay.

Lampleigh v. *Brathwait* (*1615*): Having killed a man, B asked L to do all he could to secure a pardon from the King. L spent time and money visiting places where the King was present and B then promised him £100, but failed to pay it. *Held*: there was a binding contract, as the subsequent promise fixed the sum to be paid under an implied promise (to pay a reasonable sum) in the original request.

(d) *It must normally exist to enforce waiver of rights.* If a party wholly or partially waives his rights under a contract, the waiver is not binding unless consideration is given for it (whereby the waiver becomes part of a new binding contract between the parties). Thus, if A owes B £100 and B agrees to accept £90, it would appear that he could still sue for the remaining £10 if there is no consideration for the waiver (i.e. a new element introduced at the request of the creditor, e.g. payment at an earlier time than necessary, in a different place or in a different form). This rule has, however, been modified by the *doctrine of equitable estoppel*, applied in the *High Trees House* case, cited below. This means that, if B waives his contractual rights against A, *who acts to his detriment in reliance on the waiver*, it is only fair that B should be estopped from denying that he intended the waiver to be binding. This principle is a *shield and not a sword*, i.e. it can be raised only as a defence and *not* as a cause of action (e.g. if a creditor retracts his waiver and receives payment in full, the debtor cannot later sue on the doctrine to recover the money paid)—

Foakes v. *Beer* (*1884*): Mrs. B had obtained a judgment for £2,090 against F, who asked for time to pay. The parties agreed in writing (but not by a deed) that F should pay £500 immediately and the remainder by instalments, whilst Mrs. B would "not take any proceedings whatever on the judgment". When F had paid the final instalment, Mrs. B realised that she had not charged the interest payable on judgment debts and sought to recover a further £360. *Held*: Mrs. B was entitled to the interest, as the agreement was unsupported by consideration (cf. *D & C Builders Ltd.* v. *Rees* (*1966*), XVII, 2(*d*)).

Central London Property Trust Ltd. v. *High Trees House Ltd.* (*1947*): In 1937 the plaintiffs let a block of flats to defendants at a ground rent of £2,500 per annum. In 1940, on account of the war, few flats could be let; consequently the defendants found difficulty in paying the ground rent and the plaintiffs agreed in writing to reduce it to £1,250. In 1945 the whole block became full again and plaintiffs sued for the balance of rent at the original contract rate for the last six months of 1945, pleading that, if they had so wished, they could have claimed the full rent back to 1940. *Held*: plaintiffs were entitled to the full rent for the last six months of 1945 but, in *obiter dicta*, Denning J. rejected the possibility of a claim back to 1940, thus illustrating that the effect of equitable estoppel is *suspensory* and not extinguishing.

Combe v. *Combe* (*1951*): After plaintiff (wife) had obtained a decree nisi, defendant (husband) agreed in writing to pay her an allowance of £100 per annum. He did not do so and she sued to obtain it. *Held*: she was not entitled, as there was no consideration for the promise. The *High Trees* principle did not apply here, as it relates only to situations where there has been a contract in existence and where the plaintiff has made a promise with the intention that it should be acted upon, has gone back on it, and has then sought to recover from the defendant, who has acted to his detriment in reliance on the promise. Consequently, it cannot be argued that "the *High Trees* principle strikes at the roots of the doctrine of Consideration".

THE INTENTION TO CREATE LEGAL RELATIONS

4. The rebuttal of a legal relationship. For a simple contract to be enforceable, it is essential that there should be an intention by the parties to enter into legal relationship. The courts seek to give effect to the presumed intentions of the parties; thus, in commercial agreements, there is a rebuttable presumption that the parties intended to create legal relations. An intention *not* to create legal relations (and to prevent an agreement from being binding) may be established if:

(*a*) *It is expressed in the agreement.* An enforceable contract will not exist if an agreement is stated to be *subject to contract* (cf. *Eccles* v. *Bryant & Pollock* (*1948*), 2(*b*)) or *binding in honour only*—

Rose & Frank Co. v. *J. R. Crompton & Bros. Ltd.* (*1925*): CB (an English company supplying carbon paper) had entered into an agreement with RF, appointing them sole agents in the USA. The document stated: "This arrangement is not entered into, nor is this memorandum written, as a formal or legal agreement . . . but . . . is only a definite expression and record of the purpose and intention of the . . . parties concerned, to which they each honourably pledge themselves". CB later ended the agreement and RF sued for its enforcement. *Held*: the usual presumption that commercial agreements constitute enforceable contracts was rebutted by the clear words used, although individual orders given and accepted were enforceable contracts.

Jones v. *Vernon's Pools Ltd.* (*1938*): Plaintiff sued on a football pool coupon, which he alleged he had posted and that defendant had lost. It contained a condition to the effect that the sending in and acceptance, together with all associated transactions, should be "binding in honour only". *Held*: this was a bar to any action at law.

(*b*) *It is implied from the agreement.* In social or domestic agreements there is a presumption that the parties did not intend to create legal relations. This also applies to vague promises in advertising puffs, etc. and in *Carlill* v. *Carbolic Smoke Ball Co.* (*1893*)(*see* 2c)) the presumption was rebutted by the fact that the defendants stated that they had deposited £2,000 "to show their sincerity" and, consequently, it could be concluded that they had contemplated legal liability. It has been held that a public body under a statutory duty to supply electricity, etc. does so in pursuance of that duty and *not* under a contract.

Balfour v. *Balfour* (*1919*): Defendant (husband) had agreed to pay plaintiff (wife) £30 a month whilst he was away in India. Plaintiff obtained a divorce and the defendant refused to make any further payments. *Held*: no enforceable contract, as the promise was intended to fulfil a moral and not a legal obligation (the plaintiff also had not given any consideration).

PROGRESS TEST 9

1. Distinguish between an offer and an invitation to treat. (1)

2. Having advertised plastic gnomes for sale at a quoted price, Jeremy received an order for 200 from George and posted a reply agreeing to supply them. Half an hour later, he discovered that his stock had been vandalised and could be replaced only at a large increase in cost, so he telephoned George with a new price. Advise George. (1)

3. Knowing that Joe wanted to buy a second-hand car, Fred wrote to him, offering one at £500. Joe replied: "I can pay only £400 but, if this is OK, don't bother to reply and I will collect the car on Saturday". Hearing nothing further, he went to fetch the vehicle and found that it had been sold to someone else. Advise Joe. (2)

4. Examine the nature and scope of the doctrine of equitable estoppel. (3)

5. Do you consider that an intention to create legal relations is an essential element of a simple contract?   (4)

CHAPTER X

The Capacity of the Parties

THE MINOR

1. The capacity of minors. The term *capacity* means, in its legal context, the ability to do something (such as to make a contract) and it can be assumed that the common law was developed to apply chiefly to the sane, sober, British adult. Special conditions therefore exist for persons differing from this norm—particularly in contract if there is *inequality of bargaining power* (*see* XI, **4**(*c*)(*iv*); XII, **3**(*c*) XIII, **2**(*c*) and **4**(*b*); XV, **1**(*c*)) and the first to be considered is the *minor* (*see* VIII, **2**(*a*)). It should be emphasised that a parent is not liable for his child's contracts (unless the child was acting as his agent) nor can a minor's contracts be validated by the authorisation of his parents. Contracts involving minors fall into four classes:

(*a*) *The contracts enforceable against minors.* These are of two types:

(*i*) *The contracts for necessaries.* Under the Sale of Goods Act 1979, s. 3, a minor is obliged to pay a reasonable price (not necessarily the contract price) for goods or services necessary to him, according to his conditions in life and his requirements *at the time of sale and delivery*—

Chapple v. *Cooper* (*1844*); Defendant (minor) attempted to avoid paying for her late husband's funeral but it was held to be a necessary for which she was liable.

Nash v. *Inman* (*1908*): Plaintiff (tailor) sued defendant (minor Cambridge undergraduate) for the supply of clothes, including eleven fancy waistcoats—but it was held that these were not necessaries and the action must fail.

(*ii*) *The beneficial contracts of service.* Minors are bound by contracts of employment which are *of benefit to them in their education or training for a career* (e.g. apprenticeships), even if the agreement contains burdensome terms—

Chaplin v. *Leslie Frewin (Publishers) Ltd. (1966)*: The infant son of Charlie Chaplin contracted to tell his life story to "ghost writers", in return for the royalities on the resulting book. After he had passed the text for publication, he repudiated the contract on the ground that the book was libellous. It was held that the agreement was analagous to a contract of service and binding on the plaintiff, because it was for his benefit, enabling him to make a start as an author, also to support himself and his wife without relying on social security.

Mercantile Union Guarantee Corporation Ltd. v. *Ball (1937)*: Defendant (minor haulage contractor) was sued for arrears on the hire purchase of a lorry. It was held that this was *not* a contract for necessaries or beneficial service—but a trading agreement which was *not* binding on defendant.

(*b*) *The contracts voidable by minors.* Certain contracts are binding on minors unless expressly repudiated by them before (or within a reasonable time of) attaining majority. The principal examples are agreements *to buy or rent land, to purchase shares* and *to form partnerships.* Complete repudiation can be made only on attaining majority—as it is merely suspensive up till then and can be cancelled at eighteen. The minor is responsible for any liabilities accrued at the time of avoidance and cannot recover anything paid unless there has been a total failure of consideration—

Corpe v. *Overton (1833)*: Plaintiff (minor) contracted to form a partnership in the following January, paying £100 down and agreeing to pay a total of £1,000. On coming of age, he repudiated the agreement refused to sign the partnership deed and sought to recover his £100. *Held*: it had been paid for a future partnership, which never existed, therefore there was a total failure of consideration and he was entitled to repayment.

Steinberg v. *Scala (Leeds) Ltd. (1923)*: The (minor) plaintiff applied for, and was allotted, shares in the defendant company. She paid the amount due on allotment but repudiated the contract eighteen months later and sued to recover her payment. *Held*: since the shares had some value, there was no failure of consideration and she was not entitled to recover.

(*c*) *The contracts absolutely void in respect of minors.* Under the Infants Relief Act 1874, s. 1, certain contracts are *absolutely void* (i.e. are of no legal effect) and these include all agreements by minors for the *repayment of loans*, the supply of *goods other than necessaries*, also *accounts stated*. In such cases the minor cannot obtain specific performance (XVII, 5(*d*)), nor can he recover money or goods transferred to the other party unless there has been a total failure of consideration.

Though liable for his torts, a minor cannot be made liable for what is really a breach of contract by framing the action in tort—unless there is a definite independent wrong. However, a minor who obtains goods by fraud, and remains in possession, can be required to return them; it is therefore arguable whether the contracts in this category are strictly speaking "absolutely void":

Leslie v. *Shiell* (*1914*): Fraudulently stating that he was of full age, defendant (minor) had borrowed £400 from plaintiff (money-lender). He did not repay the loan and plaintiff sued for the sum as "money had and received", and also as damages for the tort of fraud. *Held*: the money could not be recovered, as an action for fraud would be an indirect way of enforcing a void contract.

Ballett v. *Mingay* (*1943*): Defendant (minor) rented public-address apparatus from plaintiff and lent it to a friend. When plaintiff required its return, defendant was unable to comply and was sued in tort. *Held*: he was liable, as the act complained of was completely outside the contract.

Pearce v. *Brain* (*1929*): Plaintiff (minor) exchanged his motor-cycle combination for defendant's car, which broke down; so he sued to recover the combination. *Held*: he could not do so, as there had not been a total failure of consideration.

(*d*) *The contracts unenforceable against adults*. Under the Infants Relief Act 1874, s. 2, actions cannot be brought to enforce agreements made by adults to pay debts which they contracted during minority or to ratify contracts made during minority irrespective of whether there was new consideration. Except in cases of debt, however, a completely new promise with fresh consideration would be binding—and the distinction between ratification and a fresh promise is very narrow.

Smith v. *King* (*1892*): Plaintiffs (stockbrokers) sued defendant (of full age) for a debt incurred during his minority. The action was settled on his agreeing to be bound to pay two bills of exchange for £50 each but, in a subsequent action on one of the bills, he pleaded minority. *Held*: he was not liable, as the transaction amounted merely to a promise to pay a debt contracted during minority.

Brown v. *Harper* (*1893*): On attaining his majority, the defendant continued in his previous employment at an increased salary. *Held*: there was a new promise by which he was bound.

THE INSANE OR DRUNKEN PERSON

2. The capacity of insane or drunken persons. Contracts made by insane persons whose property is subject to the control of the court (under the Mental Health Act 1983) are *void*, because otherwise they would interfere with the court's right of control. Apart from this, a contract is *voidable* at the option of a party who can prove that he was, through drunkenness or insanity, incapable of understanding its nature—unless the other party can establish one of the following points:

(*a*) *It was ratified during a sober or lucid moment.*

Matthews v. *Baxter* (*1873*): Defendant bought a house from plaintiff while drunk but ratified the agreement when sober. *Held*: valid contract.

(*b*) *It relates to the acquisition of necessaries.* Where necessaries are sold to a person who, by means of mental incapacity or drunkenness, is incompetent to contract, he is bound to pay a reasonable price.

(*c*) *It was entered into by the other party in ignorance of the disability.* The onus lies on the person seeking to avoid the contract to show his state of mind at the time of the agreement and *also the other party's knowledge of it*—

Imperial Loan Co. v. *Stone* (*1892*): Defendant pleaded that he was insane when he made a promissory note but he was unable to convince the jury that plaintiff knew this. *Held*: the defence could not succeed unless he was able to establish both issues.

THE CORPORATION

3. The capacity of corporations. The contractual capacity of corporations (see VIII, **1**(*a*)) depends on the manner in which they are created:

(*a*) *The chartered corporation.* There are no legal limits to the contractual capacity of a chartered corporation—thus, if it enters into a contract beyond the powers granted in the charter, the act is valid and binding. However, a member of a chartered corporation may seek an injunction to restrain an act beyond the powers granted in the charter.

(*b*) *The statutory corporation.* The contractual capacity of a statutory corporation is defined, expressly or impliedly, in the creating statute. Any contract which is *ultra vires* the statute is *void.* Thus anyone who has supplied goods to a statutory corporation under an *ultra vires* contract cannot succeed in an action to recover the price—but, if the goods can be traced and identified, he may seek to recover them.

(*c*) *The registered corporation.* A limited company has its contractual capacity defined by the *objects clause* in its *Memorandum of Association* (a public document which it must lodge with the Registrar of Companies). Formerly, any contract which was *ultra vires* the memorandum was held to be void, but the European Communities Act 1972, s. 9(1) provides that "In favour of a person dealing with a company in good faith, any transaction decided on by the directors shall be deemed to be one which it is within the capacity of the company to enter into, and the power of the director to bind the company shall be deemed to be free of any limitation under the memorandum or articles of association." Though this means that a company cannot rely on the *ultra vires* doctrine to release itself from a contract, it would nevertheless appear possible for anyone dealing with the company to invoke the doctrine if *he* wished to avoid a contract.

PROGRESS TEST 10

1. Sam, a talented guitarist aged sixteen, wanted to become a pop star and entered into a two-year contract with Grasping, an agent, who agreed to pay him £30 a week for the exclusive use of his services. After a year, Sam's performances are now netting Grasping about £5,000 a week and Sam seeks your advice, as he wishes to change agents. (1)

2. Goodbooks Ltd, supplied two "O" Level texts and a £30 work on jurisprudence to Roger, aged fifteen, who has a vague interest in law and who told the shop to send the bill to his father. The latter is not a customer of the firm and has declined to pay anything. Advise Goodbooks. (1)

3. Arthur made a loan of £500 to his nephew John, aged seventeen. Two years later John promised to repay the full sum if uncle would accept £10 per month. Arthur agreed but six months have elapsed without John paying anything. Advise Arthur. (1)

4. Having consumed too much alcohol, O'Reilly orders a new Daimler car which he cannot afford and he seeks your advice. (2)

5. Examine the contractual capacity of corporations. (3)

CHAPTER XI

The Nature of Void Contracts

THE CONSEQUENCE OF MISTAKE

1. The categories of operative mistake. The general common law rule is that *any mistake made by either or both parties does not affect the validity of a contract*. However, if a mistake of *fact* (but not law) is so *fundamental as to destroy the basis of the agreement*, it is termed an *operative mistake* and it will cause the contract to be *void ab initio* (i.e. it never existed, right from the beginning). There are three categories of operative mistake:

(*a*) *The common mistake.* In this case the same error is made by both parties—generally in relation to:

(*i*) *The existence of the subject-matter.* If, at the time of making a contract, both parties are wrong in believing that the subject-matter exists, then the agreement will be void (as it relates to *res extincta*). However, if a seller is deemed to have warranted the existence of the goods concerned, he is probably liable to the purchaser for breach of contract if they do not exist—

Couturier v. *Hastie* (*1856*): A contract was made for the sale of a cargo of corn which, unknown to the parties, had already been sold (having been damaged at sea). *Held*: no contract. The Sale of Goods Act 1979, s. 6 now provides that "where there is a contract for the sale of specific goods and the goods, without the knowledge of the seller, have perished at the time when the contract is made, the contract is void".

McRae v. *Commonwealth Disposals Commission* (*1951*): Defendants had invited tenders for the purchase of a sunken oil tanker. Plaintiffs made an offer which was accepted and they then sent out an expedition. It was later proved that the vessel had never existed. *Held*: plaintiffs were entitled to recover damages, as the defendants had promised that there was a tanker at a given locality (High Court of Australia).

It will be seen at XVII, 3, that a close relationship exists between *mistake* and *frustration*.

(*ii*) *The quality of the subject-matter.* Common mistake concerning the quality of the subject-matter is *not* operative at common law and therefore does not invalidate a contract—

> *Leaf* v. *International Galleries* (*1950*): Plaintiff bought a painting of Salisbury Cathedral from the defendants, both parties believing it to be by Constable. Five years later, the plaintiff discovered that it was not by Constable and claimed rescission of the contract. *Held*: his claim must fail, as it had not been brought within a reasonable time and, in *obiter dicta*, Denning L. J. said "There was a mistake about the quality of the subject-matter ... such a mistake, however, does not avoid a contract."

> *Bell* v. *Lever Bros. Ltd.* (*1932*): LB paid £30,000 redundancy compensation to B, not realising that they could have dismissed him without compensation, on account of his improper conduct (which he had forgotten). They claimed the return of the £30,000 on the ground that the agreement to pay it was void through operative mistake. *Held*: the mistake merely related to the quality of the subject-matter and did not invalidate the contract.

(*b*) *The mutual mistake.* In this case there is a misunderstanding between the parties, which neither realises, and they are at cross-purposes (one believing one fact and the other believing another), generally in relation to:

(*i*) *The identity of the subject-matter.* No contract will exist if the parties are not *ad idem* (of the same mind) concerning what constitutes the subject-matter—

> *Raffles* v. *Wichelhaus* (*1864*): A contract was made for the sale of cargo to arrive "Ex 'Peerless' from Bombay". Two ships of the same name left Bombay and the defendants thought that the agreement referred to the one sailing in October, whereas the plaintiff thought that it was the one in December. *Held*: no contract.

> *Scriven Bros. & Co.* v. *Hindley & Co.* (*1913*): Plaintiffs' auctioneer sold hemp and tow. Samples of each were on view before the sale but the catalogue did not explain which lots were which, and the sacks were identical. The tow was knocked down to the defendants, who thought that they had been bidding for hemp. On realising their mistake, they refused to pay. *Held*: there was no agreement between the parties and the plaintiffs' action must fail.

(*ii*) *The quality of the subject-matter.* Here again mistake concerning the value or quality of the subject-matter will generally *not* affect the validity of an agreement (but cf. *terms* at XV, **1**).

Smith v. *Hughes* (*1871*): A farmer offered to sell oats to a race-horse trainer's manager who retained samples for twenty-four hours and then accepted the offer. He later refused delivery because new oats arrived and he thought he had been buying old ones. *Held*: the manager's mistake (which was not induced by the farmer's conduct) would not invalidate the contract.

(*iii*) *The terms of the contract.* Mutual mistake concerning the terms of a contract will generally *not* affect its validity—

Wood v. *Scarth* (*1858*): Plaintiff accepted defendant's written offer of the lease of a public house for £63 per annum. Defendant incorrectly thought that his clerk had told the plaintiff that there was also a premium of £500 and refused to grant the lease without this. *Held*: the contract without the premium was valid.

(*c*) *The unilateral mistake.* In this case only one party is mis-taken and the other realises that fact. Unilateral mistake generally relates to:
   (*i*) *The identity of the other party.* Mistake concerning the identity of the person with whom a contract is made will nullify the agreement *only if the identity is of material importance* and *if the other person realises that it is not intended that he should become a party to the contract*—

Cundy v. *Lindsay* (*1878*): One Blenkarn ordered goods from Lindsay & Co., signing the order to give the impression that it came from the reputable firm of Blenkiron & Co. He did not pay for them and sold them to Cundys. *Held*: the contract between Lindsays and Blenkarn was void for mistake, consequently the property in the goods still resided in Lindsays, who were entitled to recover them from Cundys.

King's Norton Metal Co. v. *Edridge, Merret & Co. Ltd.* (*1897*): One Wallis set up the sham business of Hallam & Co., with impressive letter-headings. Using these, he obtained from plain-tiffs, without payment, goods which were subsequently pur-chased from him in good faith by defendants. *Held*: as plaintiffs had previously traded with Wallis and as he had signed the order, they could not argue that they had intended to trade with Hallam & Co., and not with him. Consequently the contract was *not* void for mistake and plaintiffs could not recover from defendants.

Lewis v. *Averay* (*1973*): Posing as Richard Green, a well-known actor, and identifying himself with a Pinewood Studio pass, a rogue acquired L's car with a worthless cheque and then sold it to A. L sued A to recover the vehicle but the Court of Appeal held that L had intended to contract with the person present in front of him, whoever he was, thus the contract was *not* void and A had a good title to the car.

(*ii*) *The expression of intention.* If the offeror makes a material mistake in expressing his intention and the other party knows (or is deemed to know) of the error, the agreement will be void—

Hartog v. *Colin & Shields* (*1939*): Defendant offered hare skins for sale at a price "per pound", in mistake for "per piece". Plaintiff accepted the offer but could not reasonably have supposed that it expressed the defendant's real intention. *Held*: as the plaintiff must have known that it was made under a mistake, the contract was void.

Centrovincial Estates PLC v. *Merchant Investors Assurance Co. Ltd.* (*1983*): Plaintiffs leased property to defendants at a rent of £68,320 per annum, subject to review, and their solicitors wrote inviting defendants to agree to the figure of £65,000, as appropriate at the review date. Defendants accepted this by letter and, five days later, the solicitors telephoned to say that the figure should have been £126,000. The Court of Appeal upheld the agreement for £65,000, as an unambiguous offer had been accepted and defendants had given consideration (by depriving themselves of the right to suggest any other figure).

(*iii*) *The nature of a document signed.* In general, a person is bound by the terms of any document which he signs, even though he did not read it or did not understand its contents. However, the old common law plea of *non est factum* (it is not his deed) may be used to make an agreement void if a person can show that, *through blindness, senility, illiteracy, trick or fraudulent misrepresentation*, he signed a document which was *radically, fundamentally or totally different from what he believed it to be* and that *he had not been careless* in failing to discover its true nature—

Foster v. *Mackinnon* (*1869*): An old man with bad eyesight signed a document, believing it to be a guarantee—although it was actually a bill of exchange. As his signature was fraudulently obtained, it was held that he was not a party to the bill.

Saunders v. *Anglia Building Society* (*1971*): A Mrs. Gallie, aged seventy-eight, was induced by her nephew P and his business colleague L to sign a document which she thought would enable the two men to raise money on the security of her house, by assigning it to her nephew as a gift, on condition that she could live there for the rest of her life. Having broken her glasses, Mrs. Gallie could not read the document and did not ask for it to be read to her. It was, in fact, an assignment to L for £3,000 and he mortgaged the house to the Building Society but did not pay anything to Mrs. Gallie. He defaulted on the mortage payments and the Society sought possession of the house. Mrs. Gallie sued for a declaration that the assignment was void because of *non est factum* but the House of Lords held that the plea must fail as the requirements were not fulfilled.

2. The forms of equitable relief. The common law rules outlined above render a contract either totally void or completely valid, even though neither solution may be entirely just. However, if a person has entered into a contract under a misapprehension which does not constitute an operative mistake, he may nevertheless be able to obtain one of the following forms of *equitable* relief:

(*a*) *The rescission on terms.* Rescission means the avoidance of a contract by the injured party but, in the case of mistake, it appears to be available only on terms (conditions) imposed by the court. It probably applies solely to a common mistake where one party, who is not at fault, can show that it would be unjust for the other to take full advantage of his contractual rights. In such circumstances, the original rights and obligations will be dissolved and relaced by fresh ones which the court considers fair and just—

Solle v. *Butcher* (*1950*): A landlord had agreed to lease a flat to a tenant at a yearly rental of £250. Both believed that the rent was not controlled by the Rent Restriction Acts (under which it would have been £140 per annum). Consequently, the landlord had not taken steps, within the required time, to have the controlled rent raised to £250, before entering into an agreement with any tenant. The tenant paid the agreed rent (£250) for over a year but then sued for a rebate on the ground that the flat was subject to rent restriction; the landlord counter-claimed for possession, arguing that the lease was therefore void for mistake. *Held*: the flat was subject to the Rent Restriction Acts; the parties had therefore been under a common mistake of fact but it was not an operative mistake. The landlord was entitled to a rescission on terms directed by the court—the terms being that he allow the tenant to enter a new lease at £250 per annum.

(*b*) *The refusal of specific performance.* Specific performance (*see* XVII, 5(*d*)), is a discretionary remedy which will not be enforced if a mistake was caused by the plaintiff's misrepresentation *or* if the plaintiff knew of the defendant's mistake. However, where specific performance is refused, the defendant may still be liable in damages for breach of contract—

> *Webster* v. *Cecil* (*1861*): Plaintiff offered the defendant £2,000 for certain land but it was rejected. Defendant then wrote offering the land for £1,250 (really intending to write £2,250) and the plaintiff accepted, subsequently seeking specific performance. *Held*: plaintiff must have known of the mistake and specific performance was refused.

(*c*) *The rectification.* If a written contract does not accurately express the agreement actually reached between the parties, the court will rectify (correct) the document so as to bring it into conformity with the actual agreement reached. It is necessary, however, for the party seeking rectification to show that *an agreement on all points* had existed between the parties and *had continued unchanged* up to the time when it was expressed in a written document, *which failed to express the agreement* (but not merely the intention) of the parties—

> *Craddock Bros. Ltd.* v. *Hunt* (*1923*): Plaintiffs agreed orally to sell defendant a house *exclusive* of an adjoining yard but the written agreement and later conveyance *included* the yard. *Held*: both documents should be rectified.

> *Rose* v. *Pim* (*1953*): Plaintiffs received an order from Egypt for "feveroles". Not knowing what these were, they inquired of the defendants, who said that they were horse-beans, which they could supply. Plaintiffs thereupon gave an oral order for the purchase of "horse-beans" and the contract was later put into writing. When they ultimately reached Egypt, it was found that they were not "feveroles". *Held*: the written contract correctly expressed the oral agreement and therefore could not be rectified.

THE CONSTRICTIONS OF THE LAW

3. The contravention of statute law. Agreements which fulfil all the requirements of a valid contract may nevertheless conflict with legal rules laid down by statute or common law. Some contracts are absolutely prohibited and are then termed *illegal*; others may merely be denied their full validity and these are said to be *void*.

Many types of contract are rendered void by different statutes but the two principal examples are:

(a) *The wagering contracts.* These are contracts in which *two parties agree that one shall win and the other shall lose a stake, dependent on the determination of a future uncertain event, in which neither has any other interest.* The limitation to *two parties* means that any competition, game, etc., in which there are three or more participants can *not* constitute a wager. The fact that *one shall win and the other shall lose* means that football pool coupons do *not* constitute wagering contracts, as the promoters take a percentage of the stake money and are not affected by the forecasts. That is why (as shown at IX, 4(a)), the pools promoters expressly prevent the formation of enforceable contracts. A *stake* may mean a sum of money or any other property. With regard to *a future uncertain event*, the uncertainty must lie in the minds of the contracting parties. A wagering contract could therefore concern, for example, the distance from Bristol to Edinburgh, as the figure finally determined by the parties is a future uncertain event. The fact that *neither has any other interest* means that, for example, a bet by a candidate on his examination result would *not* constitute a wagering contract—nor would any insurance contract (as the Life Assurance Act 1774 forbids insurance on the lives of any persons or any events in which the person seeking insurance has no interest). The effect of wagering contracts must be considered in respect of the persons concerned:

(i) *The wagerer.* Under the Gaming Act 1845, s. 18, every wagering contract is *void* (though not illegal); consequently, the winner cannot sue the loser for his winnings (even though the loser may have made a fresh promise to pay, supported by new consideration), nor can he sue on a cheque paid, and subsequently stopped, by the loser. Likewise, if the loser does pay, he cannot sue to recover his money—

> *Hill* v. *William Hill (Park Lane) Ltd. (1949):* H owed WH about £3,600 and an agreement was made whereby he would not be posted as a defaulter if payments were made by instalments; however, he failed to pay and was sued. *Held:* the promise related to the payment of a betting account (regardless of the new agreement) and was therefore void.

(ii) *The stakeholder.* Under the Gaming Act 1845, s. 18, the winner of a wager cannot bring an action against a stakeholder to recover the *loser's* deposit. However, he can demand the return of his own—and so can the loser, up till the moment when it is

handed over to the winner, and notwithstanding the result of th
event in question.

(*iii*) *The agent*. Under the Gaming Act 1892, s. 1, an agent
who has paid a bet for his principal cannot sue for reimbursement,
nor can he bring an action in respect of a commission or other
reward for his services. Conversely, he cannot be sued by his
principal for failing to carry out instructions—though an action
can succeed against him for not handing over winnings received:

Tatam v. *Reeve* (*1893*): Plaintiff had settled four debts for
defendant, without realising that they were incurred by wagering. *Held*: he could not recover the amount paid.

(*iv*) *The lender*. Money lent would not be recoverable if it
was to be repaid only in the event of a bet being won (thereby the
lender himself would be betting) or if it was paid by the lender
directly to (or for) the winner of a bet—

Re O'Shea, ex parte Lancaster (*1911*): L guaranteed O's overdraft to the extent of £500, to enable him to pay lost bets—but
the evidence disclosed no obligation binding O to use the money
only for this purpose. *Held*: the debt to L was valid and
enforceable.

(*b*) *The restrictive trading agreements*. Under the Restrictive
Trade Practices Acts 1976–77, certain restrictive and information
agreements must be registered with the Director General of Fair
Trading. Restrictive agreements between two or more parties
engaged in producing, supplying or processing goods generally
relate to prices, conditions of sale, areas of distribution, etc. Information agreements are those whereby the parties agree to inform
each other about such matters. The Director General must submit
such registered agreements to the Restrictive Practices Court and
the onus lies on the parties to rebut the presumption that they are
contrary to the public interest. It must be shown that the benefits
arising from a restriction outweigh any detriments. If the court
declares a restriction contrary to the public interest, it is rendered
void, but the rest of the agreement may remain valid if the offend-
ing part can be severed from it—

Re Chemists' Federation Agreement (*1958*): The Federation
tried to prevent proprietary medicines from being sold other than
by qualified retail chemists. It was claimed that this would
safeguard the public but the court held that the risk was too
slight to justify such a restriction.

Article 85 of the Treaty of Rome renders void (unless they are specifically exempted) agreements, decisions and concerted practices which have as their object or effect the prevention, restriction or distortion of competition within the European Economic Community.

4. The contravention of the common law. The common law has developed the principle whereby the courts will refuse relief to parties claiming under contracts which are *contrary to public policy* (i.e. injurious to the public good). Some of these (outlined at XII, 2) are *illegal*, whereas others are *void*. It should be emphasised, however, that such contracts are not totally void—but only in so far as they contravene public policy. Thus if *severance* (i.e. the deletion of the void part without, in effect, making a new contract) can be effected, the rest of the agreement will be valid. The principal contracts which are void at common law are:

(*a*) *The contracts to usurp the jurisdiction of the courts.* An agreement which purports to remove the right of either or both of the parties to submit questions of law to the courts is void. This does not, however, invalidate arbitration agreements where each party is free, after the arbitral award, to request the court to consider any points of law which are involved.

Baker v. *Jones (1954)*: The rules of the British Amateur Weightlifters' Association provided that its central council should be the only body empowered to interpret the rules and that its decision should be final. *Held*: this provision was contrary to public policy.

(*b*) *The contracts prejudicial to the status of marriage.* In this category agreements which are void include marriage brokage contracts (i.e. where a reward is received for procuring marriages or introducing persons with a view to marriage), contracts to restrain persons from marrying at all (though partial restraint, e.g. from marrying a Roman Catholic, would probably be upheld) and also contracts for future separation of married persons (unless relating to a separation intended to take place immediately)—

Hermann v. *Charlesworth (1905)*: Plaintiff entered into a contract to pay defendant £250 if a marriage took place following an introduction made by him. She also paid a fee of £52, of which £47 was to be returned if no engagement or marriage took place within nine months. She sued to recover the £52 after nine months had passed without an engagement. *Held*: public policy requires that unsuitable marriages should not take place and, as the incentive of a fee might well produce such marriages, contracts to arrange them are void and the plaintiff was entitled to the return of her fee. It would appear, however, that agreements with "dating" agencies (which limit their obligation to providing introductions) would not be void.

Lowe v. *Peers* (*1768*): Defendant covenanted not to marry anyone other than plaintiff and to pay her £1,000 damages if he did so. *Held*: the agreement was void because it restrained him from marrying at all if plaintiff did not marry him—and she was not bound to do so.

(*c*) *The contracts in restraint of trade.* At common law, contracts in restraint of trade are presumed to be void but will be upheld if it can be shown that the restraint is *reasonable as between the parties* (i.e. no wider than is necessary to protect the proper interest of the party whom it is designed to benefit) and also *reasonable with regard to the interests of the public.* Restraint of trade may be effected between:

(*i*) *Purchasers and sellers of businesses.* Sometimes the vendor of the goodwill of a business is restrained from competing with the purchaser—

Nordenfelt v. *Maxim Nordenfelt Co. Ltd.* (*1894*): N, a manufacturer of guns and ammunition, sold his world-wide business to M and promised not to manufacture such products anywhere in the world for twenty-five years. *Held*: as the area supplied by the company was practically unlimited, the restraint was reasonable and binding.

British Reinforced Concrete Co. Ltd. v. *Schelff* (*1921*): In 1918 plaintiffs purchased a small business (supplying steel reinforcements for concrete roads), the partners of which contracted not to engage in a similar business until three years after the end of the war. One partner took employment with a company as manager of its reinforced materials department and plaintiffs sought an injunction to restrain this breach of the agreement. *Held*: the restraint clause was wider than necessary to protect the plaintiffs' interests, therefore the injunction was refused.

(*ii*) *Employers and employees.* Sometimes a contract of service provides that an employee leaving the firm shall not set up (or enter the service of) another similar business within a specified area and/or for a stipulated period. Such an agreement is void unless the former employer can show that it is essential for protecting his trade secrets or business connections.

Moreover, a restraint clause purporting to restrict a departing employee from using his *skill* in competition with his former employer is always void, even if the skill was acquired in that employer's service. As illustrated below, the principle embraces partners, as well as employees—

Littlewoods Organisation Ltd. v. *Harris* (*1978*): The plaintiffs' mail-order business (confined to the United Kingdom) competed principally with that of Great Universal Stores (operating world-wide). Employed by the plaintiffs as a divisional director, the defendant possessed details of their bi-annual catalogue (crucial to the success of their business) and his contract contained a restraint clause precluding his working for GUS within twelve months of leaving the plaintiffs. He attempted to do so and, granting an injunction, the Court of Appeal held that the covenant was reasonable and valid as, by the nature of their catalogue the plaintiffs possessed trade secrets which they were entitled to protect.

Greer v. *Sketchley Ltd.* (*1979*): The defendants (operating a dry-cleaning business in London and the Midlands) employed the plaintiff as a director, with a restraint clause precluding his engaging in similar business in any part of the United Kingdom within twelve months of leaving the firm. The Court of Appeal upheld a declaration that the clause was invalid as it was unreasonably wide in its geographical application. The covenant could not be limited to London and the Midlands—though this was effectively what had been done in the Littlewoods case—and the two were distinguished by the fact that the restraint in the first related to a specific competitor, rather than an area.

Hensman v. *Traill* (*1980*): Defendant, a general practitioner, became the plaintiff's partner under an agreement which provided that, if he should leave, he would not practise within seven miles for five years. On the retirement of a third member, the partner-ship was dissolved, and the defendant joined another local prac-tice. Plaintiff sought an injunction which was refused on the grounds that the purported restriction offended against public policy (in preventing a doctor from caring for patients) and was also unreasonably wide.

(*iii*) *Suppliers and traders.* Sometimes (possibly in return for a loan or lease) a trader enters into a *solus* agreement to buy only the goods of one particular supplier, but the requirement for reasonableness will apply, as in—

Esso Petroleum Co. Ltd. v. *Harper's Garage* (*Stourport*) *Ltd.*

(*1968*). H entered into a solus agreement with E for two garages.
In the case of the first they received a discount on agreeing to buy
all motor fuel from E, to keep the garage open at all reasonable
hours, and not to sell the garage without ensuring that the
purchaser entered into a similar agreement with E; such agreement to operate for fifty-three months. The second garage was
mortgaged to E for £7,000 on terms similar to those of the first
but for a period of twenty-one years. The first agreement was
held to be reasonable and valid, but the second was not—and it
was therefore void.

(*iv*) *Users and providers of exclusive services.* Contracts *for
services* (as well as contracts *of service*, i.e. employment) can be
void for unreasonableness, particularly if there is inequality of
bargaining power—

A. Schroeder Music Publishing Co. v. *Macaulay* (*1974*): M, an
unknown songwriter aged twenty-one, contracted to supply all
his compositions to S, who were to have full world copyright in
return for a fixed percentage on royalties. S could terminate or
assign the agreement but M could not terminate it and could
assign it only with S's consent. The contract was initially for five
years and S was not bound to publish or promote any of M's
compositions. *Held*: the restraints could not be justified as
necessary and the agreement was therefore void.

PROGRESS TEST 11

1. Mary offers to sell Jane six chairs which they both believe to
be genuine Chippendale. Three months later Jane seeks your advice
as she has discovered that they are merely reproductions. (1)

2. James and Cyril are cousins who intensely dislike each other.
Learning that Cyril wishes to sell a valuable clock, James disguises
himself as a clergyman and visits his cousin. With a cheque, which
is later dishonoured, he buys the clock and then sells it to Joe.
Advise Cyril. (1)

3. In what circumstances will a person who has signed a contractual agreement be able to (*i*) avoid liability on it (*ii*) have an
inaccuracy rectified? (1, 2)

4. Give examples of contracts which are void by statute. (3)

5. Outline the circumstances in which a contract in restraint of
trade will be enforceable. (4)

CHAPTER XII

The Nature of Illegal Contracts

THE NATURE OF ILLEGALITY

1. The forms of statutory illegality. In addition to rendering certain agreements *void* (*see* XI, **3**), statutes or delegated legislation may also make contracts *illegal*; however, it is necessary to distinguish:

(*a*) *The contracts which are illegal as formed.* The actual promise, consideration or ultimate purpose of a contract may be illegal. An important example is the Resale Prices Act 1976, which renders illegal any agreement to impose a minimum price on the resale of goods. The Restrictive Practices Court is empowered to exempt particular classes of goods but has done so in only two cases ("ethical" and "proprietary" drugs, also books). When a contract is illegal as formed, and both parties were (or should have been) aware of the illegality from the outset, *no action will lie* (unless severance of the illegal part is possible) and neither party can claim any right or remedy (*ex turpi causa non oritur actio*), even in respect of a related transaction—

Fisher v. *Bridges* (*1854*): F sold B some land to be used for an illegal lottery. B paid the price apart from £630 and executed a deed promising to pay this sum. F sued on the deed. *Held*: the original transaction was illegal; the related debt and deed were therefore tainted with illegality and neither would be enforced.

(*b*) *The contracts which are illegal as performed.* A contract which is legal in itself may nevertheless become illegal by reason of the way in which it is performed. For this to be the case, however, the prohibited act must lie at the centre of the agreement and not be merely incidental to it. When a contract is illegal as performed, *a guilty party can not claim any right or remedy*, but an innocent party has full remedies—

Anderson Ltd. v. *Daniel* (*1924*): Plaintiffs sued for the price of artificial fertiliser supplied to the defendant without an invoice required by statute to show the proportion of certain constituent chemicals. *Held*: the action must fail because, although a contract to buy and sell fertilisers is not in itself illegal, the object of the statute was to protect purchasers.

St. John Shipping Corporation v. *Joseph Rank Ltd.* (*1957*): Plaintiffs sued for the full charge of carrying the defendants' cargo, despite the fact that their ship had been overloaded and the master had been fined £1,200 for a breach of the Merchant Shipping Act 1932. *Held*: the illegal loading was merely incidental to the performance and the plaintiffs were entitled to recover.

Ashmore, Benson, Pease & Co. v. *A. V. Dawson* (*1973*): Defendant hauliers contracted to carry goods for the plaintiffs whose transport manager and assistant watched the loading of vehicles to a weight five tons in excess of that permitted by the Motor Vehicles (Construction and Use) Regulations 1966. One vehicle toppled over and its load was damaged, so the plaintiffs sued for negligence. *Held*: the contract, though lawful in its inception, was illegal in its performance, to the knowledge and with the concurrence of the plaintiffs' servants; consequently damages were not recoverable.

(*c*) *The contracts which are illegal through subsequent legislation.* The doctrine of frustration (*see* XVII, 3) covers the situation where an existing contract is rendered illegal by a change in the law (*see* XVII, 3(*a*)(*iv*)). In such circumstances, the parties are excused further performance of their obligations and no action will lie for breach.

2. The types of common law illegality. In addition to the contracts which are *void* at common law (*see* XI, 4), certain others are also considered to be contrary to public policy—but of such gravity that they are held to be *illegal*. The courts will not enforce such agreements at the instance of either party and the principal examples are:

(*a*) *The contracts to commit crimes or torts.* Agreements to commit crimes, torts or frauds upon third parties are illegal and they include contracts to defraud the Revenue—

Everet v. *Williams* (*1725*): A highwayman, who agreed with another to rob a coach, sued for his share of the proceeds. *Held*: the court could not enforce a contract based on a crime.

Miller v. *Karlinsky* (*1945*): Plaintiff was employed by the defendant for £10 a week plus expenses (which included the income tax payable on the £10). He sought to recover ten weeks' arrears of salary and £21 2s. 8d. (£21.14p) for expenses (of which £17 represented tax liability). *Held*: the contract was illegal as it defrauded the Revenue; consequently plaintiff could not recover even his ordinary salary.

(*b*) *The contracts prejudicial to national security or international relations.* Any contract, detrimental to the interests of the United Kingdom is illegal (e.g. trading with the enemy in wartime) and this also applies to any agreement which might disturb relations between the United Kingdom and friendly states—

Foster v. *Driscoll* (*1929*): Parties entered into an agreement to export whisky to the United States, contrary to the Prohibition laws of that country. *Held*: the contract was illegal and void.

(*c*) *The contracts prejudicial to the administration of justice.* Examples include contracts involving the concealment of an arrestable offence, promises by an accused person to indemnify anyone who has stood bail for him (*see* VI, 3), etc—

Keir v. *Leeman* (*1846*): Having commenced a prosecution against the defendants for riot and assault, the plaintiff told them that he would drop the charges if they would pay off a debt owing to him. The defendants agreed and, as no evidence was given against them, they were acquitted but failed to pay the debt. *Held*: the plaintiff was not entitled to recover it as the compromise was an illegal contract.

(*d*) *The contracts to promote corruption in public life.* Examples include contracts involving the bribery of officials and attempts to buy honours—

Parkinson v. *College of Ambulance Ltd.* (*1925*): The College Secretary fraudulently promised to obtain a knighthood for the plaintiff in return for a donation. He paid £3,000 but did not receive a title and sought to recover his money. *Held*: the agreement was illegal and the action must fail. Such agreements are now criminal offences under the Honours (Prevention of Abuses) Act 1925.

(*e*) *The contracts to promote sexual immorality.* Any contract, however innocent, will be invalidated if it is known by both parties that it is intended to further an immoral purpose—

Pearce v. *Brooks* (*1886*): Coach builders hired a carriage to a woman, knowing that she intended to use it for plying her trade as a prostitute. She fell into arrears with the hire charges and an action was brought to recover the sum due. *Held*: the contract was illegal and the money could not be recovered.

THE EFFECT OF ILLEGALITY

3. The recovery of property. If one party (transferor) passes money or property to the other (transferee) under an illegal contract, an action will not succeed for its recovery (*Parkinson* v. *College of Ambulance Ltd.*, 2(*d*) above), except in the following circumstances:

(*a*) *If the transferor can establish his claim without relying on the contract.*

Bowmakers Ltd. v. *Barnet Instruments Ltd.* (*1945*): Having obtained machine tools from plaintiffs under illegal hire purchase agreements (which contravened wartime regulations), the defendants failed to pay the instalments and sold some of the tools. *Held*: plaintiffs' action for the tort of conversion must succeed.

(*b*) *If the transferor genuinely repents*, before the illegal purpose has been substantially performed. However, he must convince the court that his repentance is real and that he is not repudiating the contract merely for convenience—

Bigos v. *Bousted* (*1951*): In contravention of the Exchange Control Act 1947, defendant agreed to supply the plaintiff with the equivalent of £150 in Italian lire. As security for his promise, the plaintiff deposited a share certificate with the defendant, who failed to supply the currency. Plaintiff sued for the return of the certificate, arguing that he had repented. *Held*: the so-called repentance was "but want of power to sin" because, if the lire had been forthcoming, he would have gladly accepted them; consequently the action must fail.

(*c*) *If the parties are not in pari delicto* (*equally guilty*). It has been shown at **1**(*b*) that an innocent party to a contract performed illegally has full remedies. Others not *in pari delicto* include:

(*i*) *Transferors induced by force or fraud to enter into contracts—*

Hughes v. *Liverpool Victoria Legal Friendly Society* (*1916*): Plaintiff was induced by the fraudulent misrepresentation of an insurance agent to enter into an illegal life assurance contract. *Held*: the parties were not *in pari delicto* and the premium could be recovered.

(ii) Transferors belonging to classes protected by statute—

Barclay v. *Pearson* (*1893*): A newspaper ran a missing-word competition which was held to be a lottery under the Gaming Act 1802 (which had been passed to protect lottery competitors from promoters). *Held*: the competitors could recover their entry fees (but not prizes).

(iii) Transferees under a duty to protect transferors' interests. If the defendant is the plaintiff's trustee or agent, etc., he cannot retain property on the ground that it has come to him as proceeds of an illegal transaction.

PROGRESS TEST 12

1. In relation to contract, discuss the maxim *ex turpi causa non oritur actio* (no action arises from a disgraceful cause). **(1)**

2. Sid agreed to convey Henry's furniture from London to Birmingham for £100. On arriving, Sid confessed that he had been stopped for speeding and was going to be prosecuted, whereat Henry refused to pay him. Advise Sid. **(1)**

3. Bill agreed to paint Mark's house in the evenings for £300 but said that he would accept £200 in cash, "so that the tax man won't find out". Mark paid the £200 but is extremely dissatisfied with the work and seeks your advice. **(2)**

4. In respect of contracts performed illegally, explain the position of parties not *in pari delicto*. **(3)**

5. Rich hired his private aeroplane to Rogue, knowing that it was to be used for smuggling drugs into the country on a particular date. Rogue paid £1,000 in advance but the plane developed a defect and could not be flown on the required day. Rogue wishes to recover his £1,000 and consults you. **(3)**

CHAPTER XIII

The Nature of Voidable Contracts

THE FALSE REPRESENTATION OF FACTS

1. The substance of misrepresentation. Many statements may be made in the negotiations leading up to a contract. Some of these may be intended to bind a party and they are then called *terms* (*see* XV), the untruth of which would give rise to an action for breach of contract.

Other statements, which are made simply to induce the making of a contract and by which the parties do not intend to be bound, are called *mere representations*. If one of these is untrue, it constitutes a *misrepresentation* and the contract may become *voidable* at the option of the party to whom it is made. Misrepresentation can be defined as *an untrue statement of a fact which materially induced a party to enter into a contract*. Anyone seeking relief on this ground must therefore prove that:

(*a*) *It was an actual statement.* Mere silence (i.e. failure to disclose a material fact) does not constitute misrepresentation unless there is:

(*i*) *A change of circumstances.*

With v. *O'Flanagan* (*1936*): A doctor represented the takings of his practice as £2,000 per annum. This was true but, due to his illness during the negotiations, they dropped to £250. *Held*: failure to disclose the changed circumstances amounted to misrepresentation.

(*ii*) *A half-truth.*

Nottingham Patent Brick & Tile Co. v. *Butler* (*1866*): The prospective purchasers of some land asked the vendor's solicitor whether it was subject to restrictive covenants (XVI, **1**(*a*)). He replied that he was not aware of any (simply because he had not read the deeds) and plaintiffs paid a deposit. On discovering that covenants did in fact exist, they sued to rescind the contract and to recover the deposit. *Held*: although the solicitor's statement was literally true, it was a misrepresentation and the plaintiffs must succeed.

  (*iii*) *A contract of utmost good faith*. This is explained at **2** below.

 (*b*) *It was in respect of a fact*. The statement must relate to an existing *fact* (which may include an intention). However, misrepresentation can *not* be constituted by a statement of *law* or of *opinion*—

> *Edgington* v. *Fitzmaurice* (*1885*): A company invited a loan from the public, stating that the aim was to finance future expansion, whereas the intention was really to pay off debts. *Held*: this constituted misrepresentation.

> *Bisset* v. *Wilkinson* (*1927*): The vendor told a prospective purchaser that, in his opinion, a piece of land would carry 2,000 sheep, whereas it could not in fact do so. *Held*: the statement was one of opinion and therefore did not constitute misrepresentation.

 (*c*) *It was a material inducement*. A party cannot avoid a contract on the ground of misrepresentation if it can be proved that he was aware of the untruth, ignorant of its existence or made independent investigations into it. However, he will not be prevented from obtaining relief if he failed to take an offered opportunity to test the truth—

> *Attwood* v. *Small* (*1838*): Prospective purchasers of some mines and iron works employed their own experienced agents to check the vendors' answers concerning earning capacity. They reported that the representations were accurate and the sale was completed. Six months later, on discovering that the answers had been grossly inaccurate, the purchasers sought to have the contract rescinded for misrepresentation. *Held*: as they had not initially relied on the answers, it could not be said that they had been induced by them; therefore their action must fail.

> *Redgrave* v. *Hurd* (*1881*): Defendant solicitor answered plaintiff's advertisement for a partner who would also buy his house. He was told that the practice earned about £300 a year and was offered various papers but did not read them. He agreed to buy the house for £1,600 but, on subsequently discovering that the practice was worthless, he refused to complete the purchase. *Held*: the plaintiff could not enforce the contract, as the defendant had been induced to enter into it by false representations.

2. The principle of uberrima fides. It was shown at **1**(*a*) above that failure to disclose a material fact does not constitute misrepresentation, except in the case of changed circumstances or half-truth. Additionally, however, there are six main types of contract which are said to be subject to the principle of *uberrima fides* (utmost good faith). In such agreements disclosure of all material information must be made and failure to do so renders the contract *voidable* at the option of the other party. The principal examples are:

(*a*) *The contracts of insurance.* The insured must disclose all material facts that would influence a prudent insurer's decision whether to decline the risk or to increase the premium—

> *Patten* v. *Grayston* (*1977*): Plaintiff insured his car with defendant, stating on the proposal form that it was kept in a lock-up garage at a private address. When stolen, it was in fact being kept in a parking space at a public house two miles away and defendant repudiated liability. *Held*: the location of the garage was material and judgment should be given for defendant.

(*b*) *The contracts for family arrangements*, e.g. the settlement of property, etc.

> *Gordon* v. *Gordon* (*1821*): Two brothers agreed to divide the family estates and the elder thought that he was illegitimate— although the younger knew this to be untrue. Nineteen years later the elder learnt the truth. *Held*: the agreement should be set aside.

(*c*) *The contracts within a confidential or fiduciary relationship.* This is deemed to exist between persons connected by certain recognised ties (e.g. parent and child, doctor and patient, solicitor and client, guardian and ward, trustee and beneficiary, but *not* husband and wife). In such cases the person in whom confidence is reposed cannot hold the other to a contract unless he can show that it is advantageous to the other party and that he has disclosed all material facts (*see* also **4** and XVI, **1**(*b*))—

> *Tate* v. *Williamson* (*1866*): An undergraduate in debt sought the advice of another, who suggested that he should sell certain land. The other party offered half its actual value (of which he was aware) and purchased the land. Some years later the undergraduate's heir brought this action and it was held that the sale should be set aside.

(*d*) *The contracts of suretyship and partnership.* Contracts of suretyship (guarantee, *see* XIV, 1(*a*)) and partnership do not require *uberrima fides* at their formation but, once made, they impose a duty on the parties to disclose all material facts in their dealings with each other.

(*e*) *The contracts for the sale of land.* The vendor must disclose any defects in title (right of ownership) but this duty does not extend to the physical qualities of the property—

> *F & H Entertainments* v. *Leisure Enterprises* (*1976*): Plaintiffs purchased the lease of certain premises from the defendants, on the innocent misrepresentation that the landlord had not served a notice reviewing the rent. Plaintiffs went into occupation and spent £4,000 equipping the premises but, on discovering the misrepresentation, they went out of occupation and sought to repudiate the contract. *Held*: the rent review notice was a latent defect in title, which the defendants were obliged to disclose; consequently the plaintiffs were entitled to repudiate the contract and to recover their deposit.

(*f*) *The prospectuses of companies.* Directors or promoters of a company must make full disclosure of all material facts in any prospectuses inviting the public to subscribe for shares. Failure to do so makes the contract voidable.

3. The redress of misrepresentation. Misrepresentation may be *innocent* (when a false statement is made with an honest (even if groundless) belief in its truth), *negligent* (when a statement is made carelessly by a person on whom it would be reasonable to rely (e.g. an expert or professional adviser) aware that the inquirer intended to act on the information), or *fraudulent* (when a statement is made "knowingly or without belief in its truth, or recklessly, careless whether it be true or false"—*per* Lord Herschell in *Derry* v. *Peek* (*1889*)). All three forms of misrepresentation make a contract *voidable* and the misled party has recourse to the following:

(*a*) *The passive repudiation.* The misled party may simply do nothing at all (and raise the misrepresentation as a defence, if sued for breach). Desirably, he should give notice by words or conduct (if possible, but not essentially, to the other party) that he refuses to be bound by the contract. The significance of this is that a third party obtaining, in good faith and for value, any property that has passed under a voidable contract acquires a good title up to the time of avoidance, but not thereafter—

> *Car and Universal Finance Co.* v. *Caldwell* (*1965*): C sold a car to one Norris, in consideration for a cheque which was

dishonoured on the following morning. Norris disappeared so C immediately asked the police and the Automobile Association to trace the vehicle. The car subsequently changed hands several times. *Held*: the title to the car was vested in C, as he had done all he could in the circumstances and his actions had successfully avoided the contract.

(*b*) *The action for rescission*. Rescission is an equitable (therefore discretionary) remedy and its purpose is to restore the parties to their pre-contract position; consequently, each must return to the other all property, etc. transferred. However, a misled party who had not been induced by fraud would not have to return any property *if he himself were sued*.

A right to rescind will *not* exist in the following circumstances:

(*i*) *If the misled party has affirmed the agreement*. Mere lapse of time is no bar to rescission but may nevertheless indicate a waiver of the right to rescind (cf. *Leaf* v. *International Galleries* (*1950*), see XI, 1(*a*)(*ii*)). In cases of fraud, time begins to run only from the discovery of the truth.

(*ii*) *If restitution is impossible*. Under the doctrine of *restitutio in integrum*, a contract which cannot be *totally* rescinded cannot be rescinded at all. However, in such circumstances, if rescission would be just, it may be granted in equity—

Vigers v. *Pike* (*1842*): Having been granted a lease of certain mines for £16,000, a company worked them and paid part of the money. When sued for the balance, it pleaded that misrepresentations had been made prior to the lease. *Held*: the company was liable for the balance, as the agreement could not be set aside because the mines had been substantially worked and the parties could not therefore be restored to their original positions.

(*iii*) *If a third-party has acquired an interest in the subject-matter*, in good faith and for value (cf. *Lewis* v. *Averay* (*1973*), *see* XI, 1(*c*)(*i*)).

(*iv*) *If damages would be appropriate*. The Misrepresentation Act 1967, s. 2(2) provides that, where there is a right to rescission for non-fraudulent misrepresentation, the court may declare the contract subsisting and award damages in lieu of rescission, if it would be equitable to do so—

Gosling v. *Anderson* (*1972*): Plaintiff agreed to buy a flat from the defendant but only if she could have a garage. Defendant's agent, honestly believing it to be true, told her that planning permission for garages had been given, although this was not in fact the case. *Held*: plaintiff should be awarded damages in lieu of rescission.

(c) *The action for damages.* When there is *fraudulent* misrepresentation, the misled party may not only avoid the contract but also sue *in tort* ("deceit") for damages. If the misrepresentation is *negligent*, damages may likewise be sought in accordance with the principles of tort. They cannot generally be awarded at common law for *innocent* misrepresentation (but see the provision of the Misrepresentation Act 1967, s. 2(2) at (b)(iv) above). However, under the Companies Acts 1948–76, innocent misrepresentation in a prospectus inviting the public to buy shares in a company will give rise to compensation—

> *Doyle* v. *Olby* (*1969*): As a result of fraudulent misrepresentations, plaintiff purchased an ironmonger's business. On suing for damages, he was awarded £1,500 but he appealed in respect of this figure. *Held*: the damages had been wrongly calculated on the basis that they were for breach of contract. In tort they should cover the whole of the plaintiff's loss and the sum of £5,500 was awarded.

THE VITIATING FORMS OF COERCION

4. The effects of duress or undue influence. A contract may be vitiated (i.e. made invalid) if a party is coerced into it by:

(a) *The application of duress.* In this context, duress means actual or threatened violence to (or imprisonment of) the person (not the property) of the party coerced, or his wife, children or parents. A contract induced by duress is *voidable* at common law (therefore as of right) at the option of the party who has been coerced—

> *Friedeberg-Seeley* v. *Klass* (*1957*): Defendants entered the plaintiff's flat and refused to leave until she had signed a receipt for a jewel-case and contents, which they took away; afterwards she found a cheque on her table for £90. *Held*: the transaction should be set aside.

(b) *The exertion of undue influence.* In view of its restricted nature, duress is rarely pleaded but equity has extended the principle by recognising *undue influence*. This means pressure on the party coerced, not amounting to duress, whereby he is precluded from the exercise of free and independent judgment.

At the option of the coerced party, a contract induced by undue influence is *voidable in equity*—therefore the remedy is only discretionary and it may not be granted if the coerced party's conduct was devious, if he delayed unreasonably in seeking relief, if he affirmed the transaction after the influence had ceased, or if a third party acquired rights from the transaction in good faith and for value.

Normally the coerced party must prove that undue influence existed and was exerted: however, exertion will be presumed where there is a *confidential or fiduciary relationship* (*see* 2(c)). Nevertheless, this presumption may be rebutted by showing that there was a full disclosure of material facts, that consideration was adequate or that the weaker party was in receipt of independent legal advice—

Lloyds Bank Ltd. v. *Bundy* (*1975*): Defendant and his son's ailing company both banked with the plaintiffs. Defendant guaranteed the company's overdraft to the sum of £7,500, with his £10,000 house as security. Acting on the advice of the bank's assistant manager, he increased the guarantee to £11,000 (the sum total of his assets). The company went into receivership and the bank obtained possession of the house in the county court but the defendant appealed to the Court of Appeal. *Held*: a special relationship existed between the defendant and the assistant manager, the bank was in breach of its fiduciary care in obtaining the additional charge, which would be set aside for undue influence. Lord Denning said that all such cases where the courts will set aside a transaction are based on a single principle—inequality of bargaining power (*see* X, 1).

PROGRESS TEST 13

1. Roy offered to sell Tony his power-boat for a certain price, saying that there was nothing wrong with it. Two days later, Tony agreed to buy it but, after taking possession, he discovered a major engine defect which Roy had noticed developing half an hour before Tony accepted the offer. Roy had not mentioned this and Tony seeks your advice. (1)

2. Saying that he wishes to secure her future, Brown sold his shop to his daughter, Mary, for a nominal £100. Mary soon realised that outstanding debts greatly exceeded the value of the premises and stock. Advise Mary. (2)

3. What remedies are available to a person who has been induced to enter into a contract by an honest but untrue representation made by the other party? (3)

4. Peter sold David two acres of land, saying that it would produce good crops. After demolishing some old buildings on it, David sowed seed but later discovered that the high acid content of the soil made it unsuitable for crops. Advise David. (3)

5. Michael joined a religious sect whose wealthy leader insisted that all members should make over their property to it. Michael did so just before he died and his widow now seeks your advice. (4)

CHAPTER XIV

The Nature of Unenforceable Contracts

THE NECESSITY FOR WRITING

1. The want of written evidence. Certain contracts are required by law to be made by a *deed* (*see* IX, **1**) and the principal examples are conveyances of land, leases exceeding three years and transfers of shares in British ships.

Other contracts have by statute to be *in writing* (though not necessarily in the form of a deed) and the most common are those relating to share transfers, bills of exchange, promissory notes and certain consumer credit agreements.

Yet a third class are contracts which must be *evidenced in writing*; this means that they are *unenforceable* unless the plaintiff can produce an adequate note or memorandum concerning the agreement. The memorandum need not be in any special form (a telegram or letter to a third party has been held to be adequate) and it may consist of several documents, provided that there is evidence to connect them. However, it must be signed by the defendant or his agent and it must contain the material terms of the agreement, i.e. the parties, the subject-matter, the date of commencement and, for contracts in (*b*) below, details of the consideration. Contracts which are unenforceable for lack of written evidence cannot give rise to an action for damages but can be relied on as a defence (*see* (*b*) below). There are two types of agreements in this category:

(*a*) *The contracts of guarantee.* Under the Statute of Frauds 1677, s. 4 (as amended by the Law Reform (Enforcement of Contracts) Act 1954), contracts *to answer for the debt, default or miscarriages* (i.e. *tortious liability*) *of another* must be evidenced in writing.

In the case of debts, the promise must be made by the *guarantor* (person making the promise) to the *creditor* (person to whom the debt is owed) and not merely to the *debtor* (person owing the debt). Furthermore, the agreement must be one of *guarantee* (e.g. "If A does not pay you, I will") and not *indemnity* (e.g. "Let A have some goods. I will see you are paid"). In the first case written evidence is necessary to prove liability, but the second involves original liability, for which no writing is required—

Kirkham v. *Marter* (*1819*): Defendant's son had ridden plaintiff's horse without permission and killed it. Plaintiff threatened to sue the son in tort and the father orally agreed to pay the plaintiff a sum of money in consideration of his not bringing an action. *Held*: as it related to the miscarriage of another, the agreement was unenforceable, through lack of written evidence.

Mountstephen v. *Lakeman* (*1871*): Defendant (chairman of the Brixham Local Board of Health) discussed with plaintiff (a builder) the connection of certain drains to a sewer, saying "Do the work and I will see you paid." The Board refused payment on the ground that it had never made any agreement with the plaintiff: whilst the defendant claimed that his promise was a guarantee, which could not be enforced as there was no written evidence. *Held*: defendant was liable for the debt, as his words constituted an indemnity.

(*b*) *The contracts relating to land.* Under the Law of Property Act 1925, s. 40, written evidence is necessary in respect of a contracts for *the sale or leasing or transfer of any interest in land.* A distinction must be drawn between an agreement for the sale or lease of land (which must be evidenced in writing) and the actual conveyance or transfer (which must be by deed, as explained at 1 above). The term *interest* includes all rights of way, fishing or shooting rights, etc. It must be emphasised, however, that the granting of a *licence* (e.g. permit to enter land) does *not* require written evidence, as this simply makes an action lawful, without transferring any interest.

Thomas v. *Brown* (*1876*): Plaintiff orally agreed to purchase land from the defendant and paid a deposit, which he attempted to recover when he decided to withdraw from the transaction. *Held*: the contract was unenforceable and, though the vendor could therefore not sue on it, he was entitled to rely on it as justification for keeping the deposit.

2. The doctrine of part performance. "Equity would not allow a statute to be used as an engine of fraud"; therefore, if a party to a contract relating to land (but *not* guarantee) has partly or wholly performed his part of the agreement, trusting the other party to do the same the court has a discretion to order specific performance (*see* XVII, 5(*d*)) of the contract, if this would be a proper remedy under normal circumstances, *even if there is no written evidence*. Any act of part performance is, however, subject to the following conditions:

(*a*) *It must relate to some contract and be consistent with the one alleged*. The payment of money can rarely be a sufficient act of part performance, as it can have varying explanations—

Maddison v. *Alderson* (*1883*): A man induced his housekeeper to work for many years without wages by an oral promise to leave her a life estate in his land. He died intestate and the woman sought specific performance. *Held*: this could not be granted as her conduct was not solely referable to the alleged agreement.

Wakeham v. *Mackenzie* (*1968*): An elderly widower orally agreed with plaintiff, a widow, that he would leave her his house if she would move in and look after him until he died. Giving up her council flat and paying for her board and coal, she complied but was not left anything. *Held*: plaintiff's conduct must relate to some contract and was entirely consistent with the one alleged: therefore her action against the executor for specific performance must succeed.

(*b*) *It must be such that the promisor's refusal of performance amounts to fraud.*

Rawlinson v. *Ames* (*1925*): Defendant agreed orally to lease the plaintiff's flat for twenty-one years and certain alterations were made at the defendant's request; she then changed her mind and refused to take the flat. *Held*: defendant was bound by her agreement, as the plaintiff would never have carried out the alterations unless some contract such as the one alleged did in fact exist.

(*c*) *It must relate to a contract which would be enforceable*, if the necessary written evidence existed.

(*d*) *It must be supported by adequate oral evidence* of the terms of the alleged contract.

(*e*) *It must have been performed by the plaintiff*—and *not* by the defendant.

PROGRESS TEST 14

1. Laymen sometimes believe that a valid contract needs to be in writing. How far is this belief correct? **(1)**

2. Describe the contracts which are not enforceable unless

evidenced in writing, outlining the nature of the necessary written evidence. **(1)**

3. Brian telephoned Harridges department store, where he had an account, to say that his brother Charles from Australia would be visiting them to make some purchases, adding "He's an eccentric millionaire and, if he forgets to pay you, I will." Charles ordered some expensive items which were despatched to Australia but has not paid anything and the store has charged the goods to Brian's account. Advise Brian. **(1)**

4. Margaret rented a flat from David who said that, if she agreed to move out, he would provide her with a better one. Margaret left and took a holiday in Spain where she received a letter from David denying that he had agreed to lease her the other flat. Advise Margaret. **(1, 2)**

5. Examine the equitable doctrine of part performance. **(2)**

CHAPTER XV

The Terms of a Contract

THE RIGHTS AND OBLIGATIONS OF A CONTRACT

1. The nature of a term. It was shown at XIII, 1 that statements uttered merely to induce the making of a contract (and by which the parties do not intend to be bound) constitute *mere representations*, whereas those intended to bind a party are called *terms*. The significance of this distinction lies in the difference in remedies granted for misrepresentation—as opposed to breach of a term; consequently, it is important to be able to determine which category any statement falls into.

Each case must be individually decided and the test is simply— "What would a reasonable man understand to be the intention of the parties, having regard to all the circumstances?" As a rough guide, however, a representation (made by the *representor* to the *representee*) may well be held to constitute a *term* in the following circumstances:

(*a*) *If the representee emphasises the importance of a certain fact.*

Bannerman v. *White* (*1861*): W (hop-merchant) negotiated with B (hop-grower) for the purchase of hops and inquired whether' they had been treated with sulphur (disliked by brewers), adding that, if this was the case, he would not even trouble to ask the price. *Held*: B's (incorrect) assurance that sulphur had not been used was a term of the contract.

(*b*) *If the representor emphasises a certain fact*, so that the representee is dissuaded from confirming it—

Schawel v. *Reade* (*1913*): S considered purchasing a horse for stud purposes from R, who said "You need not look for anything. The horse is perfectly sound. If there was anything the matter with the horse, I would tell you." S terminated his examination and purchased the animal, which was found to be totally unfit for stud purposes. *Held*: R's words constituted a term of the contract.

Ecay v. *Godfrey* (*1947*): The vendor of a boat stated that it was sound but advised the purchaser to have it surveyed. *Held*: the statement was not a term of the contract.

(*c*) *If the representor has special knowledge or skill*, not possessed by the representee. This is a further illustration of inequality of bargaining power (*see* X, 1)—

Dick Bentley Productions Ltd. v. *Harold Smith (Motors) Ltd.* (*1965*): B asked S for a "well-vetted" Bentley car and was shown one which S said had done only 20,000 miles since fitted with a new engine and gearbox. It had in fact run over 100,000 miles since reconditioning. *Held*: the statement was a term of the contract.

Oscar Chess v. *Williams* (*1957*): Defendant purchased a car from the plaintiffs and traded in a Morris which he said was a 1948 model (as this date was shown on the registration book). Plaintiffs allowed him £290 but later found that the car was a 1939 model (value £175), so they sued to recover £115. *Held*: defendant's statement was not a term of the contract.

2. The derivation of a term. The terms of a contract are not only founded on statements expressed by the parties but they may also be inferred by the law. It is therefore necessary to distinguish between:

(*a*) *The express terms.* In this case the terms of a contract are expressed by the parties in speech, writing or a combination of the two. Under the *Parol Evidence Rule*, however, if the parties have reduced their contract to writing, it is not generally permissible to adduce parol (i.e. oral) evidence "to add to, vary or contradict" the written document. There are, nevertheless, numerous exceptions to this rule and, for example, oral evidence may be admissible—

(*i*) *If the parties are aware that the document does not express the whole agreement.*

Krell v. *Henry* (*1903*): Defendant agreed in writing to rent plaintiff's flat for two days for £75. The purpose (not expressed in the document) was to view Edward VII's coronation procession, which was cancelled because of the King's illness. *Held*: plaintiff could not recover the balance of the rent, as the procession was the foundation of the contract and oral evidence concerning it was admissible (*see* XVII, 3(*a*)(*iii*)).

(*ii*) *If the operation of the agreement is conditional upon some event.*

Pym v. *Campbell* (*1856*): The parties entered into a written agreement for the sale of an invention but orally arranged that it should not operate as a contract until the invention had been approved by a third party. Approval was not forthcoming and plaintiff sought to enforce the agreement. *Held*: evidence of the oral arrangement was admissible and there was no contract.

(*iii*) *If the document contains a latent ambiguity*, i.e. one which does not appear on the face of it. Thus oral evidence was admissible to resolve the latent ambiguity in *Raffles* v. *Wichelhaus* (*1864*), see XI, 1(*b*)(*i*).

(*b*) *The implied terms.* The parties to a contract do not always express all of the terms by which they intend to be bound and sometimes *implied terms* are therefore inferred by the law. These are binding in the same way as (but cannot override) express terms and they are based principally upon:

(*i*) *Customs.* There may be an assumption that the parties intended to be bound by a particular custom or usage—though this may, of course, be excluded from an agreement by an express term to that effect:

Hutton v. *Warren* (*1836*): The landlord terminated the lease of a farm and, although the lease did not provide for it, the tenant claimed a reasonable sum for his tillage, sowing and cultivation. *Held*: agricultural custom required such a payment, which would be implied into the lease.

(*ii*) *Business efficacy.* Sometimes the parties may have left no doubt as to the general scope of their obligations, but have nevertheless omitted an essential provision, the absence of which would defeat their intentions. In such a case the court may supply the necessary term to implement the presumed intention and to give "business efficacy" to the contract—

Bournemouth & Boscombe Athletic Football Club Co. v. *Manchester United Football Club* (*1980*): Plaintiffs sold a player, McD, to defendants for about £200,000 and the contract contained a term that £27,777 was to be paid when McD had scored twenty goals in first-team matches. After the transfer, McD scored four goals in eleven games but, on the replacement of the manager, he was dropped from the first-team squad. When he was subsequently transferred, he had played in eighteen matches and not scored the stipulated twenty goals. Plaintiffs claimed the extra fee and the Court of Appeal held that it was necessary, as a matter of business efficacy, to imply a term that McD should have a reasonable opportunity to score the twenty goals; by transferring him, the defendants had prevented any possibility of fulfilling the agreement and were therefore in breach of contract.

(*iii*) *Conduct of the parties.* Terms may be implied from the conduct of the parties—

Hillas & Co. v. *Arcos Ltd.* (*1932*): Plaintiffs agreed to purchase from the defendants 22,000 standards of softwood in 1930, with an option to buy 100,000 standards in 1931, but without particulars as to the kind or size of timber, or the manner of shipment. After the supply for 1930 had been completed, the defendants claimed that they were not bound to deliver the 100,000 standards as the clause was vague. *Held*: it was couched in the same language as that of the previous year, therefore details could be inferred from the course of dealing between the parties.

(*iv*) *Statutory provisions.* Certain statutes provide for terms to be implied in contracts and a notable example is the Supply of Goods and Services Act 1982, whereby the following conditions may be implied: (1) that the seller of goods has a right to sell them and that they are free of any charges or incumbrances; (2) that goods sold by description will correspond with it; (3) that, where goods are sold by sample, the bulk will correspond with the sample; (4) that goods sold in the course of a business are *of merchantable quality* (i.e. fit for the purposes for which they are commonly bought) unless, before a contract is made, the seller draws the buyer's attention to any defects, or the buyer carries out an examination which would reveal such defects.

Furthermore, if the purchaser expressly or impliedly makes known to the seller any particular purpose for which the goods are being bought, there is an implied condition that they are reasonably fit for that purpose, regardless of whether it is the purpose for which they are commonly supplied—unless it can be shown that the buyer does (or can) not rely on the skill or judgment of the seller.

Lee v. *York Coach and Marine* (*1977*): In March 1974 plaintiff purchased from defendants a seven-year-old car with a new MOT certificate. Within a fortnight of the sale it was twice returned for repairs and, when the defendants refused to carry out further work the plaintiff had the car examined. It was found to be in a dangerous condition and in September the plaintiff sought to reject the car. The Court of Appeal held that it was not of merchantable quality and, although it had been driven on the road, it was not in a condition to be safely driven. It was too late for the plaintiff to reject the car but he was entitled to damages.

3. The breach of a term. The (express or implied) terms of a contract may vary in importance and they are therefore divided into the classes outlined below. The distinction is significant because of the different remedies for breach but there is no special test for determining the classification and each case must be individually decided. Any term may therefore constitute:

(*a*) *A condition*. This is an essential and fundamental term, the breach of which empowers the other party to *terminate the contract* and *recover damages*. In such circumstances he must return the property received under the contract but, if he wishes to retain it, he can only sue for damages.

(*b*) *A warranty*. This is a minor and subsidiary term, the breach of which empowers the other party to *recover damages* but *not* to terminate the contract—

L. Schuler AG v. Wickman Machine Tools Sales (*1974*): S gave W the sole rights to sell S's panel presses in England, provided that "it shall be a *condition* of this agreement" that W's representatives should visit six named firms each week to solicit orders. On a few occasions they failed to do so and S claimed the right to repudiate the contract. *Held*: the clause could not be construed as a "condition"; therefore S was not entitled to repudiate.

(*c*) *An intermediate term*. It is now generally accepted that there is a third or "intermediate" term, the breach of which empowers the other party to *recover damages* and *possibly to terminate the contract*, depending on the gravity of the breach and its consequences—

Cehave NV v. Bremer Handelgesellschaft (*1976*): C agreed to purchase for £100,000 from B a quantity of citrus pulp for use as animal feed, a term of the contract being "shipment to be made in good condition". On arrival, part of the cargo was damaged, C rejected all of it and B disputed this. The whole cargo was bought by an importer for £30,000 and was immediately sold for the same figure to C, who used it for animal feed. The Court of Appeal held that the term was an intermediate stipulation, the breach did not go to the root of the contract and it did not justify rejection.

THE LIMITATION OF LIABILITY

4. The validity of exemption clauses. Sometimes a contract contains a term purporting to exclude or limit the liability of one of the parties in certain events; however, restrictions on the validity of such *exemption* (*exclusion* or *limitation*) *clauses* have been imposed by:

(*a*) *The common law.* It has been held that an exemption clause would not be effective—

(*i*) *If it was not clearly communicated to the other party.* The party seeking to rely on an exemption clause must be able to show that the other party was aware of it or that reasonable steps had been taken to bring it to his notice; but the other party cannot plead blindness or illiteracy—

Chapelton v. *Barry UDC.* (*1940*): Beside a stack of deck-chairs was a notice "Hire of chairs 2d per session of 3 hours". Plaintiff paid 2d and was handed a ticket, on the back of which was printed "The Council will not be liable for any accident or damage arising from the hire of the chair". When the plaintiff sat on the chair, it broke and he was injured. *Held*: the clause did not protect the Council as the ticket was a mere receipt and steps had not been taken to bring the conditions to the plaintiff's notice.

(*ii*) *If it was communicated after the contract was made.* To be effective, an exemption clause must normally be communicated to the other party before the contract is made; however, communication can sometimes be inferred from the previous course of dealing between the parties—

Thornton v. *Shoe Lane Parking Ltd.* (*1971*): Plaintiff drove his car into defendants' multi-storey car park, not having used it before, and at the entrance a machine activated by the car gave him a ticket. This stated that it was issued subject to conditions displayed inside the garage (and not visible from the entrance). Later the plaintiff was severely injured in an accident in the garage. *Held*: the conditions did not protect the defendants, as the plaintiff had no opportunity to read the ticket and reject the terms.

Daly v. *General Steam Navigation Co.* (*1979*): In January 1971 plaintiff's husband booked a passage for the family in defendants' ship for 7th July. Subsequently tickets arrived in a folder containing a clause exempting defendants from injury to passengers. Whilst the ship was unberthing in July, the plaintiff was injured when a wire whiplashed and it was held that the defendants were liable, as the contract was made in January and they were not protected by a clause communicated later.

Kendall v. *Lillico* (*1969*): Sellers sold ground-nut extractions to the buyers and, on the next day, sent a "sold note" containing an exemption clause. *Held*: this was effective, as notes containing the same clause had been sent in transactions between the parties over the previous three years.

(*iii*) *If it was ambiguous or doubtful.* Under what is called the *contra proferentum rule*, an ambiguity or doubt in an exemption clause must be resolved against the party seeking to rely on it.

(*iv*) *If it was overridden by an oral promise or by misrepresentation.*

J. Evans & Son (Portsmouth) v. *Andrea Merzario* (*1976*): Defendants (forwarding agents) imported Italian machinery for the plaintiffs, in crates shipped below decks. In 1967 they proposed to change over to containers and their contract, which contained exemption and limitation clauses, gave them complete freedom in the means of transportation. However, they gave an oral assurance that the plaintiffs' containers would be shipped below decks but, as a result of an oversight, one was shipped on deck and was washed overboard. *Held*: plaintiffs were entitled to damages, as the oral promise overrode the printed conditions.

Curtis v. *Chemical Cleaning and Dyeing Co.* (*1951*): Plaintiff deposited her wedding-dress with the defendants for cleaning and was asked to sign a "receipt", stating that clothing "is accepted on condition that the company is not liable for any damage howsoever arising". Before signing, she was told by the assistant that the document simply excluded liability for certain risks, including damage to beads but, when it was returned, the dress was stained. *Held*: the company was liable, as the innocent misrepresentation had robbed it of the protection of the clause.

(*v*) *If it was subject to a collateral contract.* A collateral contract is a device whereby the courts sometimes hold that an agreement involves a second contract, co-existing with the main one, provided that its four essential elements (*see* IX, **1**) can be shown to exist. Not only can this overcome the problem of exemption clauses but it can also provide a means of circumventing the invalidity arising from illegality (*see* XII, **1**), the requirement of written evidence (XIV, **1**), the parol evidence rule (*see* XV, **2**(*a*)) and the doctrine of privity (*see* XVI, **1**)

Webster v. *Higgin* (*1948*): To induce the defendant to enter into a hire-purchase agreement, the plaintiffs' foreman said to him: "If you buy the Hillman we will guarantee that it is in good condition and that you will have no trouble with it." The defendant then signed the agreement which expressly excluded: "any statutory or other warranty, condition, description or representation ... as to the state, quality, fitness or roadworthiness". The car was a mass of dilapidated metal and the defendant did not pay the instalments. *Held*: by signing the document, the defendant had accepted the offer of a separate, collateral agreement which, being broken, entitled him to rescind the main contract.

Over the past quarter of a century, there developed a so-called doctrine of *fundamental breach*, whereby a party could not rely on an exemption clause if he committed a breach which went to the root of the contract. Illustrated in the first case below, this principle has been overruled in the second:

Harbutt's Plasticine Ltd. v. *Wayne Tank and Pump Co.* (*1970*): Defendants contracted to install equipment at the plaintiffs' factory, for storing and dispensing stearine at a relatively high temperature and the contract contained a clause limiting the defendants' liability to £2,330. After the equipment was switched on, it burst into flames and destroyed the whole factory. The Court of Appeal upheld the decision that the plaintiffs were entitled to the full sum claimed as there had been a fundamental breach which rendered inoperative the limitation of liability clause.

Photo Production v. *Securicor Transport* (*1980*): Defendants provided a night patrol service at the plaintiffs' factory, under a contract which excluded the defendants' liability for any injurious act or default by their employees. A patrolman started a fire which burnt down the factory and the House of Lords held that the clause was adequate to exclude the defendants' liability.

(*b*) *The provisions of certain statutes.* Provisions in the following statutes render ineffective exemption clauses of the nature shown:

(*i*) *The Road Traffic Act 1960, s. 151.* Clauses purporting to negative or restrict liability for the death or bodily injury of a passenger carried in, entering or alighting from a public service vehicle.

(*ii*) *The Misrepresentation Act 1967, s. 3* (*as amended*). Clauses which would exclude or restrict the liability of a party to a contract for misrepresentation (or exclude/restrict any remedy available to the other party), unless they satisfy the requirement of "reasonableness", as stated in the Unfair Contract Terms Act 1977, s. 11(1).

(*iii*) *The Carriage of Goods by Sea Act 1971, Sched. III(8).* Clauses purporting to exclude liability for negligence by a sea carrier of goods.

(*iv*) *The Road Traffic Act 1972, s. 148(3).* Antecedent agreements purporting to negative or restrict the liability of users of motor vehicles in respect of their passengers.

(*v*) *The Defective Premises Act 1972, s. 6.* Clauses in contracts relating to the provision of dwellings which purport to exclude or restrict any provisions of the Act (requiring mainly that the work is done in a workmanlike manner, with proper materials, so that the dwelling is fit for habitation) or any liability in respect of them.

(*c*) *The Unfair Contract Terms Act 1977.* This is inapplicable to contracts made before 1st February 1978 and it does *not* cover contracts of insurance or any contract in so far as it relates to: (1) the creation, transfer or termination of an interest in land; (2) the creation or transfer of a right or interest in any patent, trademark, etc; (3) the formation or dissolution of a company or partnership; (4) the creation or transfer of securities.

Provided that the transactions take place in the course of *business* (i.e. are not of an entirely private nature), the Act negatives contractual terms which purport to exclude or limit:

(*i*) *The liability for death or personal injury resulting from negligence.* In this context negligence means the breach of any obligation to take reasonable care or to exercise reasonable skill. Personal injury includes any disease and any impairment of physical or mental condition.

(*ii*) *The liability for loss or damage resulting from negligence in the manufacture or distribution of consumer goods.* If loss or damage arises from goods proving defective whilst a person is using them (or has them in his possession for use), other than exclusively for the purposes of business, a "guarantee" will be invalid if the manufacturer promises to remedy defects free of charge or at a reduced rate, in return for the consumer's surrendering his potential rights of action.

(*iii*) *The liability for other loss or damage resulting from negligence, unless the term is reasonable.* The "reasonableness test" requires that a contract term should have been a fair and reasonable one to be included, having regard to the circumstances which were (or ought reasonably to have been) known to (or in the contemplation of) parties *when the contract was made.* A valid *non-contractual notice* (which need not be in writing) should be fair and reasonable *when the liability arises* (or, but for the notice, would have arisen).

(*iv*) *The liability for breach of consumer contracts, unless the term is reasonable.* If one party deals as a consumer or on the other party's written standard terms of business, the other party cannot rely on a term to exclude or restrict his liability for breach (or to enable him to render a performance substantially different from that expected) unless it satisfies the "reasonableness test". This also applies to certain indemnity clauses, e.g. where the contract for garaging a car requires the customer to indemnify the garage for loss or damage to third parties, arising from the negligent handling of the car.

In addition to clauses excluding or restricting liability, the Act also covers: (1) subjecting liability or its enforcement to restrictive or onerous conditions; (2) excluding or restricting any right or remedy (or subjecting a person to prejudice in consequence of pursuing any right or remedy): and (3) excluding or restricting rules of evidence or procedure.

PROGRESS TEST 15

1. How does a court decide whether a particular statement is a term of a contract? (1)

2. Arthur booked a berth for his dinghy at Safemoorings Marina but, on the first day at low water, the boat grounded on a rock and was holed. The agreement did not contain any references to liability and Arthur seeks your advice. (2)

3. White, a baker, regularly delivered bread to the Brown family, but one day a loaf was contaminated and caused Mrs. Brown a serious illness. Advise Mrs. Brown (2)

4. Robert ordered a "Freezy" refrigerator from Lectrics Ltd. and emphasised that it must be delivered by the following Friday. It did not arrive and on the Saturday Robert went out and purchased a "Freezy" elsewhere. On the Monday, Lectrics delivered the model ordered and Robert refused to accept it. Advise Lectrics Ltd. (3)

5. Eric telephoned Gardentasks who agreed to provide a man at £2 per hour for weeding and grass-cutting. Two days later, Eric received a confirmation form on which was printed: "Gardentasks shall not be liable for any wrongful acts by their employees". An inexperienced man was sent and, being unable to identify weeds, he destroyed some very rare and valuable plants. Eric seeks your advice. (4)

CHAPTER XVI

The Privity of Contract

THE INVOLVEMENT OF THIRD PARTIES

1. The doctrine of privity. Basically, only the parties to a contract can receive rights or be bound by duties under it. This is known as the *doctrine of privity* and it is merely an aspect of (and cannot really be distinguished from) the rule that "consideration must pass from the promisee" (*see Tweddle* v. *Atkinson (1861)*, IX, 3(*b*)). Thus a contract cannot normally confer benefits or impose liabilities on a stranger (third party).

However, the doctrine can conflict with other principles and exceptions to its operation may therefore be found in the following circumstances:

(*a*) *If there is a restrictive covenant*. If someone purchasing land covenants not to use it in some stipulated manner, there is said to be a *restrictive covenant*. This will bind persons who later buy the land with notice of the covenant, but the principle does not extend to anything other than land—

Tulk v. *Moxhay* (*1848*): Plaintiff sold the garden in the centre of Leicester Square to one Elms, who agreed not to build upon it. Eventually the defendant bought the garden and, despite knowledge of the restriction, he planned to erect a building. *Held*: equity would not permit him to disregard the covenant and an injunction should be granted.

(*b*) *If there is a constructive trust*. A *trust* is a relationship whereby property is held by one party (the *trustee*) on behalf and for the benefit of another (the *beneficiary*).

In order to satisfy the demands of justice and good conscience, equity will sometimes recognise the existence of what is called a *constructive trust*, even though there has been no stated intention to create it. Such a trust could be held to exist, for example, where a person makes a profit in a fiduciary position (*see* XIII, 2(*c*)). For a long time this principle enabled a third party to claim a benefit under a contract by pleading that one of the actual parties acted as his constructive trustee; however, since 1933 such an argument has been virtually discarded, but it cannot be regarded as completely defunct—

> *Re Flavell* (*1883*): F entered into a partnership agreement with another solicitor and it provided that, if one died, his widow should receive an annual sum from the net profits. F died insolvent and his creditors argued that the widow was not entitled to the annuity, as she was not a party to the agreement. *Held*: the agreement had created a trust in favour of the widow, who was entitled to the annual sum.

> *Re Schebsman* (*1944*): S left his employment under a contract providing that the employers would pay him £2,000 immediately (which they did) and a further £5,500 in six annual instalments payable, in the event of his death, to his wife and daughter. S died insolvent before the payments were completed and his trustee in bankruptcy sued for the outstanding instalments, claiming that they were part of S's estate. *Held*: as the former employers were willing (though not legally bound) to pay the widow, this was due performance of the contract. However, there was *not* a trust in favour of the widow or daughter, as the wording of the contract was insufficiently explicit to create one. Also, during S's lifetime, both parties could have varied the contract by agreement—something which cannot be done to the terms of a trust, once it is created.

(*c*) *If there is statutory authority.* Under the following statutes contracts for the benefit of a third party are enforceable by that party

(*i*) *The Married Women's Property Act 1882, s. 11.* This enables spouses to effect life assurance policies in favour of each other and their children.

(*ii*) *The Marine Insurance Act 1906, s. 14(2).* This enables contracts of marine insurance to be made for the benefit of third parties.

(*iii*) *The Bills of Exchange Act 1882, s. 27(2).* This enables anyone who has given value for a bill which is dishonoured to sue any prior party who has signed it as drawer, indorser or acceptor.

(*iv*) *The Law of Property Act 1925, s. 47(1).* This requires the vendor of any property to pay the purchaser any insurance money received in respect of the property after the sale.

(*v*) *The Road Traffic Act 1972, s. 148(4).* This requires motor vehicle insurers to indemnify all persons or classes of persons whom a policy purports to cover.

(*vi*) *The Defective Premises Act 1972, s. 1.* This requires that the duty of care by persons contracting for the provision of a dwelling (*see* XV, 4(*b*)(*v*)) shall be owed not only to the party ordering the work but also to anyone who acquires an interest in the dwelling.

(*d*) *If there is a collateral contract.* As explained at XV, 4(*a*)(*v*), it may be possible to show that one of the parties is bound by another contract to the third party. In such circumstances, liability (both for and against the third party) will arise on the second contract. Strictly speaking, this is not an exception to the doctrine of privity but it is appropriate to mention it in this context—

Shanklin Pier v. *Detel Products* (*1951*): Plaintiffs (pier owners) required their contractors to use paint manufactured by defendants, who had expressly warranted to the plaintiffs that it had a life of seven to ten years. In fact it lasted only about three months and the plaintiffs were put to extra expense. *Held*: although the plaintiffs' main contract was with the contractors, they could nevertheless recover from the defendants on the collateral contract to insist on the use of the paint in consideration for the warranty.

Charnock v. *Liverpool Corporation* (*1968*): Plaintiff's car was damaged and the second defendants gave an estimate for repairs to the plaintiff and his insurance assessor. The latter authorised the work but it took three weeks more than was reasonable. The plaintiff sued the second defendants for the hire of another car over that period. *Held*: although the second defendants' main contract was with the insurance company, there was a collateral contract with the plaintiff to carry out the repairs within a reasonable time; therefore his action must succeed.

(*e*) *If there is a relationship of principal and agent.* An *agent* is a person authorised to act on behalf of another (his *principal*) and the relationship may be created in various ways, e.g. by express appointments, by implication from conduct or necessity, by subsequent ratification of an act, etc.

Under the maxim *qui facit per alium facit per se*, all acts which a person can do (except those which from their nature can only be performed personally) can be done by his agent. Thus, on behalf of his principal, an agent can make or perform contracts (except those which can only be performed personally), make or receive payments, and sign memoranda in respect of contracts of guarantee, etc. (*see* XIV, 1(*a*)). However, a principal with limited contractual capacity (e.g. a minor) cannot make by an agent a contract which he is not capable of making himself.

Contracts made by agents are subject to the following rules:

(*i*) *If the agent discloses that he is acting as such*, the principal (but *not* the agent) can sue and be sued on the contract, regardless of whether the principal was actually named. Exceptionally, the agent may become a party to the contract if it is the express intention of the parties, if the agent puts his own name to a deed, or if there is some relevant trade usage.

(*ii*) *If the agent does not disclose that he is acting as such*, the "doctrine of the undisclosed principal" will apply and the party, on discovering the principal, may elect to treat either the principal or the agent as liable—but, having chosen one, he cannot then elect for the other. However, if he commences proceedings, against the agent before becoming aware of the principal, he does not lose his right of choice.

Either the principal or the agent can normally sue on the contract but an undisclosed principal cannot intervene if this would be inconsistent with the terms of the contract or if the third party can show that he wished to deal only with the agent—

Cyril Lord Carpet Sales v. *Browne* (*1966*): Plaintiffs issued a county court summons against the defendant's agent for the price of goods sold. Discovering that the agent was in America, they then obtained judgment against the defendant, who appealed. *Held*: the institution of proceedings against the agent was a definite election; therefore the plaintiffs could not recover from defendant.

(*iii*) *If the agent names his principal but acts without authority*, the principal can ratify the contract, so that it becomes binding as between himself and the other party. If the principal does not do so, the agent becomes liable to the other party for the breach of a separate collateral contract (*see* XV, 4(*a*)(*v*) and 1(*d*) above) with a promise that he had authority in consideration for the other party's entry into the contract—

Olorunkoya v. *McCarthy* (*1965*): Plaintiff claimed £6,000 pools winnings from the defendant who acted as her agent in investing 2s. 6d (15p) per week for her. On one occasion he showed her a coupon with a stake of £96 and she paid him £150. *Held*: the defendant had embarked on an action outside the scope of his authority but the plaintiff had ratified it and was entitled to the winnings.

Chitholie v. *Nash & Co.* (*1973*): Plaintiff wished to purchase a particular house and the vendor's solicitors signed and exchanged contracts without authority. The vendor repudiated the contract and the plaintiff sued the solicitors for breach of warranty of authority. *Held*: he was entitled to damages.

(*f*) *If there is a transfer of contractual rights or liabilities.* This is outlined in 2 below.

2. The transfer of rights and liabilities. The transfer of contractual rights and liabilities to a third party is subject to the following rules:

(*a*) *The assignment of rights.* In law the term *property* means basically anything which belongs to a person and it may be classified as *real property* (relating to land) and *personal property* (everything other than real property).

One form of personal property is *chattels personal*, which comprise *choses in possession* (physical things, such as cars, books, etc.) and *choses in action* (intangible things such as debts, patents, copyright, business goodwill, etc., a right to which can be effectively asserted only by court action). (*See* XXII, 1(*c*) below.)

A right or benefit arising under a contract is a chose in action and, in certain circumstances, it may be transferred (by the *assignor*) to a third party (the *assignee*) by a transaction known as *assignment*. It is, however, *not* possible to assign a bare right of action (e.g. solely the right to sue for a breach of contract or for a tort) or contractual rights of a personal nature (e.g. contracts for personal service).

A valid assignment of a chose in action may be effected in the following ways:

(*i*) *The statutory assignment.* The Law Of Property Act 1925, s. 136 empowers the assignment of a chose in action provided that it is *in writing, signed by the assignor, absolute* (i.e. relating to the whole chose and not merely part of it) and *communicated by express notice in writing to the party from whom the assignor was entitled to claim.*

The assignee need not give the assignor any consideration and the assignment takes effect from the date when the written notice was given to the other party.

The assignment transfers the full legal obligation, the right to enforce it (in the assignee's own name) and the power to give a good discharge without the consent of the assignor.

Amalgamated General Finance Co. v. *C. E. Golding & Co.* (*1964*): Defendant brokers effected insurance on vessels owned by shipowners, who assigned the benefits from their policies to the plaintiffs. The latter sought to recover claims moneys from the defendants. *Held*: as no written notice of the assignment had been given to the insurers, the plaintiffs had no right to sue in their own name.

(*ii*) *The equitable assignment.* If there has been an intent to assign a chose in action but the requirements outlined above have not been fully complied with, there may nevertheless be a valid assignment in equity. However, in the case of contractual rights, the assignee must show that he gave consideration to the assignor (unless the assignment was complete and perfect) and, in any action, he must join the assignor as co-plaintiff (or co-defendant if he refuses).

Both statutory and equitable assignments are "subject to the equities" which means that any defence or counter claim available to the other party at the time of the assignment is available against the assignee; also that, if there have been two or more assignments of the same chose, the rights of the second and subsequent assignees are postposted to the first.

(*iii*) *The involuntary assignment.* Choses in action are assigned automatically on the death (to the personal representatives) or the bankruptcy (to the trustee in bankruptcy) of the owner.

(*b*) *The transfer of liabilities.* Contractual obligations can *not* be assigned and may be transferred only by *novation* (i.e. the discharge of the old contract and the making of a new one, *see* XVII, 2); unlike assignment, this necessitates the consent of both contracting parties and also the third party. That does not, however, preclude the possibility of *vicarious performance*—whereby A contracts to do some work for B but transfers the task to C; in such circumstances, B cannot object—provided that the work is not of a personal nature and that performance is in accordance with the terms of the contract (with A remaining liable to B until completion).

PROGRESS TEST 16

1. Outline the doctrine of privity of contract and consider any ways in which you think it should be modified.   (1)

2. Cedric wished to purchase anonymously a painting from Artreasures Ltd., so Mark bought it on his behalf but has since disappeared with the money given to him by Cedric. Advise Artreasures.   (1)

3. Ronald wished to buy a particular cabin-cruiser from Boatco, because they had told him that it was "thoroughly sound". As he was short of cash, his wealthy brother Alec agreed to pay for it and to resell it to him by instalments. The boat leaks badly and Ronald seeks your advice. **(1)**

4. How may contractual rights be assigned? **(2)**

5. Ronald agreed to sell his cabin-cruiser to Frank, on condition that he might have the use of it free of charge for two weeks each July. Frank later sold the boat to Bernard, subject to this right in favour of Ronald. The latter again seeks your advice, as Bernard will not allow him to use it. **(1, 2)**

CHAPTER XVII

The Discharge of a Contract

THE TERMINATION OF CONTRACTS

1. The discharge by performance. A contract is discharged (i.e. comes to an end) when the promisor *completely and precisely* performs his *exact* obligation. Thus, if he does something less than, or different from what he promised, the other party may reject *the entire agreement*; furthermore, if the promisor only partially performs the contract, he has no right of action *for any reimbursement at all*.

The strictness of this rule is, however, relaxed and the promisor can sue for *pro rata* remuneration (*quantum meruit*—"as much as he deserved") in the following circumstances:

(*a*) *If the contract is severable* (*divisible*). If consideration is not promised in relation to an entire work and the promisor agrees to carry out a requested task by instalments, or without any definite arrangement regarding remuneration, he will be able to recover—

Cutter v. *Powell* (*1795*): P agreed to pay C thirty guineas for performing duties as second mate in a ship for a ten-week voyage but, after seven weeks, C died. *Held*: C's widow could not recover anything.

Roberts v. *Havelock* (*1832*): R agreed to carry out repairs to a ship for reasonable remuneration but there was no agreement for a specific sum to be paid only on completion. After doing some of the work, he sought payment. *Held*: he was entitled to recover.

(*b*) *If the promisee accepts partial performance.* If the promisee had full freedom of choice but nevertheless accepted less than complete performance, the promisor may recover reasonable remuneration, provided that it is possible to infer an implied agreement by the parties to abandon the old contract and to make a new one (*see* **2** below)—

Christy v. *Row* (*1808*): C contracted to carry R's coal from

Shields to Hamburg but the ship was prevented from reaching its destination by a state of war. At the request of the consignee, the master delivered some of the coal at a different port. *Held*: C was entitled to remuneration, as partial performance had been accepted.

(c) *If the promisee prevents performance*. If the promisor cannot complete the contract because of some act or omission by the promisee, he may sue either for damages or on a *quantum meruit*. In an action for breach of contract, it is a good defence for the defendant to prove *tender of performance* (i.e. that he offered to perform his part of the agreement and the plaintiff refused to accept this)—

Planché v *Colburn* (*1831*): Plaintiff agreed to write a book to form part of a series, published by the defendant but, after the plaintiff had completed part of it, the defendant abandoned the project. *Held*: plaintiff could recover £50.

(d) *If the promisor effects substantial performance*. If there have been only minor omissions or defects in performance, the promisor can sue on the contract, subject to a counter-claim in respect of them—

Dakin & Co. v. *Lee* (*1916*): Plaintiff builders sought payment for repairs to the defendant's house but the work did not accord with the specification in certain respects. *Held*: plaintiff could recover, but with a deduction for the cost of rectifying the defects.

Bolton v. *Mahadeva* (*1972*): Plaintiff contracted to install a heating system in the defendant's house for £560. On completion, the house was 10 per cent less warm than it should have been and there were fumes in the living rooms; the cost of remedying these defects would have been £174. *Held*: plaintiff had not substantially performed the contract and therefore could *not* recover anything.

2. The discharge by agreement. As contracts are created by agreement between the parties, they may consequently be discharged in a similar way. A subsequent agreement between the parties may thus have the following effects:

(a) *The termination*. This means the extinction of an *executory* contract (i.e. one not wholly performed on either side) without replacement by a new agreement. It is, in effect, a simple contract whereby each party relinquishes his rights in consideration of a similar action by the other. An *oral* agreement is sufficient to dissolve *all* contracts—including those which must be in (or evidenced in) writing (*see* XIV, 1).

(*b*) *The substitution.* This means the extinction of an executory contract and its replacement with a new agreement (*see* XVI, 2(*b*) and 1 above). Substitution may be effected orally in respect of all types of contract—

> *Berry* v. *Berry* (*1929*): In a deed of separation, the defendant (husband) covenanted to pay his wife £18 a month. Subsequently, by an agreement not under seal, he promised to pay £9 a month plus 30 per cent of his earnings if they exceeded £350 a year. *Held*: the wife could not recover the sum fixed by the deed, as it had been replaced by the simple contract.

(*c*) *The variation.* This means an *alteration* of an *existing* contract. If it is one which has to be evidenced in writing, the variation must likewise be supported by written evidence. It is thus important to be able to distinguish between substitution and variation—and it should be assumed that the parties intended the former *only if the terms of the later agreement are fundamentally inconsistent with those of the original one*—

> *Goss* v. *Lord Nugent* (*1833*): Plaintiff was selling land to the defendant and contracted in writing to make a good title, but failed to do so. Defendant orally agreed to accept the defective title but did not complete the sale. Plaintiff sought to enforce the written contract as orally varied. *Held*: the oral agreement could not be enforced through lack of written evidence and, as the plaintiff could not supply a good title, the defendant could not be made to complete the sale.

(*d*) *The waiver.* This means a unilateral discharge whereby only one party has executed his part of a contract and then agrees to release the other from his obligation. To be enforceable such release necessitates *accord and satisfaction*, i.e. agreement and consideration, as explained at IX, 3(*d*).

> *Elton Cop Dyeing Co.* v. *Broadbent & Son* (*1919*): A, having purchased from B machinery which proved defective, sought damages for breach of warranty. Both parties then agreed to compromise the dispute by A withdrawing his claim and B remedying the defects. Changing his mind, A then sued on the original contract. *Held*: his claim must fail as there had been true accord and satisfaction.

> *D & C Builders Ltd.* v. *Rees* (*1965*): Plaintiffs, in serious financial difficulties, were owed £483 by the defendant. She offered

them £300 in full settlement and they accepted this to avoid bankruptcy. *Held*: there was no true accord (as the plaintiffs had been under pressure) or consideration; consequently the plaintiffs could recover the residue of the debt.

3. The discharge by frustration. The case of *Paradine* v. *Jane* (*1647*) (in which the defendant was held liable for the rent of property which he could not occupy on account of enemy invasion) established the rule that, if a person binds himself by contract unconditionally to do something, he cannot escape liability for damages by proving that performance became impossible (it being arguable that unforeseen contingencies should have been provided for by express stipulation). However, this rule has been mitigated by the *doctrine of frustration*, whereby a contract will be discharged if certain types of impossibility arise after it was made.

(*a*) *The application of the doctrine.* Examples of circumstances in which the doctrine may be invoked are as follows:
   (*i*) *If there is non-availability of the subject-matter.*

Taylor v. *Caldwell* (*1863*): Defendant contracted to hire a music hall to the plaintiff for a series of concerts but, before they took place, the building was destroyed by fire. *Held*: the parties were discharged from their obligations.

   (*ii*) *If there is unavoidable non-availability of a party.*

Condor v. *The Barron Knights* (*1966*): Plaintiff, aged sixteen, contracted to play as a drummer in a group for five years but a month later he had a nervous breakdown and could not undertake the full programme of engagements. The agreement was terminated and he sued for wrongful dismissal. *Held*: his action must fail as the contract had been frustrated.

Hare v. *Murphy Bros.* (*1974*): H, a foreman employed by M for twenty-five years, was sentenced to twelve months' imprisonment for unlawful wounding. On his release he was told that his post had been filled and that there was no vacancy for him. He claimed unfair dismissal. *Held*: the prison sentence was a frustrating event and the contract of employment was automatically terminated when it was imposed.

   (*iii*) *If there is complete non-occurrence of a fundamental event.* This has been illustrated in *Krell* v. *Henry* (*1903*) at XV, 2(*a*)(*i*), but a comparison must be drawn with—

Herne Bay Steamboat Co. v. *Hutton* (*1903*): A boat was hired on a specified date "for the purpose of viewing the Naval Review and for a day's cruise round the Fleet". The Review was cancelled but the Fleet remained to be seen. *Held*: there had not been sufficient change of circumstances as to amount to a frustration.

(*iv*) *If there is supervening illegality.* This has already been mentioned at XII, 1(*c*) and it is illustrated in *Avery* v. *Bowden* (*1855*) at 4(*b*) below.

(*b*) *The limits of the doctrine.* The doctrine of frustration may not be invoked in the following instances:

(*i*) *If the frustration was self-induced.* A party cannot sustain a claim for frustration if he was himself responsible for it or if he made it impossible for the other party to perform his obligations—

Maritime National Fish Ltd. v. *Ocean Trawlers Ltd.* (*1935*): M chartered from O a trawler which was useless unless fitted with an otter-trawl and, to the knowledge of both parties, this could be used only under licence. M, who had four other ships, applied for five licences but only three were granted. In naming the ships to which these should apply, M excluded the trawler chartered from O. *Held*. M could not claim frustration and would therefore be liable for the hire charge.

(*ii*) *If an obligation is merely made more onerous.* The impossibility must make any attempted performance amount to something quite different from what was originally contemplated by the parties. It is not sufficient for an event merely to make an obligation more onerous—

Davis Contractors Ltd. v. *Fareham UDC* (*1956*): Plaintiffs contracted to build seventy-eight houses for defendants at a cost of £85,836, the work to be completed in eight months. On account of weather and labour problems, the work took twenty-two months. Plaintiffs received the contract price but claimed that, because of the delay, they were entitled to treat the contract as discharged and to be paid on a *quantum meruit. Held*: though the delay was greater in degree than was to be expected, it was not caused by any new and unforeseeable event. The work had merely proved more onerous than expected and this did not constitute frustration.

(*iii*) *If the event was (or should have been) foreseen by one party.*

Walton Harvey Ltd. v. *Walker & Homfrays Ltd.* (*1931*): Defendants granted the plaintiffs the right to display an advertisement on the defendants' hotel for seven years. Within the period the hotel was compulsorily purchased and demolished. *Held*: as the defendants had been aware of this risk, the contract was *not* frustrated and they were liable in damages.

(*iv*) *If the contract relates to a lease.*

London & Northern Estates Co. v. *Schlesinger* (*1916*): The tenant of a flat was prohibited from residing in it because he was an enemy alien. *Held*: lease *not* terminated thereby.

(*c*) *The effects of the doctrine.* Where frustration is established, a contract is discharged for the future but is not void *ab initio*. The Law Reform (Frustrated Contracts) Act 1943 provides that:

(*i*) Money paid before frustration is recoverable.

(*ii*) Money due (but not in fact paid) before frustration ceases to be payable.

(*iii*) A party who has incurred expenses is entitled to reimbursement up to the value of the sums paid or due to him at the time of frustration. If, however, nothing was paid or due at that moment, he could not recover.

(*iv*) A party who has gained a valuable benefit under the contract at the time of frustration may be required to pay a just sum for it.

4. The discharge by breach. A *breach* of contract occurs if a party fails to perform one or more of his obligations, renders defective performance, makes an untrue statement in a term of the contract, repudiates his obligations or disables himself from performing them. In the last two instances, the breach may occur before the date fixed for performance; it is then called an *anticipatory breach* and it immediately entitles the other party to seek remedies, even though there is still time for the breach to be revoked.

When a breach occurs, the innocent party always has a right to an action for damages but, if *both* the following conditions are fulfilled, he may also treat the contract as discharged (i.e. refuse to perform his own obligations and decline to accept further performance by the other party):

(*a*) *If the breach creates an option to treat the contract as discharged.* Not every breach can be regarded as a cause of discharge and the simple test is *whether it is of such a nature as to render further performance of the contract purposeless*. This situation would exist if one party either indicates expressly or impliedly that he no longer intends to be bound by the contract *or* breaks a stipulation which is so essential that the very foundation of the contract is destroyed—

Hochster v. *De La Tour* (*1853*): Defendant agreed to employ the plaintiff as from 1st June 1852 but subsequently, in May, he stated that he would not do so. *Held*: plaintiff was entitled to damages, even though defendant might have again reversed his decision before the specified date.

Decro-Wall International SA v. *Practitioners in Marketing* (*1971*): In 1967 the plaintiffs (French manufacturers) orally granted defendants (English marketing company) the sole right of selling their products in the United Kingdom, it being agreed that payments should be made within ninety days of invoice. Of the twenty-seven invoices issued over three years, twenty-six were paid between two and twenty days late and there was never any doubt about the defendants' ability to pay. In 1970 the plaintiffs wrote to the defendants alleging that they had wrongfully repudiated the agreement by failing to pay bills on time and that the contract was therefore discharged. *Held*: the defendants' breach did not go to the root of the contract and could result only in damages; the plaintiffs' breach did not oblige the defendants to treat the contract as at an end.

(*b*) *If the other party exercises the option to treat the contract as discharged.* If he wishes, the innocent party may give the party in breach an opportunity to change his mind and perform his obligations. However, in such circumstances, the right to treat the contract as repudiated will be lost if the agreement is discharged in some other manner—

Avery v. *Bowden* (*1855*): Defendant chartered the plaintiff's ship at a Russian port and agreed to load her with cargo within forty-five days. Before this period had elapsed, he informed the plaintiff that he could not provide a cargo but the plaintiff kept the ship at the port, hoping that the defendant would carry out his obligation. During the forty-five days the Crimean War broke out, making it illegal for the defendant to load a cargo at a hostile port. *Held*: as the plaintiff had not exercised his option to treat the contract as discharged, the supervening illegality provided the defendant with a good defence to an action for breach.

THE FORMS OF REDRESS

5. The remedies for breach. Depending on the type of breach, the innocent party may initiate the legal proceedings outlined below (*see* (*a*)–(*e*)). However under the Limitation Act 1980, actions in respect of *simple contracts* must be brought within *six years*, while those for agreements by *deed* must be commenced within *twelve years*. The limiting periods begin as from the date on which the cause accrued—but, if the plaintiff is suffering from a legal disability (e.g. is a minor) on that date, it will be postponed until the removal of the disability. Similarly, if the action is based on fraud (or is for relief from the consequences of mistake), the period commences when the injured party discovers (or should have discovered) the fraud, etc.

As a result of a breach of contract, the innocent party has recourse to the following proceedings—the first three of which are at common law, while the last two are in equity (hence discretionary).

(*a*) *The action for unliquidated damages.* Damages are termed *unliquidated* when the amount has *not* been agreed by the parties at the time of making the contract and the different types have been outlined at VI, 2(*a*).

In assessing damages, the question of *remoteness* must be considered and the rule in respect of contract was stated in *Hadley* v. *Baxendale* (below), as refined in later cases. It is to the effect that: the party in default will be liable for such damage as a reasonable man would have foreseen as a likely result of the breach and in the light of the actual or implied knowledge which he had at the time of the contract.

Nevertheless, the aggrieved party must take all reasonable and prudent steps to mitigate the loss and he cannot obtain compensation for any damage arising from his neglect to do so (but he can claim for expenses reasonably incurred in mitigation); the onus of proving such neglect rests on the party in default—

Hadley v. *Baxendale* (*1854*): Plaintiff miller sent a broken crankshaft by the defendant carrier to an engineer who wanted it as a pattern for a new one. On account of the defendant's delay, there was a longer stoppage of work than would otherwise have been the case and the plaintiff sued for breach of contract, claiming loss of profits. *Held*: as the defendant had no actual or implied knowledge that the breach would cause the long stoppage, he could not be found liable for the outcome.

Koufos v. *Czarnikow* (*1969*): Appellant shipowners contracted to carry respondent sugar merchants' cargo from Constanza to Basrah. They were aware that there was a sugar market at Basrah but they did not know that respondents intended to sell the cargo immediately upon arrival. In breach of contract, the ship deviated and arrived nine days late, during which time the price at Basrah fell sharply and respondents lost £4,000 profits. *Held*: respondents were entitled to recover the £4,000 because appellants were aware of the sugar market and it was *not unlikely* that the cargo would be sold at market price on arrival; furthermore, they must be held to have known that market prices fluctuate.

Brace v. *Calder* (*1895*): Plaintiff had been employed by four partners, two of whom died. The remaining pair wished to continue the business and gave the plaintiff notice, terminating his employment by the four but offering immediate re-employment by the surviving two. Resenting the technical dismissal, plaintiff refused the offer of re-employment and sought damages from the original firm for wrongful dismissal. *Held*: only nominal damages should be awarded, as the plaintiff could have mitigated the breach by accepting the reasonable offer of fresh employment.

Hoffberger v. *Ascot International Bloodstock Bureau* (*1976*): After the defendants had broken their contract to buy a horse, the plaintiff vendor incurred considerable expense in keeping the animal in the hope of selling advantageously, but eventually it was sold for a much reduced figure. *Held*: plaintiff had acted reasonably and was entitled as part of his damages, to the expenses of attempting to mitigate his loss, even though his final claim exceeded the original sale price.

(*b*) *The action for liquidated damages.* Liquidated damages constitute a specific sum, agreed between the parties beforehand, as a pre-estimate of possible damage arising from a breach. They may be recovered in full but they must not be confused with a *penalty* (i.e. a threat to be held over the other party *in terrorem*). In the latter case, the plaintiff may recover only for the actual damage suffered (which may be more or less than the penalty).

It was held in *Dunlop Pneumatic Tyre Co.* v. *New Garage & Motor Co.* (*1915*) that the use of the words "penalty" or "liquidated damages" in a contract is relevant but not decisive, furthermore, a sum may be presumed to constitute a *penalty* if it is an excessive figure in relation to the greatest possible damage *or* if it is an increased amount for failing to pay a smaller sum *or* if it is a single figure relating to various breaches of differing gravity.

Cellulose Acetate Silk Co. v. *Widnes Foundry* (*1925*) *Ltd.* (*1933*): A contract contained a *penalty* of £20 for each week's delay but, after a thirty-week delay, plaintiff's loss was far greater than £600 and he sued for the full deficit. *Held*: plaintiff was entitled only to the stipulated figure, which comprised liquidated damages and not a penalty.

Forrest v. *Davies* (*1971*): The parties negotiated for the sale of a house with a poor water supply and the contract provided that a supply would be established at the vendor's cost. The installation proved more difficult than anticipated and it was then agreed that the vendor should pay the purchaser £800 if a supply was not established within six months. *Held*: this sum was a penalty and should not be forfeited.

(*c*) *The action on a quantum meruit*. Instead of suing for damages for breach of contract, a plaintiff may in the following circumstances seek remuneration *for work actually done*:

(*i*) *If the plaintiff's performance is on the understanding that there shall be some consideration*, although it is not fixed at the time of the agreement (cf IX, 3(*c*)).

(*ii*) *If plaintiff discovers that he is party to a void contract* (cf. XI).

(*iii*) *If plaintiff's performance is incomplete*. Here a *quantum meruit* action will succeed only in the circumstances outlined at XVII, 1.

(*d*) *The action for a decree of specific performance*. By this means a person can be compelled to carry out a promise which he has made. It is an appropriate remedy in cases of breach of contract for the sale or lease of land or the sale of something not available on the market. It will *not* be granted in the case of void, voidable and unenforceable contracts, simple contracts lacking any of the requirements described in IX, certain situations involving nonoperative mistake (*see* XI, 2) and also in the following circumstances:

(*i*) *If damages provide an adequate remedy*. Specific performance will not be decreed in, for example, agreements relating to the loan of money or the sale of mass-produced items—

Cohen v. *Roche* (*1927*): Plaintiff sued the defendant auctioneer for the delivery of eight Hepplewhite chairs which he claimed to have bought at an auction. *Held*: plaintiff was entitled to damages for breach of contract but not specific performance, as the chairs were "ordinary articles of commerce".

Verrall v. *Great Yarmouth Borough Council* (*1980*): The Conservative-controlled council granted the National Front a licence to hold an annual conference at their hall for £6,000. After the local government elections, the council became Labour-controlled and purported to cancel the agreement, offering to refund the money. Unable to find alternative accommodation, the National Front sought specific performance. The order was granted and an appeal by the council was dismissed by the Court of Appeal.

(*ii*) *If the contract is unfair or imposes hardship.* Specific performance may, however, be decreed if the hardship could have been anticipated by foresight and the party concerned apparently decided to take the risk. Mere inadequacy of consideration (*see* IX, 3) cannot normally constitute hardship.

(*iii*) *If there is a lack of mutuality.* Specific performance will not be decreed against one party if it is not available against the other (e.g. because he is a minor).

(*iv*) *If it concerns personal services or performance requiring supervision.* Specific performance will not be decreed in respect of agreements concerning personal services (but cf. (*e*) belcw), nor where the performance involves continuous successive acts necessitating constant superintendence—

Ryan v. *Mutual Tontine Westminster Chambers Association* (*1892*): Defendants leased a flat to the plaintiff, agreeing that a resident porter would be employed, but he was never engaged and the plaintiff sued for specific performance. *Held*: damages would be an adequate remedy and, in any event, specific performance would not be granted if it involved "the constant superintendence of the court".

(*v*) *If there has been undue lapse of time.* "Delay defeats the equities" and undue delay, sufficient to cause the court to withhold an equitable remedy, is known as *laches*.

(*e*) *The action for an injunction.* This remedy has been outlined at VI, 2(*b*) and it will *not* be granted in contract if the effect would be to grant a decree of specific performance in circumstances where it would not be given. However, it *will* be granted with contracts of personal service, but only to enforce a *negative* stipulation (i.e. where someone is doing something which he promised *not* to do) and it is also a suitable remedy to enforce the negative element of restraint of trade clauses (*see* XI, 4(*c*)).

Page One Records Ltd. v. *Britton* (*1968*): Plaintiffs (pop group managers) sought an injunction to restrain the Troggs from engaging another person as their manager. *Held*: the injunction could not be granted, as it would in effect amount to ordering specific performance of the contract to compel the Troggs to employ the plaintiffs as their managers.

Warner Bros. Pictures Inc. v. *Nelson* (*1937*): Defendant (actress Bette Davis) contracted to give her services exclusively to the plaintiffs and not to engage in any other occupation without their consent. In breach of the contract, she undertook to work for another film producer. *Held*: an injunction should be granted.

Sky Petroleum v. *VIP Petroleum* (*1974*): Plaintiffs had agreed to buy all their petrol from defendants for ten years but, after three years, defendants purported to determine the agreement. *Held*: an injunction should be granted, as the plaintiffs had little prospect of obtaining an alternative supply and damages would not be adequate compensation.

Previous chapters have shown that, in addition to providing the last two of the above remedies, equity has made other contributions to the law of contract in creating the doctrine of equitable estoppel (*see* IX, 3(*d*)), the actions for rescission on terms and rectification (in respect of mistake, see XI, **2**), the action for rescission (in respect of misrepresentation, see XIII, 3(*b*)), the concept of undue influence (*see* XIII, **4**), the doctrine of part performance (*see* XIV, **2**), the principle of the constructive trust (*see* XVI, 1(*b*)), and the equitable assignment of rights (*see* XVI, **2**(*a*)).

6. The alternatives to contractual remedies. Quite apart from the law of contract, the consumer also has recourse to:

(*a*) *The law of tort.* In relation to defective goods, a contract exists (and an action for breach will lie) only between the purchaser and the vendor. If, however, the tort of negligence can be established, it is possible to sue a manufacturer. For an action to succeed in negligence, it is necessary to establish three elements:

(*i*) that the defendant owed the plaintiff a duty of care;

(*ii*) that the defendant broke this duty; and

(*iii*) that the plaintiff suffered damage in consequence of the breach.

There then arises the question as to how widespread is the extent of such duty and it was in the case below that Lord Atkin propounded the general rule that "you must take reasonable care to avoid acts or omissions which you can reasonably foresee would be likely to injure your neighbour". He then posed the rhetorical question "Who, then, in law, is my neighbour?" to which he gave the answer "Persons who are so closely and directly affected by my act that I ought reasonably to have them in contemplation as being so affected when I am directing my mind to the acts or omissions which are called in question."—

Donoghue v. *Stevenson* (*1932*): A friend bought a ginger-beer for Mrs. D in Minchella's Cafe, Paisley and, when she refilled her glass, the decomposed remains of a snail floated out of the dark, opaque bottle. Mrs. D claimed that she suffered from shock and severe gastro-enteritis as a result of the nauseating sight and the impurities she had already consumed. She could not sue Minchella in contract, as her friend had bought the drink, so she brought an action against the manufacturer, on the ground that he had been guilty of negligence, and the House of Lords held that he owed her a duty of care.

Though a duty of care may be established, it can be more difficult to prove a breach thereof—as was shown when the Distillers Company marketed a drug containing thalidomide for pregnant mothers which caused gross deformities in their children. This reinforces proposals for the statutory creation of *product liability*, whereby manufacturers would become strictly liable for injury caused by their products to anyone (not only contractual purchasers). Were this to be introduced, it has been argued (notably by the pharmaceutical and chemical industries) that liability should not accrue if it could be shown that the product could not be considered defective in the light of scientific and technological knowledge at the time when it was put into circulation. This proposition, sometimes referred to as the *state of the art* defence, would largely nullify the intended improvement of consumers' rights.

(*b*) *The Trade Descriptions Act 1968*. This makes it a criminal offence for a trader or business-man to apply a false trade description to any goods, or to supply (or offer to supply) any goods to which a false trade description has been applied. A trade description includes a description as to:

    (*i*) quantity and size;
    (*ii*) method, place and date of manufacture;
   (*iii*) other history;
   (*iv*) composition;
    (*v*) other physical characteristics;
   (*vi*) fitness for purpose;
   (*vii*) behaviour or accuracy;
  (*viii*) testing or approval.

It is also an offence to make a statement known to be false (or recklessly to make a false statement) regarding the provision (in the course of trade or business) of services, accommodation or facilities. The Trade Descriptions Act 1972 also requires the indication of the origin of goods bearing a United Kingdom name or mark but manufactured outside the United Kingdom. Prosecutions are brought by local authorities—

Hackney London Borough v. *Measureworth and Newman* (*1981*): Magistrates had convicted defendants under the 1968 Act for selling a car after halving the odometer reading, and placing a disclaimer over it, but leaving the mileage legible. The Crown Court upheld the conviction, considering that the false description was not neutralised by the disclaimer and that offenders should not be able to disclaim their own deliberate fraud.

PROGRESS TEST 17

1. Alfred, a skilled carpenter, agreed to make six chairs for Bob but, after three had been completed, Bob said that he had decided to emigrate and would not require the chairs. Advise Alfred.   **(1)**

2. Having completed the six chairs, Alfred agreed to sell them to Colin, who paid him the quoted price of £150 but, before they were delivered, they suffered severe damage through a flood. At no extra charge, Alfred therefore offered Colin a £200 table in lieu of the chairs and Colin agreed to take it. As his wife does not like the table, Colin has returned it and is seeking performance of the original agreement. Alfred seeks your advice.   **(2)**

3. Reading that the Foreign Secretary liked to stay at the Grand Hotel, Muddysea, Elsie inquired when he would be there and booked a room for the same period, as she wished to meet him. It was later announced that the minister would have to forgo his holiday, on account of a summit conference, and Elsie cancelled her booking, claiming that the contract had been frustrated. Advise the Grand Hotel.   **(3)**

4. Awaiting the delivery of a medicinal drug which they had purchased in bulk in the Far East, Importco contracted to sell the whole consignment to Magicures. A week later the latter purported to cancel the agreement and Importco took no immediate action. It was then discovered that the drug had harmful side-effects and its sale was banned in the United Kingdom. Importco seek your advice.   **(4)**

5. Having agreed to buy Frank's car for £2,000, Keith arranged a continental tour and booked a passage on a car ferry for £50. Frank then decided to keep the vehicle and Keith tried to find a similar model elsewhere. Eventually he obtained one for £2,300 but by now the date of the ferry passage had passed. Advise Keith.   **(5)**

PART THREE

THE CRIMINAL LAW

CHAPTER XVIII

The Principles of Criminal Liability

THE GENERAL LIABILITY

1. The elements of general liability. A crime is any act or omission which is declared criminal by law, generally if it threatens the security, well-being or good order of society, and which is punishable as a result of proceedings usually initiated on behalf of the state. Crimes may be classified in various different ways—dependent principally upon their source (statutory and common law offences (*see* II, 1 (*b*) and (*c*)), mode of trial (summary and indictable offences (*see* III, 2(*a*)) or nature (arrestable and non-arrestable offences (*see* VIII, 6(*a*)(*vii*)). A basic tenet of English criminal law is the maxim *actus non facit reum nisi mens sit rea* (an act does not itself constitute guilt unless the mind is guilty). This means that, unless a statute provides otherwise, a person can be convicted of a criminal offence only if he or she has voluntarily, and without justification, pursued a course of conduct creating a situation which the criminal law is framed to prevent, and accompanied by a certain condition of mind. Consequently, the following two requirements must generally be established:

(*a*) *The existence of an actus reus* (*"guilty act"*). Criminal liability does not accrue simply from the intention of the accused—as there must be some "guilty act", which may be a positive action or an omission, thus it is necessary to consider:

(*i*) *The substance of the actus reus.* The forbidden act must embrace all the consequences that must occur (e.g. death in the case of murder), all the circumstances that must exist (e.g. a valid marriage in the case of bigamy) and all the conditions that must be fulfilled (e.g. the requirements for theft—*see* XXII, 1)—

R. v. *Deller* (*1952*): Having signed a document purporting to mortgage his car to a finance company, D traded in the vehicle, representing it as free from mortgage. The document was actually void in law and D had (unintentionally) told the truth. The Court of Appeal therefore held that, as there was no *actus reus*, D was not guilty of false pretences.

R. v. *Taaffe* (*1983*): T was convicted of being *knowingly* concerned in the importation of cannabis, a prohibited substance. He had in fact agreed to import currency, which he mistakenly thought to be a prohibited substance. Quashing his conviction, the Court of Appeal held that, as no offence would have been committed if the goods had been currency, T's incorrect belief did not convert the importation into a crime.

    (*ii*) *The voluntariness of the actus reus.* The defences of duress and automatism are considered at XIX, 2 and 4 below.
    (*iii*) *The lack of justification.* The defence of self-defence is considered at XIX, 5 below.
    (*iv*) *The criminality of omission.* An omission can constitute an *actus reus* only when there is a legal (and not merely moral) duty to act—thus no crime would result from passively watching a stranger drowning. However omissions can give rise to certain statutory offences—e.g. failing to stop in the event of a road accident (Road Traffic Act 1972, s. 25) or wilful neglect of children by their parents (Children and Young Persons Act 1933, s. 1). The same applies if anyone undertakes a duty upon which the safety or welfare of others depends—

R. v. *Dytham* (*1979*): A police officer near a club exit did not intervene or summon assistance when a man was ejected, beaten and kicked to death in the gutter. The Court of Appeal upheld his conviction of "misconduct of an officer".

R. v. *Instan* (*1893*): I lived with her elderly, helpless aunt and failed to give her food or seek medical aid. The Court of Criminal Appeal upheld her conviction of manslaughter (XXI, 3(*c*)).

    (*v*) *The chain of causation.* An *actus reus* may comprise actual conduct (e.g. the giving of false evidence on oath, which constitutes perjury) or the result of conduct (e.g. the causing of death in murder). In the latter case, a nexus (link) must be established between the act and the result. The fact that this may not be attributable solely to the conduct of the accused does not necessarily absolve him from liability but an unforeseeable intervention might, in certain circumstances, preclude his conviction—

R. v. Smith (1959): In a barrack-room fight, S stabbed a fellow soldier, who was twice dropped to the ground while being taken to the medical reception centre. Because of the pressure of other cases, he was incorrectly treated and died—though his chances of recovery would have been as high as 75 per cent. if he had been given a blood transfusion. S's conviction of murder was upheld.

R. v. Blaue (1975): B stabbed a woman who declined to have a blood transfusion as she was a Jehovah's Witness. The Court of Appeal upheld B's conviction of manslaughter (through diminished responsibility) as "it does not lie in the mouth of an assailant to say that his victim's religious beliefs...were not reasonable".

R. v. Malcherek, R. v. Steel (1981): In both cases, victims of assault were placed on life support systems which the doctors disconnected after diagnosing brain death. Dismissing appeals against conviction, the Court of Appeal held that the discontinuance of treatment had not broken the chain of causation and the original injury was the operating cause of death.

(*b*) *The existence of mens rea ("guilty mind")*. With the exception outlined in 2 below, this is an essential element of every crime, but it does not mean moral wickedness or criminal depravity. *Mens rea* can be defined as an intention to commit a criminal act or recklessness as to the consequences of that act and, in a few instances, it can include mere negligence; thus it is necessary to consider:

(*i*) *The nature of intention*. Certain offences (e.g. wounding with intent to cause grievous bodily harm, contrary to the Offences Against the Person Act 1861, s. 18), and also attempts to commit any offence, are *crimes of specific intent*, in which case a definite intention must be proved, and mere recklessness does not constitute *mens rea*. Other offences may be termed *crimes of basic intent* and in such circumstances the intention implies foresight coupled with the desire for certain consequences. The Criminal Justice Act 1967, s. 8 provides that, in determining whether a person has committed an offence, a court or jury shall not be bound in law to infer that he intended or foresaw a result of his actions by reason only of its being a natural and probable consequence of those actions, but it shall decide whether he did intend or foresee that result by reference to all the evidence, drawing such inferences from the evidence as appear proper in the circumstances.

R. v. *Mohan* (*1976*): A police officer signalled to M to stop his car but he accelerated towards the officer who was forced to jump out of the way. He was charged, *inter alia*, with attempting to cause bodily harm by wanton driving and the judge directed the jury that it was sufficient to prove that he realised that his conduct was likely to cause bodily harm, or was reckless as to whether it was caused. Quashing M's conviction, the Court of Appeal held that there needed to be proof of specific intent (i.e. a decision to commit the alleged offence) and recklessness was insufficient to constitute the necessary *mens rea*.

See *Hyam* v. *DPP* (*1975*) at XXI, 1 (*d*)(*ii*) and *R.* v. *Belfon* (*1976*) at XXI, 7.

   (*ii*) *The nature of recklessness.* This connotes conduct which creates a risk of harmful consequences, obvious to an ordinary prudent person, and the accused must have either not given any thought to the possibility of such a risk or recognised that one existed and continued with his actions. If recklessness means failing to see an obvious risk, the reason for the failure is irrelevant and it is necessary simply to show that there was an obvious risk which the accused failed to foresee.

R. v. *Miller* (*1983*): M, a vagrant sleeping in an unoccupied house, accidentally set a mattress alight but did not extinguish the fire and moved to another room. £800 damage was done and he was convicted of arson. The House of Lords upheld the conviction as, on becoming aware of the situation, M had been reckless as to the risk of further damage.

Elliott v. *C* (*a minor*) (*1983*): a fourteen-year-old girl of low intelligence entered a garden shed at 5 a.m., poured white spirit on the floor and set it alight, destroying the shed. The justices dismissed a charge of arson, finding that in view of her age, understanding, inexperience and exhaustion, she had not given thought to the risk. On appeal by the prosecutor, the Divisional Court held that the correct test was what a reasonably prudent person would have thought.

   (*iii*) *The culpability of negligence.* Negligence (as distinct from recklessness) is rarely a ground for criminal liability. Apart from manslaughter (XXI, 3(*b*) below), it does not arise in common law offences and it is found in relatively few statutory crimes (e.g. driving without care and attention, contrary to the Road Traffic Act 1972, s. 3). In general, the test is one of objectivity, based upon the conduct to be expected of a normal, prudent person—

R. v. *Lowe* (*1973*): His child having died of dehydration and gross emaciation, L was charged with wilful neglect and manslaughter. The judge directed the jury that wilful neglect which caused death must necessarily result in a conviction of manslaughter. The jury convicted L but exonerated him of gross negligence or recklessness. Quashing the conviction, the Court of Appeal held that manslaughter by negligence required proof of a high degree of negligence, amounting to recklessness, and mere neglect was not enough.

R. v. *Preston Justices, ex parte Lyons* (*1982*): A learner driver was convicted under s. 3 of the 1972 Act after he practised an emergency stop without checking his rear-view mirror, causing a motor cyclist to collide with the car. Refusing application for judicial review, the Divisional Court held that the standard of driving required was the objective standard required of all drivers.

(*iv*) *The principle of transferred malice.* If A attempts to stab B but misses and kills C, it is accepted that the malice towards B is transferred to C, whom A can be convicted of murdering—

R. v. *Latimer* (*1886*): Quarrelling with another man in a public house, L attempted to hit him with his belt but injured an innocent bystander. The Court of Criminal Appeal upheld his conviction of unlawful and malicious wounding.

R. v. *Pembliton* (*1874*): Outside a public house, P threw a stone at an adversary but missed him and broke a window. His conviction of unlawful and malicious damage under the Malicious Damage Act 1861, s. 51 was quashed, as it was held that the Act was worded to cover conduct of the *kind* prohibited.

(*v*) *The irrelevance of motive.* Mens rea must not be confused with motive (the reason why someone wishes a particular event to happen), which is usually irrelevant to the question of criminal liability. Thus an innocent motive does not preclude the existence of *mens rea* and a wicked motive without *mens rea* will not constitute a crime—

Hills v. *Ellis* (*1983*): H saw a police officer arresting a man whom he thought was the innocent party in a fight. He took the officer's arm to draw attention to the fact and was convicted of obstruction. The Divisional Court upheld the conviction, as all the requirements of the offence had been established and the motive was irrelevant.

See Hyam v. *DPP* (*1975*) at XXI, **1** (*d*)(*ii*).

THE STRICT LIABILITY

2. The elements of strict liability. Proof of the existence of *mens rea* is *not* required in certain *absolute* offences where statutes impose *strict liability* and, to obtain a conviction, it is necessary merely to prove the existence of prohibited circumstances. It may seem unjust to convict someone who has not knowingly acted improperly but it is argued that strict liability is essential when there is an over-riding need to prevent conduct detrimental to the welfare of the community and there are difficulties in proving intent. Crimes of strict liability are not easily identifiable. If the definition of an offence contains words such as "knowingly", "wilfully", "maliciously", "with intent", etc., *mens rea* will probably be necessary. In the absence of express provisions, the need for *mens rea* should be presumed but it can be rebutted. In many cases strict liability is of a regulatory nature, often applying to "victimless crimes" (I, 2 (*c*)) and tending to reflect topics of public concern at any given time. Common areas in which it is found therefore include:

(*a*) *The possession of prohibited items.* Examples include controlled drugs, uncertificated firearms, explosives, forgery equipment, offensive weapons in public places etc. It would be a defence for the possessor to establish that he was ignorant of the nature (but not merely the quality) of the item—

Warner v. *Metropolitan Police Commissioner (1969)*: W, a floorlayer who sold scent as a sideline, was found driving a lorry containing a box of 20,000 amphetamine tablets. He was convicted of possessing a prohibited drug, contrary to the Drugs (Prevention of Misuse) Act 1964, s. 1(1), although he claimed that he thought the box contained scent. On the facts of the case, the House of Lords upheld the conviction but stated that genuine belief that a parcel contained an innocent substance—also no reasonable opportunity of examining the contents—would have entitled a person to acquittal, because he would have been in possession of the parcel but not the contents.

R. v. *Hussain (1981)*: H was convicted of possessing a firearm without a certificate, contrary to the Firearms Act 1968, s. 1(1)(*a*). It was in fact a metal tube with a striker pin, which H claimed was a toy used by his son to fire corks, but tests showed that it was capable of firing .32 cartridges. The Court of Appeal upheld H's conviction.

Gibson v. *Wales (1983)*: G was charged with carrying an

offensive weapon (a flick knife) in a public place, contrary to the Prevention of Crime Act 1953, s. 1(1)(4). The magistrate held that it was not an offensive weapon *per se* and dismissed the case, as there was no proof of an intent to injure. Allowing the prosecutor's appeal, the Court of Appeal held that a flick knife is offensive *per se* and the onus is on the carrier to show that he had it with him for an innocent purpose.

(*b*) *The regulation of road traffic.* Examples include speeding, driving with excess alcohol, failure to wear a seat-belt, etc., and sometimes special reasons may provide a defence—

Strowger v. *John* (*1974*): A motorist left his car locked on a public road and, whilst he was away, the licence holder fell to the floor. He was convicted of failing to display an excise licence, contrary to the Vehicles (Excise) Act 1971, s. 12(4), but successfully appealed. On appeal by the prosecutor, the Divisional Court restored the conviction as no *mens rea* was necessary— though it might have been different if the licence had been removed by a third party.

R. v. *Newton* (*1974*): N was convicted of driving with alcohol over the prescribed limit, having unsuccessfully pleaded that his drinks had been laced—as a special reason for non-disqualification. The Divisional Court dismissed his appeal, in view of the heavy and important duty on a driver to watch the amount of drink taken.

(*c*) *The standards of food and drink.* Here strict liability relates not only to the maintenance of hygiene and the giving of proper measures but also the licensing of public houses—

Meah v. *Roberts, Lansley* v. *Roberts* (*1977*): A customer in a restaurant ordered two glasses of lemonade for his children and, by mistake, they were served with caustic soda solution. This was because a brewery employee had used the bottle while cleaning the beer supply equipment, had written "cleaner" on it in small letters and had told the waiter but not the manager. The Divisional Court held that the proprietor was guilty of offences under the Food and Drugs Act 1955, ss. 2 and 8, as there had been a sale of "food " which was not the substance demanded and unfit for human consumption: furthermore, although not concerned with the sale, the third party was also guilty of the offences.

See *Sopp* v. *Long* (*1970*) at **4**(*a*) below.

(*d*) *The protection of the environment.*

Alphacell v. *Woodward* (*1972*): A paper mill discharged waste into two tanks beside a river and two pumps were used to remove effluent. However, an overflow occurred when foliage blocked the pump inlets and, although he had not been negligent, the mill owner was convicted of "causing" polluted matter to enter the river, contrary to the Rivers (Prevention of Pollution) Act 1951, s. 2(1). The House of Lords held that, in the absence of any intervention by a trespasser or act of God, he had caused the pollution.

Maidstone Borough Council v. *Mortimer* (*1980*): M was charged with an offence under the Town and Country Planning Act 1971, s. 102(1), in that he cut down an oak tree which, unknown to him, was the subject of a preservation order. The case was dismissed on the grounds that knowledge of the order was a necessary ingredient of the offence. Allowing the prosecutor's appeal, the Divisional Court held that knowledge was not a necessary ingredient.

THE SECONDARY LIABILITY

3. The elements of secondary liability. It is necessary to consider not only *principal offenders* (i.e. those who by their own conduct, or through an agent, directly bring about an *actus reus*) but also *secondary parties* (those who "aid, abet, counsel or procure" a crime, without being the actual perpetrators). Under the Accessories and Abettors Act 1861, s. 8 (as amended by the Criminal Law Act 1977), these are liable to trial and punishment just as if they were principal offenders—though the following factors are relevant to their prosecution:

(*a*) *The existence of an offence.* If no offence is actually committed, it is not possible to convict anyone of aiding and abetting; however, it is an offence to aid and abet an attempt to commit a crime (*see* XX, **1** below)—

R. v. *Quick, R.* v. *Paddison* (*1973*): Q, a mental hospital nurse, assaulted a patient and his defence was that his conduct resulted from diabetes. As the judge ruled that this could support only a plea of insanity, he pleaded guilty. Holding that a defence of automatism (XIX, **2** below) should have been left to the jury, the Court of Appeal quashed his conviction. Consequently the conviction of P for aiding him by encouragement was also quashed.

R. v. *Dunnington* (*1984*): A and B intended to commit a robbery, with C driving the car in which they would escape. The plan misfired when A and B were put to flight and all three were charged with attempted robbery. Upholding their conviction, the Court of Appeal held that, under the Criminal Attempts Act 1981, s. 1(1)(4), to aid and abet a criminal attempt is an offence (whereas to attempt to aid and abet is not one).

(*b*) *The actus reus of aiding and abetting.* Encouragement in some form is a minimal requirement before anyone can properly be regarded as involved in an offence—

R. v. *Jones and Mirrless* (*1977*): J and M were convicted of aiding and abetting an assault, having been present at a street fight. Allowing their appeal, the Court of Appeal held that mere presence was not enough, even if it did encourage the offence. It must be shown that there was an intention to encourage and some wilful encouragement of the crime committed.

R. v. *Bentley* (*1953*): Accompanied by one Craig, B was in a rooftop chase and, after being taken into custody, he shouted "let him have it, Chris", whereat Craig shot and killed a police officer. Both were convicted of murder and Craig, being too young for the death penalty, was committed to life imprisonment, whilst B was hanged.

(*c*) *The mens rea of aiding and abetting.* It must be shown that the accused knew that his conduct would be of assistance to the principal offender and that the latter would cause the *actus reus* with the appropriate *mens rea*—

R. v. *Bainbridge* (*1960*): B had purchased oxy-acetylene cutting equipment and had supplied it to others who used it to cut the bars of a bank window. B stated that he suspected that it might be used for some illegal purpose but did not know that it was to be used for a bank robbery. Upholding his conviction, the Court of Criminal Appeal held that it was sufficient to show that the accused knew that a crime of the *type* committed was intended but, if an offence of a totally different nature had been undertaken, the supplier would not have been a party to it.

R. v. *Anderson and Morris* (*1966*): A and M went in search of one Welch, A being armed with a knife of which M denied any knowledge. Welch died of stab wounds after A had been seen punching him, with M standing behind Welch's back, apparently not taking any part. A was convicted of murder and M of manslaughter. Quashing M's conviction, the Court of Criminal

Appeal held that, where two persons embark on a joint enterprise, each is liable for acts done in pursuance of it (including any
unusual consequences) but, if one of them goes beyond what has
been tacitly agreed as part of the common enterprise, his co-
adventurer is not liable for the consequences of the unauthorised
act.

(*d*) *The impeding of apprehension.* Under the Criminal Law Act
1967, s. 4(1), it is an offence for anyone, knowing or believing
another to be guilty of an arrestable offence, to do "without lawful
authority or reasonable excuse, any act with intent to impede his
apprehension or prosecution"—

R. v. *Brindley, R.* v. *Long* (*1971*): B and L were at a garage when
two lorries containing brass ingots were stolen from a yard at the
rear and driven across the forecourt. B denied having seen the
vehicles (though she must have done so), whilst L first denied and
then admitted to seeing them. Both were convicted of contravening s. 4(1) of the 1967 Act. Dismissing applications for leave to
appeal, the Court of Appeal held that the requirements of the
offence had all been established and that the prosecution did not
have to prove that the accused knew the identity of the person(s)
committing the arrestable offence.

R. v. *Morgan* (*1971*): Two men, Phillips and Walsh, had stabbed
one Cunningham to death, with a Miss Kiley present but taking
no part. Knowing what had happened, M arranged a hideout for
P and K. In the trial of P, W and K for murder, K was acquitted
and P claimed provocation (XXI, 2(*a*)), so the count was altered
to "unlawful killing". Convicted of contravening s. 4(1) of the
1967 Act, M appealed on the ground that there is no arrestable
offence of "unlawful killing". Dismissing the appeal, the Court
of Appeal held that it is not necessary to show that the accused
knew the nature of the offence.

THE VICARIOUS LIABILITY

4. The elements of vicarious liability. As shown in VIII, 5(*c*),
vicarious liability means the responsibility of one person for the
acts of another and, in so far as the criminal law is concerned, it
relates principally to:

(*a*) *The liability of employers.* In general an employer is not
criminally responsible for conduct by employees unless a statute is
construed as imposing strict liability. He then becomes liable for

acts which he had not authorised and may even have forbidden—provided that they were committed within the general scope of the employment—

Sopp v. *Long* (*1970*): The licensee of the Windsor Station Buffet was the Secretary of British Transport Hotels, who delegated his authority through a chain of managers to a manageress. When whisky was sold in short measure at the buffet, he was convicted of an offence contrary to the Weights and Measures Act 1963. Upholding the conviction, the Divisional Court held that only the licensee could sell and, by being absent from the premises, he sold through his servant.

See Meah v. *Roberts, Lansley* v. *Roberts* (*1977*) at **2**(*c*) above.

(*b*) *The liability of companies.* A limited company is as criminally liable as a human being for offences punishable with a fine (i.e. all offences except those for which a non-pecuniary sentence is fixed by law). Invariably certain persons control the actions of a company and anything that they do on its behalf is treated as having been done by the company—

R. v. *I. C. R. Haulage Co. Ltd.* (*1944*): The company was charged with a common law conspiracy to defraud and the Court of Criminal Appeal held that the acts of the managing director were those of the company. Thus his fraud was its fraud.

Tesco Supermarkets v. *Nattrass* (*1972*): Although it had set up an elaborate system of supervision, the company was convicted of an offence under the Trade Descriptions Act 1968, as a "special offer" poster had been unjustifiably displayed, because a store manager had failed to check the work of his staff, in accordance with his duties. The House of Lords held that, as the store manager was not involved in the central direction of the company's activities, it was entitled to be acquitted.

(*c*) *The liability of parents.* Though not guilty of an offence, parents can be held responsible for fines and compensation orders on offenders under seventeen, also conditions attached to probation orders on offenders aged over seventeen.

PROGRESS TEST 18

1. Explain the significance of the maxim *actus non facit reum nisi mens sit rea.* (**1**)

2. Explain how an omission can constitute an *actus reus.* (**1**)

3. Distinguish between crimes of specific intent and those of basic intent. **(1)**

4. What is the difference between recklessness and negligence? **(1)**

5. Explain the principle of transferred malice. **(1)**

6. "*Mens rea* must not be confused with motive". Discuss. **(1)**

7. Justify strict liability and give examples. **(2)**

8. Outline the actus reus of aiding and abetting. **(3)**

9. What must be shown to establish the *mens rea* of aiding and abetting? **(3)**

10. Define vicarious liability with illustrations. **(4)**

CHAPTER XIX

The Nature of the General Defences

THE EFFECTS OF INSANITY

1. The defence of insanity. "Insanity from a medical point of view is one thing; insanity from the point of view of the criminal law is a different thing" (*per* McCardie J.). Moreover, when the sanity of an accused person is in question, medical evidence is given but the issue is determined by the jury. The matter arises in the following circumstances:

(*a*) *The issue of fitness to plead.* In criminal prosecutions, at any time before the opening of the defence case, the accused may be found "unfit to plead" (i.e. incapable of understanding the proceedings). The issue may be raised by the defence (in which case the burden of establishing unfitness is on the accused and must be proved on a balance of probabilities), the prosecution (in which case the burden is on the prosecution and must be proved beyond reasonable doubt) or the judge (with the burden on the prosecution). The matter is tried by a specially empanelled jury and if the accused is so found, an order may be made detaining him "during Her Majesty's pleasure" and the power to discharge him from such detention may be exercised only with the consent of the Home Secretary. Under the Criminal Appeal Act 1968, s. 15, the accused may appeal against a finding that he is unfit to plead—

R. v. *Podola* (*1960*): P was charged with murdering a police officer and the defence contested his fitness to plead, in that he was suffering from hysterical amnesia which prevented him from remembering events during the material period; otherwise it was not suggested that his mind was abnormal. The jury found that he was not suffering from genuine loss of memory and was fit to stand trial. He then pleaded not guilty, was convicted and sentenced to death. The Home Secretary referred the case to the Court of Criminal Appeal which held that, even if the loss of memory had been genuine, it would not have rendered the accused unfit to stand trial.

R. v. *Berry* (*1977*): B, a paranoid schizophrenic, was found unfit to plead by a jury which had not been directed as to the matters that they should consider. Allowing his appeal, the Court of Appeal held that the judge must give clear directions to the jury that they must consider the accused's ability to challenge jurors, to instruct counsel, to understand the evidence and to give evidence himself. A state of high abnormality is not necessarily conclusive of unfitness.

(*b*) *The issue of guilt.* Every person is presumed to be sane and to possess a sufficient degree of reason to be responsible for his crimes—but this presumption may be rebutted by the defence with evidence which satisfies the jury, on a balance of probabilities, that the accused was insane at the time of the offence charged. The question is determined in accordance with the criteria set out in the *M'Naghten Rules*, which arose after the acquittal in 1843 of Daniel M'Naghten (who had killed Sir Robert Peel's secretary, Drummond). The matter caused such wide dissatisfaction that the House of Lords (not in its appellate capacity) sought the opinion of the judges. Their view was that, *to establish a defence on the ground of insanity, it must be clearly proved that at the time of the committing of the act, the party accused was labouring under such a defect of reason, from disease of mind, as not to know the nature and quality of the act he was doing; or, if he did know it, that he did not know what he was doing was wrong. If the accused was conscious that the act was one which he ought not to do and if that act was at the same time contrary to the law of the land, he is punishable.* When the accused is thus found to be insane, the Criminal Procedure (Insanity) Act 1964 provides that a verdict of "not guilty by reason of insanity" shall be returned and there is detention during Her Majesty's pleasure; however, under the Criminal Appeal Act 1968, s. 12, there is a right of appeal against this verdict. Judicial interpretation of the M'Naghten Rules has related to:

(*i*) *The disease of mind.*

R. v. *Kemp* (*1957*): K was charged with causing grievous bodily harm to his wife by striking her with a hammer. Two doctors gave as their opinions that, at the time of committing the act, K was suffering from a congestion of blood in the brain which caused him to act irrationally. It was therefore argued that the defect of reason arose from a physical cause and not a mental disease but Devlin J. rejected this proposition, saying "The law is not concerned with the brain but with the mind, in the sense that 'mind' is ordinarily used, the mental faculties of reason, memory and understanding.... . In my judgment, the condition of the brain is irrelevant and so is the question of whether the condition of the mind is curable or incurable, transitory or permanent."

R. v. *Clarke* (*1972*): C was charged with shoplifting but attributed it to diabetes, which led to her actions in a fit of absent-mindedness and depression. The recorder ruled that her defence amounted to one of not guilty by reason of insanity but the Court of Appeal held that there was no sufficient defect of reason. *Per* Ackner J.: "The M'Naghten Rules relate to accused persons who by reason of a disease of the mind are deprived of the power of reasoning. They do not apply and never have applied to those who retain the power of reasoning but who, in moments of confusion or absent-mindedness, fail to use their powers to the full".

R. v. *Smith* (*1982*): Charged with having an offensive weapon and threatening to kill, S pleaded that her conduct was attributable to pre-menstrual syndrome but she was convicted. Dismissing her appeal, the Court of Appeal held that there was no defence in law of irresistible impulse.

R. v. *Sullivan* (*1983*): Charged with inflicting grievous bodily harm on a friend, S pleaded that he was recovering from an epileptic seizure at the time. The judge ruled that the defence amounted to a plea of insanity and S changed his plea to one of guilty. The House of Lords held that the verdict was correct. Although in medical terms epilepsy might not be considered a disease of the mind, the effect was such as to cause a defect of reason so that S did not know the nature and quality of the act he was doing and was thus insane for the purpose of a verdict of "not guilty by reason of insanity". This case has confirmed the widely held view that the M'Naghten Rules constitute an unsatisfactory basis for the law of insanity.

(*ii*) *The nature and quality of the act.* It is necessary to show that the accused did not know the physical quality of his act. However, if a person commits an offence under an insane delusion as to existing facts but is not in other respects insane, his liability will be the same as if the facts were real.

(*iii*) *The unawareness of wrongfulness.* If the accused was aware of the nature and quality of his act, insanity can be established only if it can be shown that he did not know that it was contrary to the law or wrong "according to the ordinary standard adopted by reasonable men"—

R. v. *Windle (1952)*: W gave his certifiably insane wife a fatal dose of 100 aspirins. There was some evidence that he was suffering from a form of communicated insanity but, after telling the police what he had done, he added that he supposed he would hang for it. Devlin J. ruled that there was no evidence of insanity to go to the jury and the Court of Appeal held that this was correct.

(c) *The issue of diminished responsibility.* In cases of murder only, it is possible, under the Homicide Act 1957, s. 2(1), to plead "diminished responsibility" (enabling the accused to be convicted of manslaughter) if it can be shown that *he was suffering from such abnormality of mind (whether arising from a condition of arrested or retarded development of mind or any inherent causes or induced by disease or injury) as substantially impaired his mental responsibility for his acts and omissions in doing or being a party to the killing.* If the accused pleads diminished responsibility, the prosecution may adduce evidence to prove insanity (Criminal Procedure (Insanity) Act 1964, s. 6)—

R. v. *Byrne (1960)*: B, a sexual psychopath, killed a young woman and pleaded diminished responsibility. Stable J. directed the jury that, if they found only that B suffered from perverse sexual urges which were impossible or very difficult to resist, that would not bring the case within s. 2(1) of the 1957 Act. Allowing B's appeal against conviction of murder and substituting a verdict of manslaughter, the Court of Criminal Appeal held that "abnormality of mind" meant a mind so different from that of ordinary human beings that the reasonable man would term it abnormal. That was sufficiently wide to cover the ablity to exercise willpower to control physical acts.

R. v. *Fenton (1975)*: F, a psychopath, was charged with four murders and pleaded diminished responsibility but the medical evidence was that the killings would not have occurred but for excessive drink. Upholding F's conviction, the Court of Appeal held that self-induced intoxication cannot of itself produce the necessary abnormality of mind.

R. v. *Kiszko (1978)*: Charged with murder, K pleaded diminished responsibility and a psychiatrist gave evidence on his behalf. No medical evidence was adduced in contradiction but the jury rejected the plea and the Court of Appeal held that they were entitled to do so, as they had to decide the issue on all the evidence and not merely that of one side.

THE EFFECTS OF AUTOMATISM

2. The defence of automatism. Automatism has been defined (by Lord Denning in *Bratty* v. *A. G. for Northern Ireland* (*1963*)) as "An act done by the muscles, without any control by the mind, such as a spasm, a reflex action or a convulsion, or an act done by a person who is not conscious of what he is doing, such as an act done whilst suffering from concussion or whilst sleep-walking". If an *actus reus* involves some positive act on the part of the accused, it must be willed by him; therefore in a state of automatism his actions would be involuntary and consequently not punishable. Automatism due to mental disease constitutes *insane automatism* (with the M'Naghten Rules applying and the burden of proof upon the accused). If, however, it is due to some other cause (e.g. sleep-walking) it is *non-insane automatism* and, once it is raised, the burden of disproving it is on the prosecution—

R. v. *Burns* (*1973*): Under the influence of alcohol and morphine, B indecently assaulted another man and he had no recollection of the incident. The issues of insanity and automatism were raised and medical evidence for the defence effectively equated the two. The judge did not clearly differentiate them, in particular with regard to burden of proof, and the Court of Appeal held that the distinction should have been clearly made.

R. v. *Stripp* (*1978*): S, who had been drinking heavily, fell asleep on a bus and, on awakening, drove it off, leaving a trail of destruction. Charged with various offences, he pleaded automatism—stating that, before falling asleep, he had banged his head and become concussed when the bus went round a corner. There was no corroboration of the blow on the head but ample evidence of intoxication. Dismissing his appeal, the Court of Appeal held that, before the question of automatism is left to the jury, a proper foundation for it must be laid by the defence.

R. v. *Bailey* (*1983*): In a hypoglycaemic state, having failed to take food after insulin, B, a diabetic, wounded another person. The recorder directed the jury that B could not rely on the defence of automatism, as his state was self-induced. The Court of Appeal held that there had been a misdirection. Self-induced automatism, other than that brought about by alcohol or dangerous drugs, may be a defence to crimes of basic intent, unless the prosecution can prove the necessary element of recklessness. The prosecution should have been prepared to show that B knew of the effects of failure to take food after insulin, or that such effects were common knowledge.

THE EFFECTS OF DRUNKENNESS

3. The defence of drunkenness. If it deprives the accused of the requisite *mens rea*, voluntary drunkenness can be a defence to crimes of specific intent (XVIII, 1(*b*)(*i*) above) but not to those of basic intent; consequently it could succeed in prosecutions for murder or wounding with intent, but not in the case of manslaughter, unlawful wounding or assault occasioning actual bodily harm. In such circumstances it could therefore be argued that the existence of drunkenness absolves the prosecution from the need to establish *mens rea*—

> *DPP* v. *Majewski* (*1976*): M was convicted of various assaults and his defence had been that he was suffering from the effects of drink or drugs at the time. Dismissing his appeal, the House of Lords held that the rule at common law was that self-induced intoxication could not be a defence to a criminal charge in which no special intent was necessary; that rule was not altered by the Criminal Justice Act 1967, s. 8 (XVIII, 1(*b*)(*i*)).

> *R.* v. *Garlick* (*1981*): G was charged with murder; there was evidence of drunkenness at the time of the offence and the jury were directed to decide whether he was capable of forming the intention to inflict serious harm. Quashing the conviction of murder and substituting a verdict of manslaughter, the Court of Appeal held that it was not a question of G's capacity to form the necessary intent—but simply whether he did form such an intent.

> *A. G. for Northern Ireland* v. *Gallaher* (*1963*): Having formed the intention to kill his wife, G bought a knife and a bottle of whisky, which he drank before the act. He pleaded insanity and drunkenness, which rendered him incapable of forming the intent for murder, but he was convicted of this. Upholding the verdict, the House of Lords held that, where a man, while sane and sober, forms the intention to kill, knowing it to be a wrong thing to do, he cannot thereafter rely on self-induced drunkenness as a defence to a charge of murder.

THE EFFECTS OF DURESS

4. The defence of duress. The accused may claim that the voluntariness of his act was vitiated by the fact that another person threatened him with serious harm (e.g. death or serious physical injury to him or his family, but not merely damage to property, business interests, etc.), unless he perpetrated the offence. If such evidence is adduced, the onus is on the prosecution to negative the defence of duress (and not on the accused to establish it). In the first case below, the Court of Appeal stated that the jury should be directed to consider, first, whether the accused's will—subjectively considered—was overborne and, secondly, if the answer is or might be affirmative, whether the accused's action under duress was reasonable. Duress will not be accepted as a defence if the accused had the opportunity to escape from the threat—

> *R.* v. *Graham* (*1982*): Under the influence of drink or drugs and in fear of his homosexual partner, G participated in the strangling of his wife. The Court of Appeal held that the correct approach on the facts was to direct the jury to consider (1) whether, as a result of what he reasonably believed, G had good cause to fear that the partner would kill him or cause serious physical injury if he did not so act and, if the answer was in the affirmative, (2) whether a sober person of reasonable firmness, sharing G's characteristics, would have taken part in the killing. The fact that the accused's will to resist had been eroded by the voluntary consumption of drink or drugs was irrelevant to the second question.

> *R.* v. *Fitzpatrick* (*1977*): F, a member of the IRA, had tried to leave the organisation but had been threatened and told that he could not do so. He was convicted of murder and robbery committed as a member and, upholding his conviction, the Court of Appeal held that the defence of duress was not available to him, as he had associated himself with violent criminals and voluntarily exposed himself to the risk of compulsion to commit criminal acts.

THE EFFECTS OF SELF-DEFENCE

5. The defence of self-defence. Under the Criminal Law Act 1967, s. 3, "A person may use such force as is reasonable in the circumstances in the prevention of crime"—and the crime could well relate to the person or property of the accused. The main problem arises in determining what is reasonable in a particular case and this is a question of fact to be decided by the jury; furthermore, when the accused claims to have acted in self-defence, the onus is on the prosecution to disprove it—

> *R.* v. *Cousins* (*1982*): In making a threat to kill, C claimed that he was acting in self-defence, by seeking to forestall what he reasonably believed was a planned attack on himself. The judge directed the jury that no question of lawful excuse (within the Offences Against the Person Act 1861, s. 16, as amended) could arise because his life was not in immediate jeopardy. Quashing C's conviction, the Court of Appeal held that a lawful excuse may exist for a threat to kill, if made for the prevention of crime or for self-defence, provided that it is reasonable in the circumstances to make such a threat. The question of what was reasonable should always be left to the jury which must be directed that it is up to the prosecution to prove absence of lawful excuse.

> *Albert* v. *Lavin* (*1981*): Attempting to "jump" a bus queue, A was stopped by L who reasonably believed that a breach of the peace was about to occur and who identified himself as a police constable. Not believing him, A punched him in the stomach and was convicted of assaulting a constable in the execution of his duty. Upholding the conviction, the House of Lords held that the assault was not justified as an act of self-defence, even if the other person had not been a police officer.

> *R.* v. *Shannon* (*1980*): S was convicted of manslaughter, having killed a person by stabbing. The defence was self-defence and the judge had merely directed the jury to consider whether S used more force than was necessary. Quashing the conviction, the Court of Appeal held that necessary self-defence should be judged by standards of common sense; the jury had found no intent to cause really serious harm but seemed to have excluded S's state of mind in considering self-defence.

THE EFFECTS OF MISTAKE

6. The defence of mistake. Under the maxim *ignorantia facti excusat, ignorantia juris non excusat* (ignorance of the fact excuses; ignorance of the law does not excuse), any mistake pleaded in respect of a criminal offence must be one of fact and not of law. Mistake will afford a defence if it negates intention or recklessness required in the *actus reus*, or if it deprives the accused of the requisite *mens rea*; consequently it is not a defence in crimes of strict liability (XVIII, 2 above), where *mens rea* does not have to be proved—

DPP v. *Morgan* (*1976*): M invited McDonald, McLarty and Parker to his house to have intercourse with his wife—telling them that she was kinky and, if she appeared to resist, it was just a pretence. Although she struggled and protested, all four had intercourse with her and were charged with rape. The judge directed the jury that, if they were satisfied that the wife had not consented, the men's belief that she consented was no defence unless it was based on reasonable grounds. The House of Lords held that this was a misdirection. So long as the accused held the belief, it did not matter that there were no reasonable grounds for doing so—though the reasonableness or otherwise of the alleged belief was important evidence as to whether or not it was truly held. (*See* XXI, 9(*b*) below.)

R. v. *Phekoo* (*1981*). P visited a house he owned, found two men in occupation and asked them to leave. They said that he threatened them and he was charged with harassing a residential occupier, contrary to the Protection from Eviction Act 1977, s. 1(3)(*a*). P said that he believed the house to be unoccupied and that the men were not residential occupiers, though he conceded that they were in fact so. The judge ruled that his belief did not matter if the person harassed was in fact a residential occupier. Allowing P's appeal against conviction, the Court of Appeal held that the offence was one where the prosecution had to prove *mens rea*; thus, if the accused honestly believed that the person harassed was not a residential occupier, the prosecution had to negative that.

PROGRESS TEST 19

1. Explain how an accused person may be found "unfit to plead". (1)

2. Outline the M'Naghten Rules. (1)

3. What is meant by "diminished responsibility" and where lies the burden of proving it? (1)

4. Distinguish between automatism and insanity. (2)

5. When may drunkenness be a defence to a criminal charge? (3)

6. In what circumstances may the defence of duress be pleaded and where lies the burden of proof? (4)

7. Discuss self-defence. (5)

8. How can a mistake affect the *actus reus* or *mens rea* of a criminal offence? (6)

CHAPTER XX

The Nature of Inchoate Offences

THE OFFENCE OF ATTEMPT

1. The elements of attempt. In the case of certain offences (e.g. driving or attempting to drive a motor vehicle, contrary to the Road Traffic Act 1972, s. 6), attempt is expressly prohibited. However, every indictable offence gives rise to liability for attempt to commit it, with the possible sentence being that for the completed offence. This includes attempts at incitement but *not* at conspiracy, aiding and abetting, or assisting offenders. Under the Criminal Attempts Act 1981, a conviction for attempt necessitates proving that "with intent to commit an offence, a person does an act which is more than merely preparatory to the commission of the offence"; thus it is necessary to establish:

(*a*) *The existence of an actus reus.* There must be some act and the question of proximity may then arise—i.e. whether it was sufficiently connected with a crime to be "more than merely preparatory". In *R.* v. *Ilyas* (*1984*) the Court of Appeal held that it must be proved that the accused had done every act necessary for achieving the result he intended.

(*b*) *The existence of mens rea.* It would appear that the prosecution must prove an intent by the accused to commit the prohibited act—but he may be guilty of attempt even if the commission of the offence is impossible (e.g. attempt to kill with a defective gun or to steal from an empty pocket) because, if the facts had been as he thought they were, he could be regarded as having the necessary intent.

Kelly v. *Hogan* (*1982*): H was convicted of an offence contrary to the Road Traffic Act 1972, s. 5(1), having been found unfit to drive, sitting in the driving seat of a car and attempting to insert keys in the ignition (although none fitted it). He appealed on the grounds that the act was not sufficiently proximate to constitute an attempt and also that the commission of the full offence was impossible, but the Divisional Court dismissed his appeal.

R. v. *Whybrow* (*1951*): W was charged with the attempted murder of his wife by electrocuting her in her bath and the Court of Criminal Appeal pointed out the distinction between the directions to be given to the jury in a case of murder, on the one hand, and of attempted murder, on the other. With murder the necessary intent (XXI, 1(*d*) below) could be to kill the deceased or to cause him grievous bodily harm; with attempted murder, however, only the intent to kill would suffice.

THE OFFENCE OF INCITEMENT

2. The elements of incitement. In the case of certain offences (e.g. incitement to disaffection—(VIII, **6**(*b*)(*i*) above)), incitement is expressly prohibited but it is also a common law crime to incite the commission of any indictable offence; thus it is necessary to establish:

(*a*) *The existence of an actus reus.* A conviction necessitates proof that the accused committed a definite act of solicitation (persuasion, encouragement or threats), expressly or impliedly, by word or deed, to induce another person to commit a criminal offence. It is immaterial whether the incitement is successful or if the crime proves impossible to commit.

(*b*) *The existence of mens rea.* It is necessary to establish an intent by the accused whereby his persuasion would result in another person committing an act which would be a criminal offence.

R. v. *Fitzmaurice* (*1983*): F incited three others to rob a woman who, according to F's father, would be carrying her firm's cash near a bank. The story was a hoax, as a security van was due to visit the bank at that time and the father, seeking a reward, had told the police that a raid on the van was being planned. The Court of Appeal set aside the conviction of the three of conspiracy to rob a person, as the crime they had conspired to commit was impossible of fulfilment, but F's conviction of incitement to rob a woman was upheld.

Invicta Plastics v. *Clare* (*1976*): Advertisers of a device to detect police radar traps were convicted of inciting people to use unlicensed apparatus, contrary to the Wireless Telegraphy Act 1949, s. 1(1), and the Divisional Court upheld the conviction.

THE OFFENCE OF CONSPIRACY

3. The elements of conspiracy. As this has two forms, it is necessary to consider:

(*a*) *The common law offence of conspiracy.* Formerly this comprised an agreement (and not mere intention or acquiescence) by two or more persons to do an unlawful act, or a lawful act by unlawful means, with the requisite *mens rea* being the intention to carry out the agreement, coupled with knowledge of those facts which make it unlawful. The Criminal Law Act 1977, s. 5(1)(*a*) abolished the offence of conspiracy at common law apart from:

(*i*) *The conspiracy to defraud.*

R. v. *Longman, R.* v. *Cribben* (*1981*): L(A garage salesman) and C were charged with conspiracy to defraud an insurance company with a false claim for the theft of a car. C made a full confession, stating that he conspired with L, who denied any involvement. In accordance with the judge's direction to the jury, both were convicted but the Court of Appeal quashed L's conviction and upheld that of C. It was held that, where the strength of the evidence is markedly different, A can be convicted of conspiring with B, although B is acquitted of conspiring with A. This may appear illogical but accords with the rules of fairness of evidence. In *R.* v. *Roberts* (*1984*) it was held that it is for the judge (and not the jury) to decide whether the evidence against each accused is markedly different.

(*ii*) *The conspiracy to corrupt public morals or outrage public decency—*

See Knuller (Publishing) v. *DPP* (*1973*) at I, 2(*c*)(*ii*) above.

(*b*) *The statutory offence of conspiracy.* The Criminal Law Act 1977, s. 1(1) and the Criminal Attempts Act 1981, s. 5(1) provide that a person shall be guilty of conspiracy to commit an offence if he agrees with anyone else to pursue a course of conduct which, if the agreement is carried out in accordance with their intentions, will constitute an offence by one or more of the parties, or would do so but for the existence of facts which would render the commission of the offence impossible; thus it is necessary to establish:

(*i*) *The existence of an actus reus.* This is the agreement which must involve two or more persons and it cannot exist if the accused is the intended victim of the offence or if the only other person(s) with whom he agrees are (both initially and at all times during the agreement) his spouse, a person under the age of criminal responsibility (VIII, 2(*a*)(*i*) above) or an intended victim of the offence.

(*ii*) *The existence of mens rea.* This is the intent to pursue the course of conduct which would constitute an offence. If the offence can be committed without knowledge of "a particular fact or circumstance" (e.g. sexual intercourse with a girl who is not known to be under 16), there can be no conviction of conspiracy unless the fact or circumstance is known to the accused.

R. v. *McDonnell* (*1966*): It was held that M could not be guilty of conspiracy with a company of which he was a director and the sole person responsible for its acts.

See R. v. *Fitzmaurice* (*1983*) at **2** above.

PROGRESS TEST 20

1. What must be established for a conviction of attempt?   (1)
2. Outline the *actus reus* and *mens rea* of incitement.   (2)
3. Distinguish between the common law and statutory offences of conspiracy.   (3)

CHAPTER XXI

The Nature of Offences against the Person

THE OFFENCES OF A FATAL NATURE

1. The elements of murder. Murder can be defined as *the unlawful killing of any human creature in being within the Queen's peace, with malice aforethought, so that death occurs within a year and a day.* A person convicted of murder must be sentenced to imprisonment for life (custody for life, if under the age of twenty-one) and it is necessary to consider:

(*a*) *The meaning of "unlawful killing".* Causing death is the *actus reus* and the chain of causation is considered at XVIII, 1(*a*)(*v*). As shown in XIX, 5, the Criminal Law Act 1967, s. 3 provides that "A person may use such force as is reasonable in the circumstances in the prevention of crime". This can cover self-defence and if, in the circumstances, force considered to be reasonable caused death, the killing would not be unlawful.

(*b*) *The meaning of "a human creature in being".* An infant is considered as "in being" when it has an existence independent of its mother—i.e. when totally extruded from the mother's body and alive—though the umbilical cord need not have been cut. Death of an infant born alive from injuries inflicted in the womb may constitute murder or manslaughter. The infliction of injuries which prevent an infant from being born alive is a separate offence (child destruction).

(*c*) *The meaning of "the Queen's peace".* Nowadays all persons in the realm are "under the Queen's peace" i.e. have a right to freedom from violence. However, regardless of where the alleged killing occurred, any citizen of the United Kingdom and Colonies accused of murder or manslaughter may be tried in Britain and this also applies to non-British subjects charged with such offences committed in the United Kingdom, its ships or aircraft—

R. v. Page (1954): Having killed an Egyptian national in Egypt, P, a British soldier, was convicted of murder by a court martial.

Upholding the conviction, the Courts Martial Appeal Court criticised the statement in the *Manual of Military Law* that it must be proved in the case of murder that the victim was under the Queen's peace, and that the army carries the Queen's peace with it, wherever it goes.

(*d*) *The meaning of "malice aforethought"*. In *Hyam* v. *DPP* (*1975*) below, the House of Lords held that malice aforethought, the *mens rea* of murder, comprises either of the following:

(*i*) *The intent to kill or to cause grievous bodily harm*. It can be presumed that a person intends to kill if he desires the death of another and deliberately takes steps towards that end. However an intent merely to cause grievous bodily harm is sufficient for a conviction of murder. "Grievous bodily harm" simply means "serious injury" and what constitutes it is a matter of fact for the jury to decide.

(*ii*) *The foresight of death or grievous bodily harm*. If the accused knew that there was a serious risk that death or grievous bodily harm would ensue from his acts, and committed those acts deliberately and without lawful excuse, the intention to expose a potential victim to that risk results from those acts. In such circumstances it does not matter whether or not the accused desired the consequences to ensue. To eliminate cases of negligence, the act and intention must be aimed at someone but, under the principle of transferred malice (XVIII, 1(*b*)(*iv*) above), it does not matter if the potential victim was not the one who succumbed.

Hyam v. *DPP* (*1975*): As her lover, Mr Jones, had formed a liaison with a Mrs Booth, H drove to the house where Mrs B lived with her son and two daughters. There, she poured petrol through the letter box, inserted a lighted newspaper and left without giving any alarm. A serious fire resulted and Mrs B's daughters were killed by asphyxiation. At her trial for murder, H claimed that her motive had been to frighten Mrs B so that she would leave the area. Ackner J. directed the jury that the motive was irrelevant and, if the prosecution proved that it was highly probable that the fire would cause death or serious bodily harm, this would establish the necessary intent. H was convicted of murder and the House of Lords dismissed her appeal.

(*e*) *The occurrence of death*. It must be proved that the victim died within a year and a day of the acts committed by the accused and, if there was a series of acts, the time runs from the last one.

2. The elements of voluntary manslaughter. Voluntary manslaughter connotes an unlawful killing with the necessary *mens rea* for murder, but with some mitigating factor, such as:

(a) *The defence of provocation.* Under the Homicide Act 1957, s. 3, "where on a charge of murder there is evidence on which the jury can find that the person charged was provoked (whether by things done or by things said, or by both together) to lose his self-control, the question whether the provocation was enough to make a reasonable man do as he did shall be left to be determined by the jury; and in determining that question, the jury shall take into account everything, both done and said, according to the effect which, in their opinion, it would have on a reasonable man". It should be emphasised that provocation is a defence only to a charge of murder and, if successful, it results in a conviction of manslaughter but not an absolute acquittal. Furthermore, if the judge decides that there is some evidence of provocation, he must direct the jury to decide whether the accused was actually provoked and whether a reasonable man so provoked would have responded in a similar way—

> *DPP* v. *Camplin* (*1978*): C, aged fifteen, claimed that a Pakistani committed a sexual offence against him, despite his resistance, and then laughed at him; resultantly, he lost his self-control and split the man's skull with a chapati pan, causing death. At his trial, the judge directed the jury that the test for provocation was its effect on a reasonable man, not on a reasonable boy, and C was convicted of murder. The Court of Appeal substituted a verdict of manslaughter and the House of Lords upheld this, stating that the reasonable man referred to is one of the sex and age of the accused, sharing such of his characteristics as the jury think would affect the gravity of the provocation.

> *R.* v. *Ibrams, R.* v. *Gregory* (*1982*): Having been terrorised by a man for several weeks, I and G planned to attack and injure him, carrying out the attack several days later when he was asleep or drunk. Charged with murder, they pleaded provocation but the judge withdrew the issue from the jury and they were convicted. Upholding the conviction, the Court of Appeal held that, in view of the delay, there was no evidence of sudden and temporary loss of self-control.

(b) *The survival of a suicide pact.* Under the Homicide Act 1957, s. 4(3), a suicide pact is "a common agreement between two or more persons, having for its object the death of all of them, whether or not each is to take his own life". If a party to such a pact survives, s. 4(1) of the 1957 Act (as amended by the Suicide

Act 1961) provides that "It shall be manslaughter and shall not be murder for a person, acting in pursuance of a suicide pact between him and another, to kill the other or be party to the other being killed by a third person".

(c) *The plea of diminished responsibility. See* XIX, 1(c) above.

3. The elements of involuntary manslaughter. Involuntary manslaughter connotes an unlawful killing *without* the necessary mens rea for murder, normally resulting from:

(a) *The commission of an unlawful and dangerous act.* What can be termed "constructive manslaughter" derives from death resulting from an unlawful act directed at someone (but not necessarily the deceased), being an act which a reasonable person would consider likely to cause some (but not necessarily serious) harm—

R. v. *Lamb* (*1967*): In jest L pointed a revolver at a friend and pulled the trigger. The chamber opposite the barrel had been empty and L mistakenly thought that rotation occurred after (rather than before) firing. Resultantly the friend was killed and L was convicted of manslaughter. Quashing the conviction, the Court of Appeal held that there was no intent of assault (*see* **4** below), therefore no unlawful act.

DPP v. *Newbury, DPP* v. *Jones* (*1977*): From the parapet of a railway bridge, N and J pushed part of a paving stone into the path of a train, causing the death of the guard sitting in the cab. They were convicted of manslaughter and the House of Lords upheld the conviction as there was no need to prove that they had foreseen that harm might result to someone.

R. v. *Mitchell* (*1983*): Forcing his way into a post office queue, M struck a Mr Smith, causing him to fall against a Mrs Crafts, an old lady of eighty-nine, who fell to the ground. She suffered a broken femur, which led to pulmonary embolism from which she died. M was convicted of manslaughter and the Court of Appeal upheld the conviction, as the unlawful and dangerous act did not have to be directed at the victim.

(b) *The culpability of gross negligence.* Criminal negligence is of a much more serious nature than that which might ground liability in tort (XVII, 6(a) above). The test is what a reasonable person would have foreseen as a consequence of the accused's conduct— and death must be a strong probability—because, if it were merely a possibility, the negligence would be insufficiently serious for manslaughter—

R. v. *Seymour (1983):* Having caused death by reckless driving on a public road, S was convicted of manslaughter. Upholding the conviction, the House of Lords held that, in such circumstances, the jury should be directed that they must be satisfied that the accused drove in such a manner as to create an obvious and serious risk of causing physical injury to some other person who might happen to be using the road.

See R. v. *Lowe (1973)* at XVIII, **1**(*b*)(*iii*) and *R.* v. *Cato, R.* v. *Morris, R.* v. *Dudley (1976)* at **8**(*c*) below.

(*c*) *The criminality of omission. See* XVIII, **1**(*a*)(*iv*) above.

THE NON-FATAL OFFENCES OF A PHYSICAL NATURE

4. The elements of common assault. The common law has distinguished between *assault* (causing another to fear immediate and unlawful personal violence) and *battery* (using unlawful force on another, without his consent). Over the years the word "assault" has acquired a broader connotation (embracing battery) but this has not prevented it from being applied in its narrower sense (as in *R.* v. *Lamb (1967)* at **3**(*a*) above). In such circumstances the *actus reus* is the creation in the mind of a person (possibly even by mere words) the belief that unlawful force is to be used immediately against him—and the *mens rea* is the intention to create the belief. It is therefore a crime of basic intent and consequently drunkenness is no defence—

Logdon v. *DPP (1976):* Demanding the payment of money which he alleged was owed to his client, L showed a gun (which he said was loaded) to a VAT official and threatened to hold her hostage. When he saw her shaking, he handed over the weapon which was a replica. He was convicted of assault and, upholding the conviction, the Divisional Court held that the offence involved a threat of unlawful force committed when, by a physical act, the threatener intentionally or recklessly caused the threatened person to believe that such force was about to be inflicted on him.

R. v. *Beasley (1981):* Having hit a friend in the eye with a round fired from a .22 air rifle, B was charged with malicious wounding but, as it was accidental, the judge directed the jury that a verdict of common assault could be returned—and he distinguished assault and battery. B was convicted of assault and, quashing the conviction, the Court of Appeal held that causing the apprehension of immediate and personal violence was not an element of malicious wounding, thus a verdict of assault in its narrower sense was not an alternative.

Fagan v. *Metropolitan Police Commissioner (1969)*: Asked by a constable to move his car, F drove forward; one of the wheels came to rest on the officer's foot and the engine stopped. Later F reluctantly reversed the vehicle. He was convicted of assault and, upholding the conviction, the Divisional Court held that it was a continuing offence and it was sufficient for the *mens rea* to be formed during its continuance.

5. The elements of assault occasioning actual bodily harm. Under the Offences Against the Person Act 1861, s. 47, it is an offence to commit an assault (in the broader sense) on another, thereby causing actual bodily harm. The *actus reus* is the assault or battery leading to the harm and the *mens rea* is an intention to commit the assault, or recklessness. "Bodily harm" means any hurt or injury calculated to interfere with a person's health and comfort—

R. v. *Roberts (1972)*: R made unwanted sexual advances to a lady who was travelling in his car. He attempted to remove her clothing and, being terrified, she jumped from the car. R was convicted of assault occasioning actual bodily harm and, upholding the conviction, the Court of Appeal held that the proper test of causation was whether the injury was something that could reasonably have been foreseen as the consequence of what the accused said or did. R was therefore guilty of causing the injuries which ensued.

6. The elements of unlawful and malicious wounding. Under the Offences Against the Person Act 1861, s. 20, it is an offence *unlawfully and maliciously to wound or inflict any grievous bodily harm upon any other person, either with or without any weapon or instrument*. The *actus reus* is the unlawful wound or infliction of grievous bodily harm, and the *mens rea* is the fact that the accused acted maliciously. It is therefore necessary to examine:

(*a*) *The meaning of "unlawfully"*. This simply means that the accused was not acting in self-defence or that the victim had not consented.

(*b*) *The meaning of "maliciously"*. This does not imply a wicked or evil intent but merely that the accused acted with the foresight that some harm (not necessarily serious) would result—as enunciated in—

R. v. *Cunningham* (*1957*): Having entered a house, wrenched out the gas meter and stolen the contents, C failed to turn off a tap and left the pipe discharging gas. He was charged with "maliciously causing to be taken a noxious thing" and Oliver J. defined "malicious" as "wicked". Quashing C's conviction, the Court of Criminal Appeal held that "maliciously" in a statutory crime postulates foresight of consequence.

R. v. *Mowatt* (*1968*): Convicted of unlawful wounding, M appealed on the ground that, in the course of his summing up, the judge had not dealt specifically with the meaning of "maliciously". Dismissing the appeal, the Court of Appeal held that, if the physical act by the accused was a direct assault which any ordinary person would be bound to realise was likely to cause some physical harm, and if the accused did not claim that it was an accident or that he had not realised that harm might result, then it is not necessary to deal specifically with the meaning of "maliciously".

R. v. *Sullivan* (*1981*): S was convicted of unlawful wounding, the judge having directed the jury that an intention to frighten the victim and resultant injury were sufficient to establish the offence. The Court of Appeal held that this was a misdirection and it must be shown that the accused was aware that the probable consequences of his voluntary act would be to cause some injury to the victim.

(*c*) *The meaning of "wound"*. It is necessary to prove a breaking of the whole skin (both outer and inner)—thus scratching or burning does not necessarily constitute wounding—

C (*a minor*) v. *Eisenhower* (*1984*): E had shot another youth with an air pistol, causing a bruise below the eyebrow and a bloodshot eye, resulting from internal rupturing of the blood vessels. The Juvenile Court convicted him of unlawful wounding but, allowing his appeal, the Divisional Court held that there could be no wounding without breaking of the whole skin.

(*d*) *The meaning of "inflict"*. There has been much discussion as to whether "inflicting" harm differs from "causing" harm (as in s. 18 of the 1861 Act) and the courts have tended to interpret "inflicting" as connoting an element of assault, as in—

R. v. *Wilson* (*Clarence*) (*1983*): W was charged with unlawful wounding and the jury were directed that they could convict him of the alternative offence of assault occasioning actual bodily harm. They returned this verdict and the Court of Appeal quashed the conviction but, restoring the conviction, the House of Lords held that both charges impliedly included allegation of assault occasioning actual bodily harm.

(e) *The meaning of "grievous bodily harm".* This has been defined in 1(*d*)(*i*) above—

R. v. *Hamilton* (*1980*): H was charged with inflicting grievous bodily harm and with assault occasioning actual bodily harm. The judge directed the jury that whether the injury was really serious bodily harm should be determined by assessing the degree of seriousness of the assault. The Court of Appeal held that this direction was wrong, as very serious assaults could result in no injury.

7. The elements of wounding with intent. Under the Offences Against the Person Act 1861, s. 18, it is an offence unlawfully and maliciously, by any means whatsoever, to wound or cause any grievous bodily harm to any person, with intent to do some grievous bodily harm to any person or with intent to resist or prevent the lawful apprehension or detaining of any person. The *actus reus* is thus virtually identical with that of unlawful and malicious wounding, though the use of the word "cause" (as opposed to "inflict") removes the need to establish an assault. With regard to *mens rea*, it must be proved that the accused acted maliciously (*see* 6(*b*) above), with the specific intent of causing grievous bodily harm, or resisting or preventing arrest. Mere recklessness would not be sufficient, as enunciated in—

R. v. *Belfon* (*1976*): B was charged with wounding with intent and the jury were directed that, if he foresaw the likely consequences of his act (i.e. serious injury) but committed the act recklessly, that would provide the necessary intention. Allowing B's appeal, the Court of Appeal held that the direction was incorrect and that a specific intention to cause grievous bodily harm must be proved.

8. The defence of consent. As merely touching a person could constitute battery, consent is constantly being impliedly given to potential offences against the person. Participation in various sports and acceptance of school discipline are but two common examples. However, consent can not be a defence to a charge of assault occasioning actual bodily harm or in the following circumstances:

(*a*) *If there is unreasonable conduct.*

R. v. *Billinghurst (1978):* In an off-the-ball incident during a rugby match, B punched another player and fractured his jaw. The judge directed the jury that rugby players consent to reasonable force, that sometimes the force exceeds that to which they consent and that a decisive distinction may be drawn between force inside and outside the course of play. B was convicted of assault occasioning grievous bodily harm.

R. v. *Taylor (1983):* The Court of Appeal held that a schoolmaster has a right to chastise his pupils in a reasonable and controlled way. Throwing missiles is neither and, if a pupil is injured in the process, there is no defence to a charge of assault occasioning actual bodily harm.

(*b*) *If there is vitiation by fraud or ignorance.*

Burrell v. *Harmer (1967):* H was convicted of assaulting two boys, aged twelve and thirteen, by tattooing their arms. Upholding his conviction, the Divisional Court held that, if the boys were unable to appreciate the nature of the act, their apparent consent was no consent.

(*c*) *If there is likelihood of resultant death.*

R. v. *Cato, R.* v. *Morris, R.* v. *Dudley (1976):* Accused was convicted of manslaughter, having injected heroin into another man who died from failure of the respiratory system, on account of intoxication from drugs. Upholding the conviction, the Court of Appeal held that the victim's consent was not generally a defence to a charge of manslaughter—though it might be relevant to consideration of whether there was recklessness or gross negligence.

THE NON-FATAL OFFENCES OF A SEXUAL NATURE

9. The elements of rape. Under the Sexual Offences Act 1956, s. 1, it is an offence for a man to rape a woman and the Sexual Offences (Amendment) Act 1976 provides that a man commits rape if (*a*) he has unlawful sexual intercourse with a woman who, at the time of the intercourse, does not consent to it (the *actus reus*) and (*b*) at the time he knows that she does not consent to the intercourse or he is reckless as to whether she consents to it (the *mens rea*). In a prosecution for rape it is therefore necessary to prove:

(*a*) *The act of unlawful sexual intercourse.* The intercourse is deemed complete upon proof of penetration of the vagina by the penis and it is not necessary for the hymen to be ruptured or for there to be emission of seed. The slightest penetration will suffice and, if none is proved, the accused may be charged with attempt. The intercourse must be unlawful and therefore, as a general proposition, a husband cannot be guilty of rape on his wife unless there exists a decree nisi (but not merely a petition for divorce), a judicial separation, a matrimonial order (or an agreement) containing a non-molestation clause—

> *R. v. Reeves* (*1983*): The Court of Appeal held that it is possible for a husband to be guilty of raping his own wife if there is in force an injunction restraining him from contacting or cohabiting with her. The injunction can be terminated by mutual agreement (whereby the parties voluntarily resume the matrimonial relationship) and it is for the jury to decide whether this has happened.

There is an irrebuttable presumption that males under the age of fourteen are incapable of committing rape or any other offence involving sexual intercourse—though they can be convicted of aiding and abetting rape, or of indecent assault (**10** below).

(*b*) *The absence of consent.* Consent may range from actual desire to reluctant acquiescence and the issue should not be left to the jury without further direction. A conviction does not require proof that the victim put up any resistance or that force or threats were used, but consent is vitiated in the following circumstances:

(*i*) *If the rape was effected by fraud, force or the inducement of fear—*

> *R. v. Olugboja* (*1981*): O and another man forced two girls to a bungalow where O told one that he was going to have intercourse with her. She asked him to leave her alone but did what he told her. The House of Lords held that, although no specific threats had been made, the girl had submitted through fear of what might happen if she did not, and the intercourse was non-consensual.

(*ii*) *If the victim did not understand the nature of the act.* This situation might arise on account of tender years, drunkenness or mental deficiency—

> *R. v. Lang* (*1976*): During L's trial for rape, the defence suggested that the victim had been drinking and may have been less inhibited than usual. The judge invited the attention of the

jury to the question of how she came to take the drink but did not direct them as to the state of her mind (which had to be proved to show that her apparent consent was not real). Quashing L's conviction, the Court of Appeal held that the failure to direct the jury as to this critical question amounted to a misdirection.

(c) *The existence of knowledge or recklessness.* A conviction of rape requires proof that the accused either knew that the woman was not consenting to intercourse or was reckless as to whether she consented. However, as shown in *DPP* v. *Morgan* (*1976*) at XIX, **6** above, the accused will be acquitted if he believed, albeit mistakenly and without reasonable grounds, that there was consent—

R. v. *Bashir* (*1982*): B was convicted of rape on a count alleging recklessness, the judge having directed the jury to consider the conduct of a reasonable man. Quashing the conviction, the Court of Appeal held that the proper test was whether B had acted recklessly and not whether a reasonable man would have acted in the same way. Further, where there was evidence that the accused had reasonable belief in consent, the judge should put it to the jury, even if the accused did not give evidence.

The Sexual Offences (Amendment) Act 1976 prohibits the publication of matter likely to lead to the identification of complainants in rape cases; also, if the accused pleads not guilty, it prohibits consideration (without leave of the judge) of the complainant's sexual experiences with anyone other than the accused.

10. The elements of indecent assault. Under the Sexual Offences Act 1956 ss. 14 and 15, it is an offence for any person (male or female, including boys under the age of fourteen) to make an indecent assault upon a male or female. It is therefore necessary to show:

(a) *The existence of an actus reus.* This requires proof of:

(i) *The commission of an assault.* There must be an assault or battery within the definition of **4** above, but consent is no defence if it has been obtained by fraud, if the intended or probable consequence of the assault is the infliction of bodily harm, or if the consenting party is under the age of sixteen or mentally deficient—

R. v. *Kimber* (*1983*): Charged with indecent assault on a severely disturbed female patient in a mental hospital, K claimed that he thought she was consenting but added that he was not really interested in her feelings at all. The recorder directed the jury that K's belief was irrelevant and he was convicted. Dismissing his appeal, the Court of Appeal held that the jury should have been asked to determine whether K had in fact believed (reasonably or not on whatever grounds) that the woman was consenting: however, by his own admission, there had been no miscarriage of justice.

(*ii*) *The circumstances of indecency.* This probably means that there was an overt sexual element in the assault—

Beal v. *Kelley* (*1951*): In a wood a man exposed his penis to a fourteen-year-old boy and invited him to rub it. The boy refused and the man caught hold of him. It was held that this amounted to an indecent assault.

(*b*) *The existence of mens rea.* A conviction of indecent assault requires proof of indecent intention—

R. v. *Pratt* (*1984*): Having forced two boys to undress, P claimed that his sole motive was to search for cannabis which he thought they had taken from him. It was held that an indecent intention had to be proved by the prosecution.

11. The elements of unlawful sexual intercourse. Under the Sexual Offences Act 1956, ss. 5, 6(1) and 7(1), it is an offence for a man to have unlawful sexual intercourse with a girl under the age of thirteen (and) subject to certain exceptions... with a girl under sixteen (or) with a woman who is a defective. In the case of a girl under thirteen, the offence is one of strict liability—thus belief that she was older is no defence and her consent is immaterial (though absence of it could give ground for a rape charge). If a girl is between thirteen and sixteen, it is a defence for a man to show that he had reasonable cause for believing that she was his wife (though the marriage would be invalid) or that he was *under the age of twenty-four and had not previously been charged with a like offence and had reasonable cause for believing her to be sixteen or over*—

R. v. *Taylor, Roberts and Simons* (*1977*): T, R and S were convicted of unlawful sexual intercourse, having engaged in various repeated sexual acts with a fourteen-year-old girl, described as "undoubtedly a wanton" and "treated as the village whore". Upholding their convictions, the Court of Appeal held that consent was no defence.

12. The elements of indecent exposure. This has two possible forms and it is therefore necessary to examine:

(*a*) *The nature of the statutory offence.* Under the Vagrancy Act 1824, s. 4, it is an offence for a person wilfully, openly, lewdly and obscenely to expose his person with intent to insult any female. The *actus reus* is the exposure by a man of his penis to a woman and the *mens rea* is an intent to insult—

> *Ford* v. *Falcone* (*1971*): When his landlady came to collect the rent, F had no clothes on the upper part of his body and proferred his person. He was acquitted of an offence under s. 4, as the act took place in private. Allowing the prosecutor's appeal, the Court of Appeal held that the offence could be committed in a private place.

> *Evans* v. *Ewels* (*1972*): Having exposed part of his stomach to the complainant, with intent to insult her, E was convicted under s. 4. Allowing his appeal, the Divisional Court held that "person" meant "penis". Exposure of any other part of the body could constitute the common law offence.

(*b*) *The nature of the common law offence.* It is an offence to commit an act injurious to public morals or to outrage public decency in public. To obtain a conviction, the prosecution must prove that the act was committed in the sense that more than one person must at least have been able to see it but it is not necessary to show that the members of the public who saw the act were actually disgusted or annoyed.

PROGRESS TEST 21

1. Outline the M'Naghten Rules with particular reference to the *mens rea* of murder. **(1)**
2. Explain the defence of provocation. **(2)**
3. What circumstances give rise to involuntary manslaughter? **(3)**
4. What must be proved for a conviction of common assault and what would convert it to an assault occasioning actual bodily harm? **(4, 5)**
5. Distinguish between unlawful wounding and wounding with intent. **(6, 7)**
6. How can consent to assault be vitiated? **(8)**
7. Outline the essential elements of rape. **(9)**
8. Explain the *actus reus* and *mens rea* of indecent assault. **(10)**

9. How can sexual intercourse be unlawful and what possible defences are there?   **(11)**

10. Describe the statutory and common law provisions relating to indecent exposure.   **(12)**

CHAPTER XXII

The Nature of Offences against Property

THE ESSENTIALS OF THEFT AND ROBBERY

1. The elements of theft. Under the Theft Act 1968, s. 1 *a person is guilty of theft if he dishonestly appropriates property belonging to another, with the intention of permanently depriving the other of it*. The *actus reus* is the appropriation of property belonging to another, whilst the *mens rea* requires dishonesty and the intention permanently to deprive. It is therefore necessary to examine:

(*a*) *The meaning of "dishonestly".* As stated by Lord Lane L. C. J. in *R.* v. *Ghosh* (*1982*) (5(*a*)(*ii*) below), the judge should direct the jury that a person acts dishonestly if his conduct would be regarded as dishonest by the ordinary standards of reasonable people, and he realises that it is so regarded. It is immaterial that he may genuinely believe that he is morally justified in acting as he did. Under s. 2 of the 1968 Act, an appropriation may be dishonest even if the accused is willing to pay for the property (e.g. leaves behind money even greater than its value) but it would *not* be dishonest on:

(*i*) *The ground of belief in a legal right.* A person is not guilty of theft if he believes that he has the right in law to deprive the other of the property—

R. v. *Robinson* (*1977*): Charged with robbing a man whose wife owed him £7, R was convicted of theft, the judge having directed the jury that the defence necessitated an *honest* belief in a legal right. Quashing the conviction, the Court of Appeal held that it did not have to be an honest belief.

(*ii*) *The ground of belief in consent.* A person is not guilty of theft if he believes that he would have the other's consent if the other knew of the appropriation and the circumstances of it.

(*iii*) *The ground of belief that the owner cannot be discovered.* If property is found by a person, he is not guilty of theft if he appropriates it in the belief that the person to whom it belongs cannot be discovered by taking reasonable steps.

(*b*) *The meaning of "appropriates"*. Under s. 3(1) of the 1968 Act, "Any assumption by a person of the rights of an owner amounts to an appropriation". This means that a person is guilty of theft when he commits any act relating to the property which only an owner can do. However, if he purchases something, which he later discovers to have been stolen, and retains it, he has committed an appropriation but is not guilty of theft—

R. v. *Monaghan* (*1979*): M, a cashier, placed £3.99 from a customer in the till but did not ring it up. When arrested, she admitted that she intended to take out an equivalent sum at a later stage. The Court of Appeal upheld her conviction of theft, because appropriation existed in the fact that she had put the money in the till for her own benefit and not that of her employers.

Eddy v. *Niman* (*1981*): Two people had entered a supermarket with intent to steal. Having placed goods in a basket, one changed his mind, left the goods with his associate and walked out. The Divisional Court upheld his acquittal of theft, because the placing of goods in a basket was within the store's implied consent and there had been no assumption of the rights of an owner.

R. v. *Morris*; *Anderton* v. *Burnside* (*1983*): In supermarkets, M and B had each removed labels from goods and replaced them with ones showing lower prices, which they paid at the check-out. Both were convicted of theft and, dismissing their appeals, the House of Lords held that the changing of the labels was something which only an owner could do; therefore there had been an appropriation.

See Corcoran v. *Anderton* (*1980*) at 2(*a*) below and *R.* v. *Pitham*, *R.* v. *Hehl* (*1977*) at 7(*b*).

(*c*) *The meaning of "property"*. Under s. 4 of the 1968 Act, "property" covers money, all tangible property, choses in action (XVI, 2(*a*) above) and other intangible property. In effect, it includes gas and water but not electricity (the dishonest use of which is provided for in s. 13). Land cannot be stolen except by a person who holds property on trust for another *or* who is not in possession of the land and appropriates anything severed from it *or* who is a tenant and appropriates all or part of a fixture or structure let to be used with the land. The picking of wild mushrooms, flowers, fruit or foliage is not theft unless it is for reward. Similarly wild creatures not tamed or ordinarily kept in captivity cannot be stolen—but under Schedule 1 to the 1968 Act it is an offence to take or kill deer in enclosed land or to take fish from water which is subject to private rights; furthermore, poaching is covered by the Night Poaching Acts 1828 and 1844—

R. v. Kohn (1979): K, an accountant, drew various sums from a company account, using company cheques, for his own purposes. The Court of Appeal upheld his conviction of theft as there was appropriation of the cheques themselves, and also of choses in action (i.e. debts owed by a bank to a customer whose account is in credit or overdrawn within agreed limits).

Oxford v. Moss (1979): A university student obtained a proof of his examination paper which he photocopied and intended to return. Upholding his acquittal of theft, the Divisional Court held that confidential information was not tangible property and therefore it could not be stolen.

(*d*) *The meaning of "belonging to another"*. Under s. 5 of the 1968 Act, property is regarded as "belonging to another" if that person has possession or control of it *or* has any proprietary right or interest in it *or* if it has been received from another for a particular purpose (e.g. a contribution to a fund) *or* if it has been obtained by another's mistake (e.g. receiving a £1 coin tendered in mistake for 5p or a debt mistakenly repaid twice over).

R. v. Turner (1971): To evade payment, T removed his car from the garage where it had been repaired, without telling the proprietor. Upholding his conviction of theft, the Court of Appeal held that the property was in the possession or control of the garage.

R. v. Woodman (1974): From a disused site, W took scrap metal, of which the occupier had no knowledge, and the Court of Appeal upheld his conviction of theft.

Wakeman v. Farrar (1974): Having received cash in lieu of a lost Supplementary Benefit Giro order, the payee subsequently found the order and cashed it. The Divisional Court held that he was guilty of theft, as the Department of Health and Social Security retained a proprietary right in the order.

Edwards v. Ddin (1976): Having had his car filled up with petrol, D drove away without paying. He was acquitted of theft as the property of the petrol passed to him when it was placed in his car and the vendor did not retain a right of disposal. The Divisional Court upheld this decision.

(e) *The meaning of "intention of permanently depriving"*. Under s. 6 of the 1968 Act a person is to be regarded as having the intention of permanently depriving another of his property if he intends to treat the thing as his own, to dispose of regardless of the other's rights. The question can properly be left to a jury without a specific direction or illustrations of the intention—

R. v. Johnstone, Comerford and Jalil (1982): Johnstone and C were draymen who collected bottles from customers, who were entitled to the refund of deposits paid. Johnstone and C did not record all the bottles collected but gave some to Jalil, so that he could recover the deposits for sharing amongst all three. It was held that, as they had intended to return the bottles to the company, there was no intention permanently to deprive and consequently no theft.

R. v. Downes (1983): D lawfully held seven sub-contractor vouchers, belonging to the Inland Revenue, and sold the vouchers to others so that they could be used as forgeries to evade tax. The Court of Appeal upheld his conviction of theft as the essential character of the vouchers was destroyed when they were sold; consequently, although they would be returned to the Inland Revenue, there was sufficient intent to deprive it permanently of its property.

2. The elements of robbery. Under the Theft Act 1968, s. 8, *a person is guilty of robbery if he steals and, immediately before or at the time of doing so, and in order to do so, he uses force on any person or seeks to put any person in fear of being then and there subjected to force*. It is therefore necessary to examine:

(a) *The meaning of "if he steals"*. If any of the elements necessary for theft should not exist, then there cannot be a conviction of robbery—thus all of the defences open to one charged with theft are available also for robbery—

Corcoran v. Anderton (1980): Two men attempted to snatch a woman's handbag and, striking her in the back, the first tugged at the bag which fell to the ground. The woman screamed and the men ran away. Convicted of robbery, the second man appealed on the ground that, as there had been no appropriation of the bag, his conduct could not have exceeded attempt. Upholding the conviction, the Divisional Court held that the tugging could amount to a sufficient degree of control to constitute appropriation.

See R. v. *Robinson* (*1977*) at 1(*a*)(*i*) above.

(*b*) *The meaning of "immediately before or at the time".* Force used to acquire information needed for a theft to be committed some time later, or used after a theft has been completed, would not convert it to robbery—

> *R.* v. *Donaghy and Marshall* (*1981*): After D and M threatened the life of a mini-cab driver, he drove them to London, where they stole £22 from him. It was ruled that, in order to convict of robbery, the jury had to be satisfied that the accused gave the impression by their manner that they were continuing the threats at the time of the theft.

(*c*) *The meaning of "uses force on any person".* Accidental force or slight physical contact will not suffice but the force may nevertheless be minimal. The fact that it is used "on any person" precludes actual or threatened damage to property but means that it may be effected against someone other than the one whose property is stolen—

> *R.* v. *Dawson, R.* v. *James* (*1978*): D and J were convicted of robbery. The victim had given evidence that he had been nudged and pushed off balance so that, whilst he was trying to regain his balance, his wallet had been stolen. Upholding the conviction, the Court of Appeal held that the question as to whether force had been used to further theft had properly been left to the jury.

THE ESSENTIALS OF BURGLARY

3. The elements of burglary. Under the Theft Act 1968, s. 9(1), *A person is guilty of burglary if* (*a*) *he enters any building or part of a building as a trespasser, with intent to commit... offences of stealing anything in the building, of inflicting on any person therein grievous bodily harm or raping any woman therein and of doing unlawful damage to the building or anything therein,* also (*b*) *if having entered any building or part of a building as a trespasser, he steals or attempts to steal anything... or inflicts or attempts to inflict on any person therein any grievous bodily harm.* It is therefore necessary to examine:

(*a*) *The meaning of "enters".* The word "enters" is not defined in the Act and can give rise to various possible interpretations.

However, the natural meaning would connote a complete entry, in which case a partial entry, the use of an instrument (e.g. a pair of tongs) or the employment of an innocent agent (e.g. a boy under ten) would not fulfil the requirement.

(b) *The meaning of a "building"*. This covers not only dwellings but also offices, shops, etc., and under s. 9(3) it also applies to "an inhabited vehicle or vessel" even at times when a person having a habitation in it is not there. The words "part of a building" provide for situations where someone has a right to be in one part but not in another—

B and S v. *Leathley* (*1979*): In a farmyard B and S stole goods from a 3-ton freezer container (25 ft × 7 ft × 7 ft), which had not been moved for two years. Their convictions of burglary were upheld as the container was held to be a building in that it was "a structure of considerable size and intended to be permanent, or at least to endure for a considerable time."

R. v. *Walkington* (*1979*): W was charged with burglary, having been seen to enter the counter area of a department store and open a till drawer (which was empty). The judge directed the jury to decide whether the counter area was "part of a building", whether W had knowingly entered it as a trespasser and whether at that time he intended to steal. W was convicted and, dismissing his appeal, the Court of Appeal held that a person entering premises intending to steal is guilty of an offence regardless of the fact that there is nothing in the premises worth stealing.

(c) *The meaning of "as a trespasser"*. A conviction necessitates proving that the accused must have known (or been reckless as to the fact) that he entered a building without consent or by fraud—

R. v. Collins (*1973*): At 4 a.m. a girl awoke and saw on her window sill a naked, blond young man. Concluding that he was her boyfriend, she invited him in and sexual intercourse took place. When she turned on the light, she realised that it was not her boyfriend but C—who was convicted of burglary with intent to commit rape. The Court of Appeal quashed the conviction as the jury had not been directed to consider whether C knew he was entering without an invitation or was reckless whether he did so or not.

R. v. *Jones*, R. v. *Smith* (*1976*): J and S entered a bungalow belonging to the father of one of them and stole two television sets. They were convicted of burglary and appealed on the ground that a person such as a son, with general permission to enter, could not be a trespasser. Upholding their convictions, the Court of Appeal held that, as the permission given had been exceeded, the jury were entitled to find that they were trespassers.

R. v. *Gregory* (*1983*): G claimed that he had been invited to enter a house by two men who said that they were cleaning it after a death in the family; also he had never suspected that there was anything dishonest about the invitation to buy such of the contents as he thought appropriate. The judge directed the jury that if G had gone to the house as a fence, intending to buy on site, he would be just as guilty of the burglary as any of the main burglars. G was convicted of burglary and appealed on the ground that he was a handler (see **7** below) and not a thief. Upholding his conviction, the Court of Appeal held that a burglary may be a continuing process, involving several appropriations by different persons at different times during the incident.

(*d*) *The meaning of "grievous bodily harm"*. This has been defined in XXI, 1(*d*)(*i*) above and a lesser offence would not suffice—

R. v. *Jenkins* (*1983*): J was charged with burglary in that he "inflicted grievous bodily harm on ... therein" but he was found guilty of the lesser offence of assault occasioning actual bodily harm. Allowing his appeal, the Court of Appeal held that on such a charge it is not open to the jury to convict of the lesser offence.

4. The elements of aggravated burglary. Under the Theft Act 1968, s. 10, *A person is guilty of aggravated burglary if he commits any burglary and at the time he has with him any firearm or imitation firearm, any weapon of offence or any explosive.* A "weapon of offence" means "any article made, or adapted for use, for causing injury to or incapacitating a person, or intended by the person having it with him for such use".

R. v. *Jones* (*1979*): It was held that, if two men commit a burglary and one of them carries a weapon, then the other also has the weapon "with him" (as he has it "immediately available to" him); thus both are guilty of aggravated burglary.

R. v. *Francis* (*1982*): Two men entered a house armed with sticks and, after discarding them, stole property. The jury were directed that the prosecution needed only to prove that they were armed when they entered the premises and they were convicted of aggravated burglary. Substituting burglary convictions, the Court of Appeal held that there had been a misdirection. Unless they intended to steal when they entered, they were guilty of aggravated burglary only if they had a weapon with them at the moment when they stole.

THE ESSENTIALS OF DECEPTION

5. The elements of deception. Defined in greater detail in (*a*)(*i*) below, deception means, in effect, dishonest words or conduct which directly cause another to transfer property, accord a pecuniary advantage, provide a service or forgo settlement of a debt. The following therefore constitute criminal offences:

(*a*) *The obtaining of property by deception.* Under the Theft Act 1968, s. 15(1), *A person who by any deception dishonestly obtains property belonging to another, with the intention of permanently depriving the other of it, shall on conviction be liable to imprisonment.* It is therefore necessary to examine:

(*i*) *The meaning of "deception".* Under s. 15(4) of the 1968 Act, this means "any deception (whether deliberate or reckless) by words or conduct, as to fact or as to law, including a deception as to the present intentions of the person using the deception or any other person". There must therefore be some form of misrepresentation which the maker knows to be untrue or which he makes not caring whether it be true or false. Recklessness thus connotes indifference as to truth or falsity and consequently mere negligence would not be sufficient. A deception as to "present intentions" could arise from a situation where one person obtains money from another by falsely pretending that he will do some work for it. In all cases the deception must be the cause of the obtaining—

R. v. *Gilmartin* (*1983*): G, a stationer, obtained supplies with post-dated cheques which he knew would be dishonoured and was convicted of dishonestly obtaining goods by deception. Upholding his conviction, the Court of Appeal held that the deception was by conduct—i.e. falsely representing that each cheque was a good and valid order for the payment of the sum specified.

R. v. *Collis-Smith* (*1971*): After petrol had been put in the tank of his car, CS told the pump attendant to book it to his firm, knowing that he was not authorised to say this. The Court of Appeal quashed his conviction of obtaining petrol by deception, as the deception was made after the possession had been obtained.

(*ii*) *The meaning of "dishonestly"*. Dishonesty in this context characterises a state of mind, as opposed to a course of conduct; consequently, there cannot be a conviction if a person makes a representation which he believes to be true—even though he ought to have known it to be false. A jury should therefore be directed to determine whether, according to the ordinary standards of reasonable and honest people, what was done was dishonest; if this is so, they must then decide whether the accused must have realised that what he was doing was dishonest by those standards. This was enunciated in—

R. v. *Ghosh* (*1982*): G, a surgeon, was alleged to have falsely represented that money was due to him for an operation which had been performed on the National Health by someone else. The Court of Appeal upheld his conviction of deception.

R. v. *McCall* (*1971*): McC was convicted of obtaining property by deception, having acquired a loan of £310 by falsely stating that he had a fine of that amount to pay. He appealed on the ground that he had not acted dishonestly, having intended to repay the money. Upholding his conviction, the Court of Appeal held that this was no defence.

(*iii*) *The meaning of "obtains"*. Under s. 15(2) of the 1968 Act, "A person is to be treated as obtaining property if he obtains ownership, possession or control of it and 'obtain' includes obtaining for another, or enabling another to obtain or to retain". It is therefore sufficient to obtain ownership without possession or vice versa.

(*iv*) *The meaning of "property belonging to another"*. Property has the same meaning as in 1(*c*) above—except that, in this case, there are no exclusions in respect of land, wild flowers and wild creatures—

R. v. *Davies* (*1982*): D was convicted of obtaining property by deception, having persuaded two residents of an old people's home to endorse cheques drawn in their favour and to hand them over to him. Upholding his conviction, the Court of Appeal held that, as the residents had not appreciated what they were signing, the property in the cheques remained with them and did not pass to D—therefore he could be guilty of dishonestly obtaining "property belonging to another".

(*b*) *The obtaining of a pecuniary advantage by deception.* Under the Theft Act 1968, s. 16(1), *A person who by any deception dishonestly obtains for himself or another any pecuniary advantage shall on conviction on indictment be liable to imprisonment.* This means dishonestly obtaining credit or some other form of financial advantage. Section 16(2) of the 1968 Act now sets out two cases (a third having been repealed) in which a pecuniary advantage is to be regarded as obtained. The first covers the situation where a person is allowed to borrow by way of overdraft, or to take out any policy of insurance or annuity contract, or obtains an improvement of the terms on which he is allowed to do so. The second covers the situation where a person is given the opportunity to earn remuneration or greater remuneration in an office or employment, or to win money by betting—

R. v. *Lambie* (*1981*): Having exceeded the £200 limit of her credit card, L was asked to return it to the bank but continued to use it. She was convicted of the evasion of a debt by deception and, upholding her conviction, the House of Lords held that the presentation of the card had been a representation of her authority to make a contract on the bank's behalf.

R. v. *Alexander* (*1981*): A was convicted of obtaining a pecuniary advantage by deception, having secured an insurance policy by pretending to be someone else. Upholding the conviction, the Court of Appeal held that, until its validity was challenged, it was a "policy of insurance" which A had been "allowed to take out".

(*c*) *The obtaining of services by deception.* Under the Theft Act 1978, s. 1. (1) *A person who by any deception dishonestly obtains services from another shall be guilty of an offence.* (2) It is an obtaining of services "where the other is induced to confer a benefit by doing some act, or causing or permitting some act to be done, on the understanding that the benefit has been or will be paid for"—

R. v. *Halai* (*1983*): To obtain a mortgage, H made false statements to a building society's agent and used post-dated cheques (which he knew would be dishonoured) to pay for a survey and open a savings account. Falsely representing that cash had been paid into the account, he withdrew £100 from it. Upholding his conviction, the Court of Appeal held that by deception he had obtained a service from the agent, a benefit from the survey, and £100 from the building society.

(*d*) *The evasion of liability by deception.* Under the Theft Act 1978, s. 2, it is an offence if, by deception, a person *dishonestly secures the remission of the whole or part of any existing liability to make a payment—whether his own liability or another's* OR *with the intent to make permanent default in whole or in part of an existing liability to make a payment, or with intent to let another do so, induces the creditor or any person claiming payment on behalf of the creditor to wait for payment (whether or not the due date for payment is deferred) or to forgo payment* OR *dishonestly obtains an exemption from, or abatement of, liability to make a payment.* In this context, "liability" means a legally enforceable liability and the provisions would not apply to a liability, which has not been accepted or established, to pay compensation for a wrongful act or omission. Furthermore, a person induced to take in payment a cheque, or other security for money, by way of conditional satisfaction of a pre-existing liability, is treated not as being paid but as being induced to wait for payment—

R. v. *Sibartie* (*1983*): S had bought an underground season ticket covering the first two stations of an eighteen-station journey and another covering the last two stations (on a different line). On passing a ticket inspector at the interchange station, he waved a season ticket and subsequently said that he intended to go out at that station and pay. He was convicted of attempted evasion of a liability by deception and, upholding his conviction the Court of Appeal held that the waving of the ticket, to indicate that it authorised a journey without further payment, was dishonestly obtaining an exemption from liability to pay the excess which an honest person would have had to pay.

THE ESSENTIALS OF BLACKMAIL

6. The elements of blackmail. Under the Theft Act 1968, s. 21, *a person is guilty of blackmail if, with a view to gain for himself or another, or with intent to cause loss to another, he makes an unwarranted demand with menaces.* There can be no "attempt to blackmail" and it is necessary to examine:

(*a*) *The meaning of "with a view to gain...cause loss to another".* Under s. 34(2) of the 1968 Act, gains and losses must be in money or other property and may be temporary or permanent. Moreover, "gain" includes keeping what one has, as well as getting what one has not; also "loss" includes not getting what one might get, as well as parting with what one has—

R. v. *Parkes* (*1973*): Charged with blackmail, P claimed that there had been no demand "with a view to gain", as the money demanded constituted a debt owed to him by the complainant. This submission was rejected on the ground that P intended to obtain hard cash, as against a mere right of action for the debt.

(*b*) *The meaning of "unwarranted"*. Under s. 21(1) of the 1968 Act, "a demand with menaces is unwarranted unless the person making it does so in the belief (*a*) that he has reasonable grounds for making the demand and (*b*) that the use of menaces is a proper means of reinforcing the demand". If the accused pleads that the demand was not unwarranted, the prosecution must show that he made it not having the belief outlined above. The factual question of his belief should be left to the jury and it does not matter what a reasonable man would have believed.

(*c*) *The meaning of "demand"*. Provided that a demand is made, it is immaterial whether it is oral or written, whether it is complied with or even whether it is heard—

Treacy v. *DPP* (*1971*): T posted a letter in the Isle of Wight, threatening a woman in West Germany that, unless she sent him money, he would disclose certain photographs to her husband. He was convicted of blackmail and the House of Lords held that his trial in England had been valid as the offence was committed when the letter was posted.

(*d*) *The meaning of "with menaces"*. This does not mean that there must necessarily be threats of violence as it is sufficient for something unpleasant or detrimental to be threatened. Under s. 21(2) of the 1968 Act, it is immaterial whether the menaces relate to action to be taken by the person making the demand. The threats may be veiled, as opposed to express, but must be such as to alarm an ordinary person of normal stability and courage—though it is not necessary to show that the intended victim did in fact become alarmed—

R. v. *Harry* (*1974*): H, the treasurer of a college rag committee, wrote to 115 shopkeepers inviting them to pay £1−5 for posters to "protect you from any Rag activity which could in any way cause you inconvenience". A count of blackmail was withdrawn from the jury as the threat was not "of such a nature and extent that the mind of an ordinary person of normal stability and courage might be influenced or made apprehensive, so as to accede unwillingly to the demand".

THE ESSENTIALS OF DISHONEST HANDLING

7. The elements of dishonest handling. It is an offence dishonestly to handle stolen goods and, under the Theft Act 1968, s.22(1), *A person handles stolen goods if (otherwise than in the course of stealing), knowing or believing them to be stolen goods, he dishonestly receives the goods, or dishonestly undertakes or assists in their retention, removal, disposal or realisation by or for the benefit of another person, or if he arranges to do so.* It is therefore necessary to examine:

(*a*) *The meaning of "stolen goods"*. Under s. 34(2) (b) of the 1968 Act, "goods" should be taken to mean money and all other property except land but including things severed from land by stealing. "Stolen goods" comprise property acquired not only by theft but also by blackmail and deception. For the offence to be committed, the goods must be "stolen" at the time of handling and, under s. 24(3), stolen property may cease to be stolen if restored to the person from whom it was stolen, if transferred to some other lawful possession (e.g. that of the police) or if the person from whom it was stolen ceases to have any right to restitution. If a handler of stolen goods exchanges them for money or other property, then both the stolen goods and the money (or other property) become "stolen goods". If, however, stolen goods come into the possession of an innocent party and are then exchanged for something else, the property acquired in exchange does not become "stolen goods"—

> *Greater London Metropolitan Police Commissioner* v. *Streeter* (*1980*) A man stole four cartons of cigarettes from his employers and loaded them into a company lorry. However, the security officer found them, marked them and informed the police, who followed the lorry to S's shop. S was charged with dishonest handling but the magistrate upheld a submission of no case on the ground that the delivered goods were not stolen because the security officer had brought them back into the owner's possession. Allowing the prosecutor's appeal, the Divisional Court held that neither the security officer nor the police had purported to exercise possession or control; they had merely waited to see what would happen. The case would therefore be remitted to the magistrate to continue the hearing.

See R. v. *Marshall* (*1977*) at VII **4**(*b*).

(*b*) *The meaning of "otherwise than in the course of stealing"*. Handling cannot occur *in the course of* stealing—even by someone who is assisting another to commit a theft. However, once a dishonest appropriation has been completed, subsequent dealings in (and disposal of) the goods will constitute "handling"—

> *R.* v. *Pitham, R.* v. *Hehl* (*1977*): When a man was sent to prison, a friend decided to steal all his furniture and offered it to P and H, who went to the man's house and bought it very cheaply. They were convicted of handling and appealed on the ground that it had been in the course of stealing. Upholding their conviction, the Court of Appeal held that the burglar had assumed the rights of owner when he invited them to buy the furniture and this was a dishonest appropriation, amounting to theft. Their subsequent conduct therefore constituted handling "otherwise than in the course of stealing".

(*c*) *The meaning of "knowing or believing them to be stolen".* A person may be said to know or believe that goods are stolen if he has no substantial doubt about the matter. However, there must be more than mere suspicion and it is insufficient to show that the accused *ought to have believed* that goods were stolen—e.g. if he purchased them for a ridiculously low price and "deliberately shut his eyes" to the possibility—

> *R.* v. *Grainge* (*1974*): G went into a shop with an acquaintance who stole a pocket calculator. Later he handed it to G who said that he thought his friend was honest and that he had been handed a radio. G was charged with handling and the recorder directed the jury that a person was not entitled to shut his eyes if circumstances looked suspicious, and from such suspicion guilty knowledge could be inferred. Quashing his conviction, the Court of Appeal held that the direction was defective, also that the guilty knowledge must have existed at the moment of receipt of the goods.

> *R.* v. *McDonald* (*1980*): Charged with handling a stolen television set, M had said to the police that, in the circumstances in which he came by it, it must have been stolen—though there was no other evidence to confirm this. Upholding his conviction, the Court of Appeal held that M had admitted circumstances within his own knowledge from which the jury were entitled to infer that the set had been stolen (*R.* v. *Marshall* (*1977*) was considered—*see* VII, 4(*b*)).

(*d*) *The meaning of "dishonestly receives".* Proof of receiving requires evidence that the accused (or his agent or servant, acting on his authority) obtained possession or control of the stolen goods, or participated with others in obtaining such possession or control. It is insufficient to receive the thief who has stolen goods in his possession—furthermore, receiving cannot occur while he still retains possession (e.g. during negotiations for the disposal of the goods).

(*e*) *The meaning of "retention, removal, disposal or realisation"*. In these cases it is necessary to prove that the acts were done "by or for the benefit of another person"—thus the disposal of the goods for the thief's own benefit would not make him a handler—

R. v. *Bloxham* (*1982*): Not knowing that it was stolen, B bought a car for £1,300 but did not receive any documents; he later suspected theft and sold the vehicle for £200. Quashing his conviction for handling, the House of Lords held that a purchaser could not be "another person".

R. v. *Sanders* (*1982*): S admitted to having used certain stolen goods found in his father's garage and was charged with dishonestly assisting in their retention. The jury were directed that he was guilty of this if he had used the goods but, quashing his conviction, the Court of Appeal held that simple usage does not constitute assisting in retention.

PROGRESS TEST 22

1. In what circumstances would the appropriation of property not be considered to be dishonest?   (1)

2. In a prosecution for theft what is meant by "property belonging to another"?   (1)

3. What must be established if a person is to be convicted of robbery?   (2)

4. Examine the essential elements of burglary.   (3)

5. What is aggravated burglary?   (4)

6. Discuss the offence of obtaining property by deception.   (5)

7. How can a pecuniary advantage be obtained by deception?   (5)

8. In what ways can a liability be evaded by deception?   (5)

9. What constitutes blackmail?   (6)

10. Outline what must be established for a conviction of dishonest handling.   (7)

APPENDIX I

Selected Bibliography

PART I

Allott, A. N., *The Limits of Law*, Butterworths
Aubert, V., *Sociology of Law*, Penguin
Barnard, D., *The Civil Court in Action*, Butterworths
Barnard, D., *The Criminal Court in Action*, Butterworths
Cross, R., *The English Sentencing System*, Butterworths
Dias, R. W. M., *Jurisprudence*, Butterworths
Drewry, G., *Law, Justice and Politics*, Longman
Farrar, J. H., *Introduction to Legal Method*, Sweet & Maxwell
Freeman, M. D. A., *The Legal Structure*, Longman
Harris, J. W., *Legal Philosophies*, Butterworths
Harris, P., *An Introduction to Law*, Weidenfeld and Nicolson
Hart, H. L. A., *The Concept of Law*, Oxford
Jackson, P., *Natural Justice*, Sweet and Maxwell
Jackson, R. M., *The Machinery of Justice in England*, Cambridge U.P.
Kiralfy, A. K. R., *The English Legal System*, Sweet and Maxwell
Lawson, F. H., *Remedies of English Law*, Butterworths
Lloyd, D., *The Idea of Law*, Penguin
Phillips, O. Hood, *A First Book of English Law*, Sweet and Maxwell
Radcliffe and Cross, *The English Legal System*, Butterworths
Sawer, G., *Law in Society*, Oxford
Taylor, L., *Deviance and Control*, Nelson

PART II

Cheshire and Fifoot, *The Law of Contract*, Butterworths
Cheshire and Fifoot, *Cases on the Law of Contract*, Butterworths
Smith and Thomas, *A Casebook on Contract*, Sweet and Maxwell
Treitel, G. H. *The Law of Contract*, Stevens

PART III

Cross and Jones, *Introduction to Criminal Law*, Butterworths
Cross and Jones, *Cases on Criminal Law*, Butterworths
Williams, G., *Textbook of Criminal Law*, Stevens
Elliott and Wells, *Elliott and Wood's Casebook on Criminal Law*,
    Sweet and Maxwell

APPENDIX II

Examination Technique

1. Carefully revise for the examination—remembering that it is not devised to ascertain the full extent of your knowledge or to trap you into errors. Its purpose is to provide a reasonable range of questions to verify whether you have read, understood and absorbed the elements of the syllabus—also whether you have brought to bear on your reading some intelligent and critical appreciation of your own. More is demanded than the mere regurgitation of memorised extracts from textbooks.

2. Carefully read through the whole examination paper, including the instructions contained in the heading. Five or ten minutes spent in thoughtful assessment can save you wasted effort and subsequent anguish.

3. Carefully select the questions which you intend to answer. It is not always wise to choose those that appear to be easiest, as it is always better to select the ones on which merit can be shown.

4. Carefully divide the total time by the number of answers required, allowing five to ten minutes for reading through the script at the end. When the time apportioned to each question has elapsed, the next *must* be started. If you submit four fulsome answers when in fact five are required, you impose on yourself a handicap of twenty per cent.

5. Carefully analyse each question, making certain that you appreciate whether more than one point has been raised.

6. Carefully answer the question that has been set and do not write an answer to a question in the same field which you would have preferred to have set.

7. Carefully make a "skeleton" of each answer, with brief headings. Assemble in a logical order the principles and facts that you intend to use.

8. Carefully avoid irrelevance; this does not gain any marks and often results in a lower mark than might otherwise have been awarded for the relevant matter that is included.

9. Carefully memorise statutes and cases but bear in mind that it is always the *principle* that matters. The examiners will give credit in "problem" questions if they are tackled in the right way—even

though the answer arrived at may not be the one which is expected. You need to be able to identify the relevance of facts, to apply appropriate legal rules thereto and to evaluate judicial reasoning.

10. Carefully present your work in such a way that the examiner finds it a joy to mark. He is a human being, who appreciates legibility and clarity—combined with clear, concise and exact communication.

Specimen Test Papers

Answer any five questions in each paper.
The time allowed for each paper is three hours.

PAPER I

1. Describe the inter-relationship of law, justice and morality.
2. "Equity came to supplement, not to supplant, the common law." Discuss.
3. What are the main sources of English law?
4. Outline the jurisdiction of magistrates' courts and assess their value.
5. Examine the role and supervision of administrative tribunals.
6. Describe the two branches of the legal profession and consider whether they should be amalgamated.
7. Explain the procedure of a criminal trial in the Crown Court.
8. Consider the deterrent and reformative effects of criminal sanctions.
9. Distinguish between "binding" and "persuasive" precedent.
10. What advantages are to be gained by converting a partnership into a limited company?

PAPER I

1. Discuss the function of law as "a marker of boundaries of acceptable conduct".
2. Examine the disintegration of the Curia Regis and the jurisdiction of the courts which subsequently developed.
3. What effect has United Kingdom membership of the European Community had on Parliament and the courts?
4. Outline the value and supervision of arbitration.
5. Consider the role of the county court.
6. What are the advantages and disadvantages of trial by jury?
7. Describe the procedure for dealing with a "small claim".

8. What principles are followed by a court in the interpretation of a statute?

9. Explain the admissibility of evidence in criminal proceedings.

10. Examine the legal position of a minor.

PAPER II

1. Examine the different ways in which an offer may terminate.

2. In what circumstances, if any, can a debt be discharged by the payment of a smaller sum of money?

3. Discuss contracts in restraint of trade and the circumstances in which they may be enforceable.

4. "Some contracts which are contrary to public policy are void, whereas others are illegal." Discuss.

5. Suffering a cash-flow problem, John consulted his accountant, Cyril, who suggested that he should sell his Aston-Martin and offered him £10,000 for it. John accepted this but is now consulting you as he has discovered that the car was worth £15,000.

6. Consider the doctrine of part performance.

7. Distinguish between conditions and warranties.

8. Examine the ways in which a contract might impose liabilities upon a third party.

9. In what circumstances may a contract be discharged by frustration?

10. In September Alfred booked the Nits pop group for a performance at the Town Hall in the following February. In November they suffered bad press publicity and Alfred sent a letter cancelling the engagement. In January one of their records came high in the charts and Alfred wrote to say that the contract still stood. Advise the Nits.

PAPER II

1. In what circumstances, if any, can past consideration be valid consideration?

2. Discuss the contractual position of minors.

3. Examine the types of mistake which may affect the validity of a contract, and also those which will not.

4. Describe any circumstances in which money passed under an illegal contract can be recovered.

5. As several of his windows had been broken by an eleven-year-old, Philip telephoned the boy's father, Roger, to say that he was going to report the matter to the police. Roger offered him £30 if

he promised not to do so and Philip agreed—but after six months he has not received the money and seeks your advice.

6. Consider the rescission of contracts induced by misrepresentation.

7. Examine the validity of exemption clauses.

8. Explain what is meant by "the assignment of a chose in action".

9. Outline the circumstances in which a decree of specific performance might be sought.

10. In a shop window a video recorder bore a card with the words "compatible for all tapes". Tony signed an order-form to purchase one but, when it was delivered, he found that it would not accept several types of tape. On re-reading the form, he noticed that it contained the statement "all conditions and warranties implied by statute or common law are hereby excluded". Advise Tony.

PAPER III

1. Distinguish between EITHER *mens rea* and motive OR negligence and recklessness.

2. Examine the defences of duress and necessity.

3. What constitutes an attempt?

4. Describe, with illustrations, the essential ingredients of theft.

5. What must be proved for a conviction of aggravated burglary?

6. Being short of money, Alan persuaded Bill to "steal" his car, for which he then submitted an insurance claim. Consider the criminal liability of Alan and Bill.

7. In a drunken brawl, Colin aimed a punch at David, missed him and hit Eric, breaking his jaw. Discuss Colin's criminal liability.

8. Intending to steal his money, Frank invited George to his flat and gave him a laced drink. After taking his wallet (which contained nothing of value) he then carried out the unconscious George and left him in a park, where he was found dead on the following morning. Consider Frank's criminal liability.

9. One month a computer error caused his firm to pay Hugh two salaries. Disgruntled at not having received a rise for three years, he kept the extra money and said nothing. Discuss his criminal liability, if any.

10. Outline the requirements for a conviction of rape.

PAPER III

1. In what circumstances may statutes dispense with the need to prove *mens rea*?

2. With regard to the defences of insanity and automatism, do you consider the present situation to be satisfactory?

3. Examine the liability of a limited company for offences committed by its employees.

4. State what must be proved for a conviction of murder.

5. What is meant by robbery?

6. Alec agreed to help Brian with a burglary, on the understanding that they should not carry firearms. After entering the premises, they were disturbed by a man brandishing a poker, whereat Brian produced a revolver and shot him dead. Consider the criminal liability of Alec and Brian.

7. With a cheque which he knew would be dishonoured, Charles bought a £400 video recorder, which he sold a week later to Douglas for £100. During the next month Douglas became suspicious and resold the machine to Edward for £75. Discuss the criminal liability, if any, of all three.

8. As Fred, a vagrant, had threatened to assault Gregory's elderly mother if he was not provided with alcohol, Gregory went to the self-service shop next door and, finding that he had insufficient money, he changed the price tag on a bottle of whisky before he paid for it and gave it to Fred to drink. Examine the criminal liability of Fred and Gregory.

9. Harry supplied Ian with a quantity of explosive, suspecting that it was to be used for safe-breaking. Two weeks later, it was found intact in a device attached to the car of a foreign diplomat. Examine Harry's criminal liability, if any.

10. How can an assault be categorised as indecent?

Index

251

M&E Handbooks

Law

Business and Management

Advertising/F Jefkins
Basic Economics/G L Thirkettle
Basic of Business/D Lewis
Business and Financial Management/B K R Watts
Business Mathematics/L W T Stafford
Business Systems/R G Anderson
Data Processing Vol 1: Principles and Practice/R G Anderson
**Data Processing Vol 2: Information Systems and
    Technology**/R G Anderson
Human Resources Management/H T Graham, R Bennett
International Marketing/L S Walsh
Managerial Economics/J R Davies, S Hughes
Marketing/G B Giles
Marketing Overseas/A West
Modern Commercial Knowledge/L W T Stafford
Modern Marketing/F Jefkins
Office Administration/J C Denyer, A L Mugridge
Operational Research/W M Harper, H C Lim
Production Management/H A Harding
Public Administration/M Barber, R Stacey
Public Relations/F Jefkins
Purchasing/C K Lysons
Retail Management/R Cox, P Brittain
Selling: Management and Practice/P Allen
Statistics/W M Harper
Stores Management/R J Carter

Accounting and Finance

Auditing/L R Howard
Basic Accounting/J O Magee
Basic Book-keeping/J O Magee
Company Accounts/J O Magee
Company Secretarial Practice/L Hall, G M Thom
Cost Accounting/W M Harper
Elements of Banking/D P Whiting
Elements of Insurance/D S Hansell
Finance of Foreign Trade/D P Whiting
Investment: A Practical Approach/D Kerridge
Investment Appraisal/G Mott
Management Accounting/W M Harper
Practice of Banking/E P Doyle, J E Kelly
Principles of Accounts/E F Castle, N P Owens

Humanities and Science

European History 1789–1914/C A Leeds
Land Surveying/R J P Wilson
World History: 1900 to the Present Day/C A Leeds

'A' LEVEL
LAW
UPDATE

BARRY JONES

Since the publication of the second edition of this <u>Handbook</u> there have been numerous developments, the most significant of which are discussed fully in this update.

M&E HANDBOOKS: LAW

PART ONE: THE FOUNDATIONS AND FUNCTIONS OF LAW

1. The law of the European Community (See II, 1(d)). On 1st January 1986 Spain and Portugal were admitted to membership of the European Communities, as a result of which the Commission now has 17 members, the European Parliament has 518 MEPs and the European Court of Justice has 13 judges.

2. The prosecution of offences (See III, 1(a)(ii) and IV, 5(b)(i)). Under the Prosecution of Offences Act 1985, which came into full operation on 1st October 1986, most criminal prosecutions are now instituted by the <u>Crown Prosecution Service</u>, which comprises about 1,500 lawyers with 40 Chief Crown Prosecutors (mostly covering separate police areas), appointed by the Director of Public Prosecutions. The latter deals with only the most complex and sensitive cases, e.g. political, terrorist, official secrets, company fraud and race relations prosecutions.

3. The role of solicitors (See IV, 3(b)).

(a) Under the Administration of Justice Act 1985, the Law Society gained new powers in relation to its dealing with complaints against solicitors. Since 1st September 1986 there has existed a <u>Solicitors Complaints Bureau</u>, whose lay-dominated Investigation Committee examines all complaints concerning delays, overcharging, conflicting interest, dishonesty, deception, shoddy work, etc. There is also a solicitor-dominated Adjudication Committee which can bring serious cases of misconduct before the Disciplinary Tribunal. Complainants wishing to pursue negligence claims can be put in touch with a Negligence Panel.

(b) Solicitors now have limited advocacy rights in the High Court, whereby they can appear in formal and unopposed proceedings.

(c) Consideration is currently being given to the feasibility of fusing the two branches of the legal profession, also the possible inception of mixed practices involving other professions. Press coverage of such proposals needs to be closely followed.

4. The functions of juries (See IV, 4(a)). On 10th January 1986 the <u>Report of the Fraud Trials Committee</u> (Chairman Lord Roskill, HMSO, ISBN 0 11 380008 8) recommended that complex fraud cases should be tried, not by a judge and jury, but by a <u>Fraud Trials Tribunal</u>, comprising a judge and two skilled lay members with appropriate qualifications. The Report is discussed in the White Paper <u>Criminal Justice: Plans for Legislation</u> (Cmnd.9658, ISBN 0 10 196580 X).

5. The role of the police (See IV, 5(c)). Under Part IX of the Police and Criminal Evidence Act 1984, complaints in

1

respect of police conduct should be made to the Chief
Constable of the force concerned. He must then decide whether
the matter should be determined by an Informal Resolution
(only if the conduct complained of would not result in a
criminal or disciplinary charge), a Formal Investigation (by
an officer of the rank of Chief Inspector or above, and at
least equal in rank to the officer complained of) or Referral
to the <u>Police Complaints Authority</u>. Established on 29th April
1985, this comprises a chairman (appointed by the Queen) and
at least eight other members (who must not be serving or
retired policemen) appointed by the Home Secretary. Any
complaint alleging conduct resulting in death or serious
injury must be referred to this body, whilst other complaints
may be so referred. The Authority may then supervise an
investigation, in which case it approves the investigating
officer, who must make a report. If this shows that a serious
criminal offence may have been committed, the Chief Constable
must send a copy to the Director of Public Prosecutions.
Should the report show that a criminal offence has not been
committed, the Chief Constable must send a memorandum to the
Authority, stating whether he has preferred disciplinary
charges, and, if not, why not. The Authority may then require
him to do so. Whatever the outcome of his complaint, a
citizen always has the right to bring a civil action (e.g. for
false imprisonment or trespass) against the police.

6. The ordering of costs (See VI, **4**(b)). Under the
Prosecution of Offences Act 1985, the prosecution (except in
the case of a private one) may not now seek costs from central
funds.

7. The admissibility of confessions (See VII, **4**(c)). Under
the Police and Criminal Evidence Act 1984, s.76, confessions
are inadmissible unless the prosecution proves beyond
reasonable doubt that they were not obtained by oppression
(including torture, inhuman or degrading treatment, or the use
or threat of violence) or by any method likely to render them
unreliable. The exclusion of a confession does not affect the
admissibility of any facts discovered as a result of it.

8. The freedom of the person (See VIII, **6**(a)). Powers of
arrest, stopping, searching, detention, etc. are now specified
in the Police and Criminal Evidence Act 1984, the main
provisions of which relate to:

    (a) <u>The nature of arrestable offences</u>. An arrest will be
justified if it is supported by a warrant, which is issued by
a magistrate to a constable, ordering him to bring the person
named before the court. However, as shown in (b) and (c)
below, not only a police officer but also a private citizen
may effect a lawful arrest without a warrant, in respect of
the following which are defined in s.24 of the 1984 Act as

arrestable offences:

    (i) Offences for which the sentence is fixed by law (e.g. murder, treason, piracy with violence).

    (ii) Offences for which there is a sentence of five years imprisonment for persons aged 21 or over who have not been previously convicted.

    (iii) Offences under the Customs and Excise Acts for which a person may be detained (e.g. obstructing officers, impeding searches, destroying evidence, importing or exporting prohibited goods).

    (iv) Offences under the Official Secrets Acts 1911 and 1920 (i.e. all offences under these Acts, regardless of prescribed sentences).

    (v) Offences under the Sexual Offences Act 1956, ss.14, 22 and 23 (i.e. indecent assault on a woman, causing prostitution of women and procurement of girls under the age of 21).

    (vi) Offences under the Theft Act 1968, ss.12(1) and 25(1) (i.e. taking a motor vehicle or other conveyance without authority and going equipped for burglary, theft or cheat).

    (vii) Offences under the Public Bodies Corrupt Practices Act 1889, s.1 and the Prevention of Corruption Act 1906, s.1 (i.e. corruption of any member, officer or servant of a public body, also corrupt transactions with agents).

    (b) <u>The police powers of arrest</u>. Under ss.24-25 of the 1984 Act, a constable may effect an arrest without a warrant in the following circumstances:

    (i) If he has reasonable grounds for suspecting that an arrestable offence has been committed and that the relevant person is guilty of it. It is not necessary for an arrestable offence to have in fact been committed.

    (ii) If anyone is about to commit an arrestable offence or if he has reasonable grounds for suspecting that someone is about to do so.

    (iii) If any (i.e. non-arrestable) offence has been (or is being) committed or attempted and it appears impracticable or inappropriate for a summons to be served, because of specified doubts about the suspect's name and address or if the constable has reasonable ground for believing that arrest is necessary to prevent the suspect from causing physical injury to himself or another, suffering physical injury, committing an offence against public decency, causing an unlawful obstruction of the highway, or harming a child or other vulnerable person.

    (iv) If the offence is specified in any of 21 statutes preserved in Schedule 2 of the 1984 Act.

Anyone arrested by a constable must be informed as soon as practicable that he is under arrest and be given the grounds for it. This requirement is essential, even if the arrest and/or grounds are obvious, because the arrest is unlawful if it is not complied with.

    (c) <u>The citizen's power of arrest</u>. Under ss. 24 and 26 of the 1984 Act, a private citizen may effect an arrest (without a warrant) in the following circumstances:

(i) If a person is in the act of committing an arrestable offence or if there are reasonable grounds for suspecting that he is doing so. The arrest is thus limited in time, as it may be effected only when the person is (or is supposed to be) committing the offence.

(ii) If an arrestable offence has been committed and a person is guilty of it or there are reasonable grounds for suspecting him to be so. In this case it is necessary for an arrestable offence to have been actually committed, though not necessarily by the person arrested.

(iii) If the offence is specified in certain statutes, e.g. the Theft Act 1968, s.34 (persons making off without payment).

(d) The common law power of arrest. In addition to the above provisions of the 1984 Act, a constable or a private citizen has a common law power to arrest, without a warrant, anyone committing a breach of the peace in his presence, or threatening to commit or renew such a breach so that he reasonably and honestly believes that it will be committed in the immediate future. A breach of the peace occurs whenever harm or violence is threatened, so as to be likely, to a person or his property, or when a person is put in fear by reason of some assault, riot or affray, provided that the conduct concerned relates to violence. This was enunciated in

R. v Howell (Erroll) (1982): At 4 a.m., H was one of a group causing a disturbance outside a house where a party was being held. He was warned by a constable to stop swearing, was subsequently arrested and struck the constable. The Court of Appeal upheld his conviction.

(e) The police powers of search after arrest. After an arrest, other than at a police station, a constable may search the arrested person if he has reasonable grounds for believing that he may present a danger to himself or others or that he has concealed on him any article that might be used to assist him to escape, or which might be evidence relating to the offence for which he has been arrested. The constable may also search any premises wherein the person was, when (or immediately before) he was arrested, for evidence relating to the offence. These powers arise only if there are reasonable grounds, which must also exist if anything found is seized.

(f) The police powers of stopping and searching. Under ss.1-3 of the 1984 Act, a constable may stop and search a person or vehicle (or anything in or on it) and may detain the person or vehicle for the purpose of such a search provided:

(i) That the constable has reasonable grounds for suspecting that he will find stolen or prohibited articles. "Prohibited articles" comprise offensive weapons and articles made (or adapted) for use in burglary or theft.

4

(ii) That the power is exercised in a public place. This means any place to which the public (or any section of it) has access, with or without payment. It may include a garden or yard if there are reasonable grounds for suspecting that the person involved does not reside there and is not there with express or implied permission.

(iii) That the person involved is not required to remove any clothing in public, other than specified items. These comprise outer coat, jacket and gloves (thus the provision could enable articles to be concealed in hats).

(iv) That the search is conducted in a reasonable time. If the person involved is uncooperative, reasonable force may be used.

(v) That the constable brings certain information to the attention of the person involved, before commencing the search. If not in uniform, the constable must produce proof of identity and he has a mandatory duty to give his name and police station, also the object of (and grounds for) the search. The person searched (or the owner of the vehicle) is entitled to a copy of the record of the search, if it is requested within twelve months.

The duty to supply information applies to all searches, including those under various statutory provisions not repealed by the 1984 Act; notably the Firearms Act 1968, s.47 (suspicion of carrying a firearm in a public place), the Misuse of Drugs Act 1971, s.23 (suspicion of unlawful possession of a controlled drug), and the Prevention of Terrorism (Temporary Provisions) Act 1984, Sched.3. Failure to comply with the requirement would make a search unlawful but it does not apply to the search of an unattended vehicle, a vehicle or aircraft leaving an aerodrome/designated airport cargo area, or a vehicle before it leaves the goods area of a "statutory undertaker" (i.e. the operator of railway, road, water-borne transport, etc.), if searched by one of its own constables.

(g) The police power of road checks. Under s.4 of the 1984 Act a road check may be imposed to stop all vehicles (or those selected by any criteria), provided:

(i) That the purpose is to ascertain whether a vehicle is carrying a person whom there are reasonable grounds for suspecting of being in the area and of having committed a serious arrestable offence or of being a witness to such an offence or of intending to commit such an offence or of being unlawfully at large. The police have other powers of stopping vehicles (e.g. under the Road Traffic Act 1972, s.159) which do not constitute road checks under the 1984 Act, as illustrated in

Moss v. McLachlan (1985): Travelling in a convoy of vehicles on the M1, striking miners were stopped and an Inspector stated his reason to be fear of a breach of the peace. A group attempted to push past and the Divisional

Court upheld their conviction of obstructing a police
officer in the execution of his duty.

A "serious arrestable offence" is one listed in Schedule 5 of
the 1984 Act. Under s.116(3) other offences are serious only
if likely to lead to certain circumstances, e.g. serious harm
to the security of the State or public order, serious
interference with the administration of justice or the
investigation of offences, the death of (or serious injury to)
any person, also substantial financial loss or gain to any
person.

(ii) That the check is authorised in writing by a
Superintendent (or above). Exceptionally, as a matter of
urgency, an officer below that rank may give such authority
(except in respect of persons intending to commit serious
arrestable offences) but a written report must be provided as
soon as possible to a Superintendent.

(iii) That the written authority specifies the name of
the authorising officer, the ground for giving it (including,
where appropriate, the nature of the serious arrestable
offence), the locality to which it relates and the period for
which it is given; this may not exceed seven days but it may
be renewed.

(iv) That anyone in charge of a vehicle stopped at a
road check is entitled to obtain a written statement of its
purpose.

(h) The police powers of detention. Under s.36 of the 1984
Act, every police station which is regularly used for
detention must, at all times when it is open, have at least
one designated custody officer, not below the rank of sergeant
and not involved in the investigation of offences referred to
him. At all other stations at least one officer must be
available to perform such functions when required. On arrival
at a police station, anyone arrested without a warrant must be
brought before the custody officer, who must decide whether
there is sufficient evidence to charge him with the offence
for which he was arrested. Thereafter the procedure is as
follows:

(i) If the custody officer decides that there is
sufficient evidence to charge the arrested person, he may be
detained for as long as is necessary for the charge to be put
to him. He may then be charged, or informed that he may be
liable to prosecution and released without charge, on or
without bail.

(ii) If the custody officer decides that there is not
sufficient evidence to charge the arrested person, he must
order his release (on or without bail), unless he has
reasonable grounds for believing that detention is necessary
to secure or preserve evidence relating to the offence or to
obtain such evidence by questioning. In such circumstances,
the detained person must be informed of the grounds for his
detention (unless he is incapable of understanding what is

said to him, or violent, or in urgent need of medical attention) and a written record of those grounds must be made in his presence. If through drink, drugs or violence, the arrested person is not in a fit state to be charged or released without charge, he may be detained until fit to be dealt with.

(iii) If the arrested person is detained (having been charged or not), reviews of his detention must be made not later than six hours after its commencement and thereafter at intervals of not more than nine hours, in order to confirm that the criteria for detention are still satisfied. If the person has been charged, this function is carried out by the custody officer, but, if he has not been charged, it is the responsibility of an Inspector (or above) who is not involved in the investigation. A review may be postponed if it is impracticable for it to be performed.

(iv) If the arrested person is not charged, he may not, (subject to certain exceptions) be detained for more than 24 hours. Detention beyond that time and up to 36 hours is permitted only if authorised by a Superintendent (or above) who has reasonable grounds for believing that detention is necessary to secure or preserve evidence, that a serious arrestable offence is involved, and that the investigation is being conducted expeditiously. For extension beyond 36 hours the police must apply to a magistrates' court for a warrant of further detention. This may be granted for 36 hours and may be extended to not more than 96 hours from the time when detention commenced.

(v) If the arrested person is charged, his release must be ordered unless the custody officer is unable to verify his name and address or has reasonable grounds for believing that detention is necessary for his own protection, to prevent him from causing physical injury to others or damage to property, or that he will fail to answer to bail if it is granted, or that he will interfere with witnesses or obstruct the course of justice. Once charged, the person must be brought before a court as soon as practicable, in any event not later than the first available court sitting, which itself must be no later than the next day (excluding Sundays, Christmas Day and Good Friday).

(i) <u>The police treatment of detained persons</u>. Section 66 of the 1984 Act empowers the Home Secretary to issue Codes of Practice on police powers and procedures. These are brought into operation by statutory instrument and four such codes were approved by Parliament in December 1985. Part V of the Act, however, makes specific provisions in respect of:

(i) The searching of detained persons. The custody officer must cause to be included in the custody record particulars of property in the possession of detained persons at the station. They may therefore be searched (by a constable of the same sex) only in so far as is necessary for this duty to be performed. The custody officer may seize and retain any property other than items subject to legal privilege (e.g. lawyer-client communications). However, he may retain clothes and personal effects only if he believes that they may be used by the detained person to cause physical injury to himself or others, to damage property, to interfere with evidence or to assist him in escape or if he has reasonable grounds for believing that they may be evidence relating to an offence by anyone. The person from whom the property is seized must be told the reason, unless he is incapable of understanding what is said.

(ii) The intimate searching of detained persons. An intimate search (i.e. the physical examination of body orifices) may be conducted only at a police station, hospital, surgery or other place used for medical purposes, provided that it is authorised by a Superintendent (or above). This officer must have reasonable grounds for believing that the person has carefully concealed articles which could be used to cause harm or to assist in escape, and that they cannot be found without an intimate search. The reason must be explained to the person and every endeavour must be made to have the search carried out by a doctor; however, if one is not available, it may be performed by a constable of the same sex.

(iii) The rights of detained persons. Before questioning an arrested person, the custody officer must explain the reason for the detention. He must also inform him (and give him written notice) of his rights to have someone informed of his arrest and location, to have access to legal advice, and to consult the codes of practice. He is also entitled to a copy of the custody record and to be formally cautioned ("You do not have to say anything unless you wish to do so, but what you do say may be given in evidence"). The exercise of the rights to have someone informed and to have legal advice may be delayed for up to 36 hours (48 hours for those detained under terrorism legislation), if the detention is for a serious arrestable offence and provided that authority is given by a Superintendent (or above). The person detained must be informed of the reason, i.e. that the exercise of the rights might interfere with evidence of serious arrestable offences, alert others suspected of having committed them or hinder the recovery of property. In normal circumstances, the person detained must be supplied with writing materials, if they are requested, may speak on the telephone to one person (apart from the right to have someone informed) and, at the discretion of the custody officer, may have visitors. A 24-hour Duty Solicitor scheme ensures that detained persons can receive free legal advice from a solicitor of their own choice or one from a list which must be provided.

(iv) The taking of fingerprints. A person's fingerprints may be taken at a police station only if he gives written consent or if a Superintendent (or above) authorises the taking of them because: the person has not been charged

and the officer has reasonable grounds for believing that
fingerprints will tend to confirm or disprove his suspected
involvement in a criminal offence; the person has been charged
with, or reported for, a recordable offence (i.e. one which
will be recorded in national police records); the person has
been convicted of a recordable offence and his fingerprints
are not already on record.

(v) The taking of body samples. An intimate sample (i.e.
of blood, semen or other tissue fluid, urine, saliva, pubic
hair, or a swab from a body orifice) may be taken from a
detained person if a Superintendent (or above) authorises it
and if the person consents in writing. In the case of a young
person (14 but not yet 17), the written consent of his parent
or guardian is also required. The officer's authority may be
given only in the case of a serious arrestable offence and if
he has reasonable grounds for believing that the sample will
tend to confirm or disprove the detained person's involvement
in it. Intimate samples (apart from urine and saliva) may be
taken only by a registered medical practitioner. Refusal to
give a sample is capable of amounting to corroboration of
evidence against the person concerned. A non-intimate sample
(i.e. hair other than pubic, a sample from or under a nail, a
swab from any part of the body other than an orifice, a
footprint or similar impression other than from the hand) may
be taken if the person consents in writing and provided that
an Inspector (or above) has reasonable grounds for believing
that it will tend to confirm or disprove the suspect's
involvement in a particular offence. In the case of a serious
arrestable offence, a non-intimate sample may be taken without
the appropriate consent, provided that a Superintendent (or
above) has reasonable grounds for believing that it will tend
to confirm or disprove the person's involvement.

9. The freedom of property (See VIII, 6(d)). Entry on
property possessed by another, without lawful authority, or
remaining on it after authority has been withdrawn,
constitutes the tort of trespass, without any need to prove
actual damage. To provide the lawful authority, various
statutes (e.g. the Firearms Act 1968, the Theft Act 1968, the
Misuse of Drugs Act 1971, etc.) therefore authorise the issue
of search warrants, which permit entry on only one occasion
and can be executed by any constable within one month of
issue. The Police and Criminal Evidence Act 1984 Part II also
makes provisions regarding the entry and search of premises
(here meaning any place, vehicle, vessel, aircraft,
hovercraft, off-shore installation, tent or movable structure)
and the seizure of articles:

(a) <u>The police powers of entry and search with a warrant</u>.
Under s.8 of the 1984 Act, a Justice of the Peace may, on
application, issue a warrant authorising a constable to enter
and search premises (and seize anything specified) provided:

(i) that the Justice has reasonable grounds for believing that a serious arrestable offence has been committed; that there is material on the premises likely to be of substantial value to the investigation of the offence; that the material is likely to be admissible in evidence at a trial for the offence;

(ii) that one of the following conditions is fulfilled: that it is not practicable to communicate with anyone entitled to grant entry to the premises; or, if it is, that it is not practicable to communicate with anyone entitled to grant access to the evidence, or that entry to the premises will not be granted unless a warrant is produced, or that the purpose of the search may be frustrated or seriously prejudiced unless a constable can secure immediate entry;

(iii) that the subject-matter of the search does not constitute material subject to legal privilege, i.e. lawyer-client communications, also items enclosed or referred to therein; excluded material, i.e. material held in confidence, e.g. personal (medical, etc.) records acquired or created in an occupation, human tissue or tissue fluid taken for diagnosis or medical treatment, journalistic material (documents of records); special procedure material, i.e. journalistic material other than that which constitutes excluded material, also other confidential business material.

In certain circumstances access to excluded and special procedure material may be obtained by applying to a circuit judge for an order.

(b) **The police powers of entry to arrest without a warrant**. Under s.17 of the 1984 Act, and provided that he has reasonable grounds for believing that the person concerned is to be found thereon, a constable may enter and search any premises for the following purposes:

(i) to execute a warrant of arrest, or commitment;

(ii) to arrest a person for an arrestable offence;

(iii) to arrest a person for an offence under ss.1, 4 or 5 of the Public Order Act 1936;

(iv) to arrest for any offence under ss.6, 7, 8, or 10 of the Criminal Law Act 1977 (offences relating to entering and remaining on property). In this case the constable must be in uniform;

(v) to recapture a person who is unlawfully at large;

(vi) to save life or limb or to prevent serious damage to property.

(c) **The common law powers of entry without a warrant**. In addition to the above statutory provisions:

(i) the police are entitled at common law to enter and remain on premises, without a warrant, in order to prevent a breach of the peace, as enunciated in

Thomas v. Sawkins (1935): A meeting on private premises was advertised with the purpose of protesting against the Incitement to Disaffection Bill and also to demand the dismissal of the Chief Constable. Admission was open to the public and the police attended but were requested to leave. A constable committed a technical assault on the promoter, thinking that he was about to use force. The Divisional Court upheld the magistrates' ruling that this was not unlawful, because the police were entitled to enter and remain on the premises throughout the meeting, as they had reasonable grounds for believing that there might be incitement to violence and breaches of the peace.

(ii) a private citizen may enter premises to save life or limb, or to prevent serious damage to property.

<u>Cope</u> v. <u>Sharpe</u> (1912): The defendant entered the plaintiff's land and destroyed heather to prevent the spread of a fire. There was held to be no trespass.

(d) <u>The police powers of entry and search after arrest, without a warrant</u>. Under s.18 of the 1984 Act, a constable may enter and search any premises occupied or controlled by a person who is under arrest for an arrestable offence, if he has reasonable grounds for suspecting that there is evidence on the premises that relates to the offence, or to some other arrestable offence which is connected with or similar to it. Generally such entry and search must be authorised by an Inspector (or above) and if a constable acts without this authorisation he must inform an Inspector as soon as practicable.

(e) <u>The police powers of seizure without a warrant</u>. Under s.19 of the 1984 Act, a constable who is lawfully on any premises is empowered to seize anything if he has reasonable grounds for believing that it has been obtained through the commission of an offence, or that it is evidence in relation to an offence, and that it is necessary to seize it in order to prevent its being concealed, lost, altered or destroyed. On similar grounds he may also require information contained in a computer to be produced in a visible and legible form which can be taken away.

PART TWO: THE LAW OF CONTRACT

10. The outlines of recent judgments. Relevant decisions of the Court of Appeal have related to:

(a) <u>The restraint of trade</u> (See IX, **4**(c)(ii))

<u>Oswald Hickson Collier & Co.</u> v. <u>Carter-Ruck</u> (1984): In OHC's solicitors practice, the partnership deed provided that a retiring partner should not for two years solicit or act for any clients of the firm, other than those introduced by him. The Court of Appeal held that the words "or act" were too wide, as the solicitor-client

relationship was a fiduciary one and it would be contrary
to public policy to preclude a solicitor from acting for a
client who desired his services. (2 W.L.R. 847 C.A.)

Edward v. Warboys (1984): The Court of Appeal held that
the above decision had not been intended to lay down a
strict rule of law but that such a covenant raised a
serious issue to be tried, as to whether in any given case
it would be contrary to public policy to preclude a
solicitor from acting for a client who desired his
services. (2 W.L.R. 850 C.A.)

(b) The exercise of undue influence (See XIII, 4(b))

Goldsworthy v. Brickell (1986): The Court of Appeal held
that undue influence will be presumed in any relationship
if (i) A has ceded to B such trust and confidence that the
latter is compelled, out of public policy, to show that he
has not abused or betrayed it; (ii) B is in a position to
influence A into effecting the transaction of which
complaint is made; (iii) the transaction is so improvident
(or the gift made by A is so large) that friendship,
charity or other usual motives cannot reasonably account
for it. There is no need to prove dishonesty or conscious
abuse of power. (The Times 21 July 1986)

(c) The validity of exemption clauses (See XV, 4(c))

Phillips Product v. Hyland(T) & Hamstead Plant Hire Co.
(1985): PP hired from HPH a JCB excavator operated by
Hyland, an employee of HPH. The standard form of contract
provided that Hyland should be regarded as the servant of
PP, who would alone be responsible for all claims arising
from the operation of the excavator. Hyland refused to
tolerate interference with the way in which he operated the
machine and his negligence resulted in damage to PP's
premises, amounting to £3,043. The Court of Appeal held
that the liability condition was not fair and reasonable
and was therefore ineffective, under the Unfair Contract
Terms Act 1977. (82 L.G. Gaz. 681 C.A.)

(d) The nature of a penalty (See XVII, 5(b))

Liberty Life Assurance Co. v. Sheikh (1985): S was
employed by LLA as an insurance agent; he was paid on
commission and his contract contained a clause requiring
him to repay commission received in the event of his
dismissal. The Court of Appeal held that the clause was
penal, either because it was not a reasonable pre-estimate
of damages in the event of a breach of contract, or because
it was a forfeiture clause. (The Times 25 June 1985)

(e) <u>The action on a quantum meruit</u> (See XVII, **5**(c))

<u>Withey Robinson (a firm)</u> v. <u>Edwards</u> (1985): E employed WR, a firm of estate agents, to provide valuations, inventories and assistance in the purchase of a night-club. WR rendered an account for professional charges based on the RICS scale 17(b) and, when E denied that such a basis for payment had been agreed, they served a statement of claim for £5,980 as the cost of work done. The trial judge held that there was no term in the agreement entitling WR to payment on scale 17(b) but that they were entitled to a substantial sum by way of quantum meruit. Dismissing E's appeal, the Court of Appeal held that, whilst WR had not contended for remuneration on a quantum meruit basis, E's own case had recognised that WR were entitled to some remuneration on such a basis. (277 E.G. 748 C.A.)

PART THREE: CRIMINAL LAW

11. The outlines of recent judgments. Relevant decisions of the Court of Appeal have related to:

(a) <u>The elements of secondary liability</u> (See XVIII, **3**(a)).

<u>R.</u> v. <u>Dunnington</u> (1984): D was the driver of a car in which it was intended that two others should escape, after committing a robbery. The intended victim put the pair to flight by throwing bottles at them and all three were charged with attempted robbery. Dismissing D's appeal against conviction, the Court of Appeal held that, although there cannot be an attempt to aid and abet, it is still an offence to aid and abet an attempt. (2 W.L.R. 125 C.A.)

(b) <u>The defence of duress</u> (See XIX, **4**).

<u>R.</u> v. <u>Valderrama-Vega</u> (1985): Charged with a drug offence, VV pleaded that he and his family had been threatened with injury or death by a Mafia-type organisation, that he had been under severe financial pressure and that there had been threats to disclose his homosexuality. Upholding his conviction, the Court of Appeal concurred with the judge's direction that duress was a defence if the defendant acted "solely" as a result of threats of death or serious injury, and that the jury were entitled to convict even if they thought that VV would not have acted as he did but for the threats. (Crim.L.R. 220 C.A.)

(c) <u>The defence of self-defence</u> (See XIX, **5**).

<u>R.</u> v. <u>Bird</u> (1985): In a fight at a party, B hit her ex-boyfriend in the face with a glass, blinding him in one eye. Charged with unlawful wounding, she pleaded

self-defence and the judge directed the jury that anyone
using this defence needed to show by conduct an
unwillingness to fight. Quashing B's conviction, the Court
of Appeal held that, although it was a factor to be
considered, failure to demonstrate an unwillingness to
fight was not fatal to a plea of self-defence. (2 All
E.R. 513 C.A.)

(d) <u>The defence of mistake</u> (See XIX, **6**).

<u>R</u>. v. <u>Williams (Gladstone)</u> (1984): W was convicted of
assaulting a police officer who failed to produce a warrant
card and whom W mistakenly believed to be assaulting a
youth. Quashing his conviction, the Court of Appeal held
that the jury should have been directed that: (i) the
burden of proving the unlawfulness of W's actions lay on
the prosecution; (ii) if W had acted under a mistake as to
the facts, he should be judged according to his mistaken
view; (iii) the reasonableness of W's belief was material
to the question whether the belief was held at all but, if
it was held, its reasonableness was irrelevant to guilt or
innocence. (78 Cr.App.R 276, C.A.)

(e) <u>The offence of attempt</u> (See XX, **1**).

<u>R</u>. v. <u>Shivpuri</u> (1986): S was convicted of attempting to be
knowingly concerned with and harbouring a controlled drug,
namely heroin. In a police interview he had admitted to
possession of drugs and, in a statement under caution, he
had said that he deeply suspected the substance to be
heroin. On analysis it was found to be a vegetable
material similar to snuff but the Court of Appeal upheld
the conviction. Subsequently, the House of Lords,
over-ruling its own decision in <u>Anderton</u> v. <u>Ryan</u> (1985),
dismissed S's appeal, as the impossibility of the crime was
no defence for a person charged with criminal attempt. (2
W.L.R. 988 H.L.)

<u>R</u>. v. <u>Pearman</u> (1985): Whilst driving a car, P was stopped
by police officers in an unmarked vehicle. On learning
their identity, he reversed at high speed, collided with
the police car, went fast forward, hit one constable, then
drove off. He was convicted of attempting to cause
grievous bodily harm with intent, the jury having been
directed that he had the necessary intent if he did a
voluntary act foreseeing that really serious bodily harm
would probably result from it. Quashing the conviction,
the Court of Appeal held that foresight of consequences
should not be equated with intent, although it was
something from which intent might be inferred. (R.T.R. 39
C.A.)

(f) <u>The offence of conspiracy</u> (See XX, **3**).

<u>R.</u> v. <u>Cooke</u>, <u>R.</u> v. <u>Sutcliffe</u> (1985): Convicted of the
common law offence of conspiracy to defraud, C and S were
catering employees who had sold privately-acquired
beverages (in washed-up plastic cups belonging to the
British Railways Board), without accounting for the
proceeds. Quashing the conviction, the Court of Appeal
held that the use of the cups constituted a substantive
offence (under the Theft Act 1968), conspiracy for which
must be charged as such, and not as a common law
conspiracy. (Crim.L.R. 215 C.A.)

(g) <u>The elements of murder</u> (See XX, **1**).

<u>R.</u> v. <u>Hancock</u>, <u>R.</u> v. <u>Shankland</u> (1985): The Court of Appeal
laid down that, where death results although the
defendant's purpose was not primarily to kill or injure,
the jury should be directed to consider: (i) whether the
defendant committed the alleged acts; (ii) if so, whether
they were of such a kind as being highly likely to cause
death or serious injury; (iii) if so, whether the defendant
appreciated that he was highly likely to cause death or
serious injury; (iv) if so, the defendant may be guilty of
murder but the jury should distinguish between the desire
for a particular result and the intent required for the
commission of the offence. (135 New L.J. 1208 C.A.)

(h) <u>The elements of rape</u> (See XXI, **9**).

<u>R.</u> v. <u>Breckenridge</u> (1984): The Court of Appeal held that,
in a "reckless rape" case, the jury must be directed to
convict only if they find that the defendant could not care
less whether the complainant was consenting. (79 Cr.App.R
244 C.A.)

(i) <u>The elements of burglary</u> (See XXII, **3**).

<u>R.</u> v. <u>Brown (Vincent)</u> (1985): B was convicted of burglary,
having broken a shop window and rummaged about with the top
half of his body inside the window. Upholding the
conviction, the Court of Appeal held that there had been a
substantial and effective "entry". (Crim L.R. 212 C.A.)